A HANDBOOK OF WEAVES

A HANDBOOK

BY G. H. OELSNER

OF WEAVES

Translated and revised

by Samuel S. Dale, including

a supplement on the analysis of

weaves and fabrics and 1875 illustrations

DOVER PUBLICATIONS, INC., NEW YORK

Published in Canada by General Publishing Company, Ltd., 30 Lesmill Road, Don Mills, Toronto,
Ontario.
Published in the United Kingdom by Constable
and Company, Ltd., 10 Orange Street, London WC 2.

This Dover edition, first published in 1952, is an
unabridged and unaltered republication of the
original edition published by The Macmillan Company in 1915.

International Standard Book Number: 0-486-23169-0
Library of Congress Catalog Card Number: A52-7007

Manufactured in the United States of America
Dover Publications, Inc.
180 Varick Street
New York, N.Y. 10014

CONTENTS

A HANDBOOK OF WEAVES

A HANDBOOK OF WEAVES

DRAWING-IN DRAFTS

DRAWING the warp yarn into the harness is of special importance, as the production of the weave pattern depends upon this operation, called "drawing-in." In laying out the draft for a pattern, it is necessary to know what effect any particular drawing-in draft will have.

The order of drawing-in is so varied that it is difficult to give general directions. The number of threads in the weave pattern cannot be taken as a standard for determining the number of shafts to be used, as other conditions must be taken into consideration. When the number of shafts to be used is unavoidably large, the drawing-in draft must be arranged to keep the number as small as possible.

On the other hand, when the set of the warp is very close it is often necessary to increase the number of shafts to avoid bringing too many heddles on one shaft, which often causes difficulty in forming a clear shed.

It is frequently necessary to arrange the drawing-in draft for fancy goods, not only to make the work of drawing-in regular and convenient, but also to bring certain shafts into particular positions so as to adjust the strain to the strength of the yarn or to facilitate the formation of the shed. If the warp is composed of both cotton and wool yarn, the shafts carrying the wool warp should be placed nearest the reed. Like-

1

wise warp threads making abrupt and difficult intersections should be on shafts as near the reed as possible.

Oral instructions for drawing-in are sufficient only for
straight drafts. To avoid errors a drawing-in draft
should always be supplied to the operative. The shafts
are represented in the draft either by horizontal lines or
by spaces between the lines. In this book the spaces
between the lines are used for this purpose. The numbering of the shafts on the draft must correspond with
the shafts on the loom, and be understood by all the
operatives who have occasion to refer to the drafts.

There are two methods of drawing-in:

1. From the reed toward the whip roll (from bottom
to top, Fig. 1).

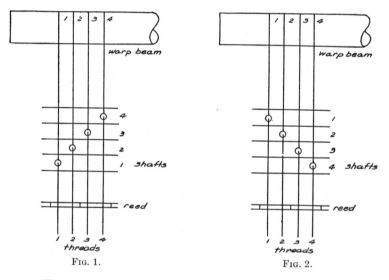

Fig. 1.   Fig. 2.

2. From the whip roll toward the reed (from top to
bottom, Fig. 2).

The first method is designated by the expression
"front to back"; the second, "back to front." Those
who prefer the "front-to-back" order claim that the
front shaft should be called the first as it is nearest
to the weaver or drawer-in and is the first to meet
the operative's eye. On the other hand, those who
prefer the "back-to-front" order insist that the back

shaft should be called the first because the yarn from the warp beam reaches that shaft first.

The first thread is at the left in both cases. Neither of these methods has any advantage over the other, but the use of both in the same mill is frequently a cause of confusion.

The warp threads at Figs. 1 and 2 are indicated by the perpendicular lines, the first thread being at the left. The shaft on which the thread is drawn is indicated by a point, circle, cross or figure. Ordinarily the drawing-in draft is marked on drafting paper, along with the weave draft.

FIG. 3.

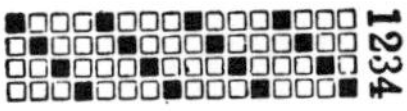

FIG. 4.

Fig. 3 is a straight draft on four harness from front to back. Fig. 4 is a straight draft on four harness from back to front.

The various drawing-in drafts may be classified as follows:

1. Straight.
2. Scattered or Satin.
3. Pointed.
4. Broken.
5. Intermittent.
6. Manifold or Corkscrew.
7. Grouped.
8. Divided.
9. Combination.

These are also classified as straight (1) and cross drafts (2 to 9).

1. STRAIGHT DRAFT

The straight drawing-in draft forms a basis for all others and proceeds in one direction only. It can be used with any number of shafts. Each succeeding thread is drawn on the succeeding shaft, the first thread on the first shaft, the second thread on the second shaft, and in this regular order until the last shaft is reached, after which the operation is repeated, beginning with the first shaft.   With eight shafts the threads will be drawn in as follows:

On shaft 1 . . . . . . threads 1, 9, 17, 25, etc.
On shaft 2 . . . . . . threads 2, 10, 18, 26, etc.
On shaft 3 . . . . . . threads 3, 11, 19, 27, etc.
On shaft 4 . . . . . . threads 4, 12, 20, 28, etc.
On shaft 5 . . . . . . threads 5, 13, 21, 29, etc.
On shaft 6 . . . . . . threads 6, 14, 22, 30, etc.
On shaft 7 . . . . . . threads 7, 15, 23, 31, etc.
On shaft 8 . . . . . . threads 8, 16, 24, 32, etc.

The number of threads in a straight draft is equal to the number of shafts, and each shaft carries one thread for every repeat of the draft.   Fig. 5 is a straight

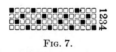

Fig. 5.

Fig. 6.

draft from back to front on four shafts.   Fig. 6 is a straight draft from back to front on eight shafts.

2. SCATTERED OR SATIN DRAFT

In this draft the order of drawing-in is disconnected and scattered so that it resembles the draft for a satin weave, from which it has derived the name, satin.

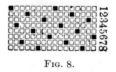

Fig. 7.   Fig. 8.

At least four shafts are required for this order of drawing-in.   Fig. 7 is a satin draft on four shafts; Fig. 8, a satin draft on eight shafts.

3. POINTED DRAFT

This order of drawing-in results from running a straight draft first in one direction and then in the other. The shaft at each point of reversal receives but one thread, the other shafts each carrying two threads for the resulting double line. The number of threads in a pointed drawing-in draft in which the draft line runs the same distance in each direction, is two less than double the number of shafts. For example, the pointed draft on eight shafts, Fig. 9, covers 14 threads. The thread at either point of reversal is called the "point thread."

By varying the length of the lines in either direction two or more points can be brought into one draft. It is not necessary that the lines cover the same number of threads. By changing the direction at irregular intervals the point threads can be brought on different shafts, and, in fact, arranged so that each shaft carries the same number of threads as in the case of a straight draft.

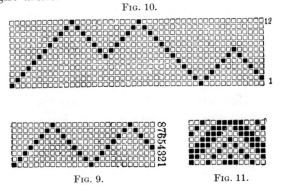

FIG. 10.

FIG. 9.

FIG. 11.

Attractive effects can be produced by varying the order in reversing a pointed draft, as shown in the draft on 12 shafts at Fig. 10. By using a twill weave with a pointed drawing-in draft the effect in the cloth is similar to that of the drawing-in draft. This causes the filling threads to float over several extra threads at the point of reversal, Fig. 11, which is objectionable in some classes of goods.

4. BROKEN DRAFT

Here one group of threads is drawn in straight in one direction and then another group is drawn in straight in the opposite direction. Where the direction is reversed the first thread of the new series is started higher or lower than the last thread of the preceding series. In a cloth woven with this draft the

Fig. 12.

Fig. 13.

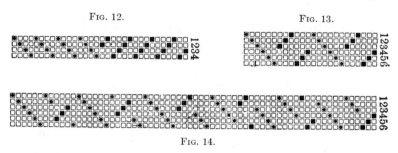

Fig. 14.

twill runs forward and backward in the order of drawing-in.

Instead of the symmetrical union of the two twill lines as obtained by the pointed drawing-in draft, a break occurs in the weave, making the point of junction distinct. The new twill line, especially in balanced twills, begins with a sharp break against the old line, Fig. 15. Where the twill reverses, the last thread of one twill line works in opposition to the first thread of the succeeding twill line. The risers of one thread come opposite the sinkers of the other thread. The twill can, of course, be run in either direction as far as desired. Figs. 12, 13 and 14 show three variations of the broken draft.

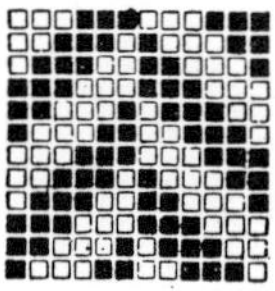

Fig. 15.

In most cases the broken draft is preferable to the pointed, and is much more frequently used. The former gives a better interlacing of the threads and a better junction of the twill lines than is possible with a pointed draft.

5. INTERMITTENT DRAFT

This is a straight draft with this difference, that at short intervals a certain number of shafts are skipped, the number depending on the weave to be used. Fig. 16 shows an intermittent draft on four shafts, in which

FIG. 16. FIG. 18.

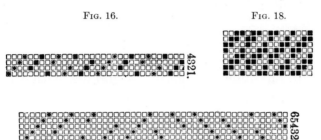

FIG. 17.

the draft is broken every four threads. This style of drawing-in enlarges the pattern to a greater or less extent, as compared with a straight draft. The direction of the intermittent draft can be changed, as illustrated at Fig. 17, which shows a draft on six shafts, reversed at the end of every twenty-four threads.

The number of shafts skipped to produce a break in an intermittent draft depends on the weave. Thus one shaft is skipped on a ^{2}—$_2$ twill; two shafts on a

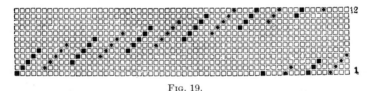

FIG. 19.

^{3}—$_3$ twill; and three shafts on a ^{4}—$_4$ twill, to obtain the desired break. Fig. 18 is the weave pattern obtained with a ^{2}—$_2$ twill and the drawing-in draft at Fig. 16. The first and last threads in an intermittent draft should break with each other.

Peculiar effects result from carrying each group of threads forward in progressive order, as shown at Fig. 19, in which the drawing-in of each group is begun 1 shaft in advance of the preceding group.

6. MANIFOLD OR CORKSCREW DRAFT

This draft is used where each twill line is formed by alternate threads, Fig. 23. It is especially effective where the warp is dressed 1 light, 1 dark, each color forming a separate twill. An even number of shafts is divided into two equal groups, one including the odd-numbered shafts, the other the even-numbered. With eight shafts each group consists of four shafts. The odd-numbered threads in the warp are drawn in straight on alternate shafts, beginning with shaft 1. The even-numbered threads are drawn in straight on alternate shafts beginning with shaft 5. Fig. 20 shows a manifold or corkscrew drawing-in draft on

FIG. 20.   FIG. 21.

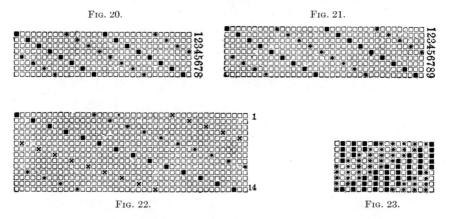

FIG. 22.   FIG. 23.

eight shafts, in which the two sets of shafts are distinguished by different marks.

A better junction of the two twill lines is obtained with an uneven number of shafts, 7, 9, 11, etc., because of the overlapping of the floats of adjacent warp threads. The drawing-in of the threads for one of the twills (threads 2, 4, 6, 8, etc.) is begun on the shaft following the larger division of the whole number of shafts. For example, when nine shafts are divided into two parts, 1 to 5 and 6 to 9, the first twill begins on shaft 1, the second twill on shaft 6, Fig. 21. Fig. 23 is the corkscrew weave obtained with a 9-leaf ^{5}—$_4$ twill and the drawing-in draft shown at Fig. 21.

To combine three twills the shafts are divided into three parts; for example, 12 shafts into 3 divisions of 4 each. The drawing-in is begun with the first thread on the first shaft of the first group, the second thread on the first shaft of the second group, the third thread on the first shaft of the third group; as, 1, 5, 9, 2, 6, 10, 3, 7, 11, etc.

A better effect is obtained by using a number of shafts that cannot be divided into three equal groups, using the largest group for the first twill. Fig. 22 shows an example of such a draft on 14 shafts, beginning 1, 6, 11, etc. If the warp is dressed 1 black, 1 gray, 1 white, three twills of different colors will be formed in the cloth, the first black, the second gray and the third white. The three twills are distinguished on the draft, Fig. 22, by three different marks.

7. GROUPED DRAFT

This style of drawing-in is often used for the production of striped, checked and other fancy effects for which two weaves are used, the threads of one

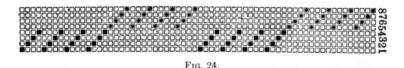

Fig. 24.

weave coming on one set of shafts, and those for another weave on a separate set. Fig. 24 shows a grouped draft on 8 shafts, 16 threads being drawn straight on each half (4) of the shafts to form the complete pattern.

8. DIVIDED DRAFT

This style of draft is much employed, both for double warp and double warp and filling fabrics. The face and back threads are drawn on separate groups of shafts. Fig. 25 shows a divided draft for which the warp is dressed 1 face, 1 back. The four front shafts carry the face warp; the other eight shafts, the back warp.

If the warp is dressed 2 face, 1 back, with the face and back each carried by five shafts, the draft will be as shown at Fig. 26, the face warp coming on the

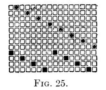

Fig. 25.

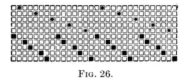

Fig. 26.

five front shafts, and the back warp on the five back shafts. The shafts carrying the face threads are usually hung next to the reed, as the weave for the back threads is generally easier than the face weave. If, however, the back warp is the weaker yarn, it should be drawn on the shafts nearest the reed.

9. COMBINATION DRAFT

The various methods of drawing-in are frequently combined in one draft for the production of weave patterns. The variety of these patterns is unlimited and it is, therefore, impossible to give a general idea of them from a few examples.

The nine classes of drawing-in drafts described above form the groundwork for all drafts. In the chapters which follow it will be shown how these methods of drawing-in should be employed. It must not be understood, however, that every possible weave pattern can be made with the examples given. Many variations, both in the number of the shafts and in the grouping of the threads, will be found necessary in practice.

Many requirements must be taken into consideration in deciding upon the number of shafts and the order of drawing-in for a particular pattern. Among them may be mentioned the following:

1. The drawing-in draft should be as simple as

possible in order to facilitate the work of the drawer-in and weaver.

2. The number of shafts should be as small as practicable. Closely set cloths require a larger number of shafts.

3. The distribution of the threads on the different shafts should be as uniform as possible.

FIG. 29.

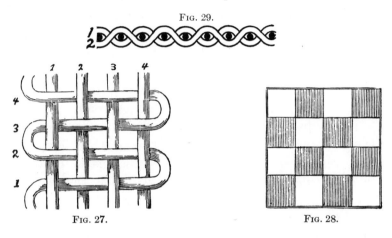

FIG. 27.

FIG. 28.

4. The draft should contribute to the formation of a clear shed.

5. Relieving the strain on the warp yarn. The threads with the least number of intersections in the weaves are drawn on the back shafts. The shafts carrying the least number of threads are placed as far back as possible. The best method of drawing-in for a particular fabric can be determined only by experience and a study of the various kinds of weaves.

DRAFTING WEAVES

The weave draft or plan for interlacing the warp and filling is drawn on cross section or "point" paper, which has upright and horizontal lines at regular intervals intersecting each other at right angles and forming small squares, each of which represents the intersection of a warp and a filling thread.

Each space between the upright lines represents a warp thread. Each space between the horizontal lines represents a filling thread. The marks or points in the small squares indicate whether the warp or filling comes to the face at that point.

Throughout this work a mark on a draft, unless otherwise stated, indicates that the warp is raised above the filling at that point of intersection. The exceptions to this rule are found when it is better to indicate the filling floats by marks, as for broché effects.

TWIST OF YARN

It is evident that a thread can be twisted in either one of two directions, Figs. 30 and 31. The simplest

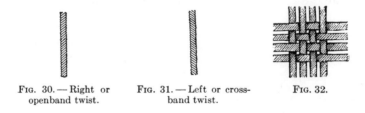

FIG. 30. — Right or openband twist.   FIG. 31. — Left or crossband twist.   FIG. 32.

method of designating the direction of the twist is by the terms "right" and "left." Unfortunately the practice in this respect is not uniform. The same direction is styled "right" by a part of the trade, and "left" by another part. The more common custom is to call the twist at Fig. 30 right-hand; that at Fig. 31, left-hand. This seems to be the almost exclusive practice on the continent of Europe and in the cotton and cordage industries elsewhere. This custom will be followed in this work when referring to "right" or "left" twist.

The twist at Fig. 30 is also called "openband"; that at Fig. 31, "crossband." This method of indicating the direction of twist was derived from the old method of spinning yarn by hand. The thread is twisted in one direction when the band running from the wheel to the spindle is straight or open, and in the opposite direction when the band is crossed. The spinner turns the wheel by hand so that the top of the wheel moves to the right or away from the spinning spindle.

SET OF THREADS

The set ordinarily should be as near as possible the same for both warp and filling. If the warp is set too close, it is impossible to drive the filling uniformly into the fabric, and the goods may show ribbed or grooved effects crossways of the cloth. This result also follows when the filling is materially heavier than the warp. On the other hand, if the warp is coarse with an open set, while the filling is fine with a close set, the streaks or ribs will run lengthways. Ribbed effects are sometimes made purposely by alternating coarse with fine yarn in warp or filling.

Broadcloth is woven very wide as the weight, handle and finish of the fabric is largely the result of shrinkage by fulling. The loom width of wool-dyed and piece-dyed broadcloths varies from 85 to 95 inches for 6/4 goods.

To facilitate the felting of broadcloths and improve the face it is better to make the warp and filling of opposite twist.

THE PLAIN WEAVE

This work will treat of the interlacing of two sets of threads intersecting each other at right angles. The yarn running lengthways of the cloth is the warp; that running crossways and carried by the shuttle is the filling or weft. The order in which the warp and filling interlace each other is the weave.

Weaves are divided into three primary classes:

1. Plain.
2. Twill.
3. Satin.

From these three classes are derived an innumerable number of other weaves, known as mixed or derivative

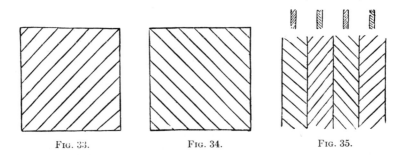

FIG. 33.   FIG. 34.   FIG. 35.

weaves. Where two or more weaves are used for the same fabric, the resulting weave is called a combination weave; and the fabric is called fancy, as distinguished from plain goods made with but one weave.

The plain weave is also called the taffeta weave in silk weaving, and is frequently designated as the "cotton" weave. It is balanced, that is, the warp and filling come to the face to the same extent. The weave covers two warp and two filling threads. At each pick each alternate warp thread is raised above the filling thread, the other warp threads being under the filling. This order is reversed at the next pick. For example, at one pick, warp threads 1, 3, 5, 7, etc., are raised and threads 2, 4, 6, 8, etc., are lowered in the shed. At the next pick, threads 1, 3, 5, 7, etc., are lowered and threads 2, 4, 6, 8, etc., are raised.

Fig. 27 shows the manner in which the threads are interlaced in a plain weave. Fig. 28 is a draft corresponding to Fig. 27, and in which the shaded squares indicate that the warp is raised above the filling. The blank squares indicate that. the warp lies under the filling. Fig. 29 is a longitudinal section of a cloth woven with a plain weave and showing two adjacent warp threads, marked 1 and 2. The black circles are the ends of the filling threads.

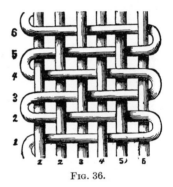

FIG. 36.

A warp set with 40 to 50 threads per inch can be woven easily with a plain weave on two shafts. A better shed can be obtained and the strain and friction on the yarn reduced by increasing the number of shafts as the set becomes closer. A general rule is to have not more than 20 to 25 threads per inch on each shaft.

Cloth woven with a plain weave has a finer appearance and harder feel, and is smoother, but possesses less elasticity than fabrics woven with other weaves.

Fig. 32 shows a plain weave in which the warp twist is right or openband twist, Fig. 30, and the filling twist is left or crossband twist, Fig. 31.

Tricot effects can be made with a plain weave by arranging the threads in both warp and filling, 1 right twist, 1 left twist. To keep the two kinds of yarn separate in weaving, one is usually tinted slightly with aniline so it can be distinguished from the other.

THE TWILL WEAVE

A characteristic of the simplest form of the twill weave is that the float of each filling thread is set one warp thread to the right or left of the float of the preceding filling thread. For example, the 3-shaft twill running to the right, Fig. 37, is formed by but one

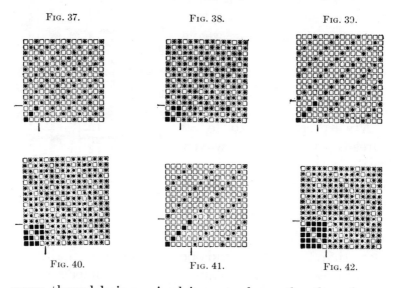

Fig. 37. Fig. 38. Fig. 39.

Fig. 40. Fig. 41. Fig. 42.

warp thread being raised in one place, the threads on both sides being lowered. The first warp thread is over the first filling thread, then the second warp thread is raised over the second filling thread, the third over the third, etc. Each filling float is one warp thread to the right of the float of the preceding pick. By this progressive order of interlacing the warp and filling, raised or ribbed lines are formed, running in a diagonal direction.

The slant of this twill line is influenced by the set

16

of the warp and filling. If the threads per inch in the warp are equal to the threads per inch in the filling, the line of this twill will be at an inclination of 45°. If the warp set is closer than that of the filling, the twill line will approach the perpendicular; if the filling set is closer, the twill line will approach the horizontal.

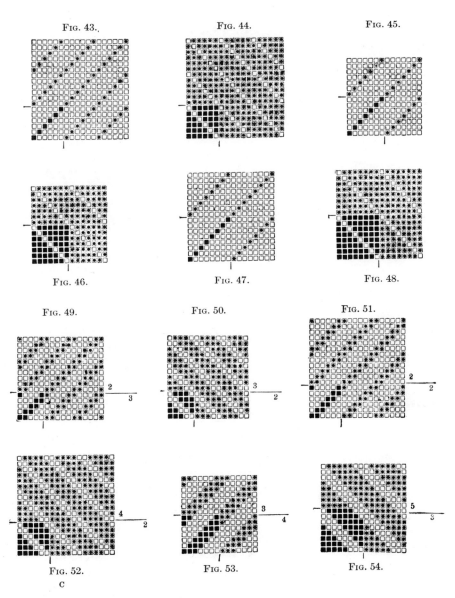

FIG. 43. FIG. 44. FIG. 45.

FIG. 46. FIG. 47. FIG. 48.

FIG. 49. FIG. 50. FIG. 51.

FIG. 52. FIG. 53. FIG. 54.

C

Twill weaves are classified as follows:

> 1. Uneven.
> 2. Balanced.

Uneven twills are those in which the warp comes to the surface to either a greater or less extent than does the filling. If the warp predominates on the face,

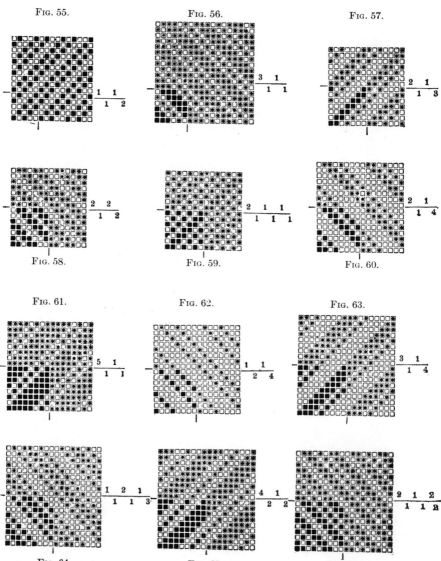

FIG. 55.

FIG. 56.

FIG. 57.

FIG. 58.

FIG. 59.

FIG. 60.

FIG. 61.

FIG. 62.

FIG. 63.

FIG. 64.

FIG. 65.

FIG. 66.

the weave is called a warp twill.   If the filling predominates, it is called a filling twill.

Fig. 36 shows the intersection of the warp and fill-

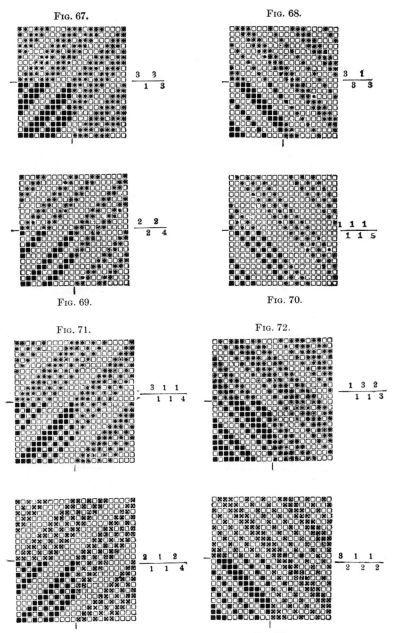

FIG. 67.

FIG. 68.

$$\frac{3\quad 3}{1\quad 3}$$

$$\frac{3\quad 1}{3\quad 3}$$

$$\frac{2\quad 2}{2\quad 4}$$

$$\frac{1\quad 1\quad 1}{1\quad 1\quad 5}$$

FIG. 69.

FIG. 70.

FIG. 71.

FIG. 72.

$$\frac{3\quad 1\quad 1}{1\quad 1\quad 4}$$

$$\frac{1\quad 3\quad 2}{1\quad 1\quad 3}$$

$$\frac{2\quad 1\quad 2}{1\quad 1\quad 4}$$

$$\frac{3\quad 1\quad 1}{2\quad 2\quad 2}$$

FIG. 73.

FIG. 74.

ing in the 3-leaf filling twill at Fig. 37. Other examples of uneven twills are shown at Figs. 37 to 82.

Balanced twills are those in which the warp and filling come to the surface to the same extent.

Fig. 83 shows the intersection of the warp and filling for the 4-leaf balanced twill at Fig. 84. Other examples of balanced twills are shown at Figs. 85 to 99.

All regular twills covering an uneven number of

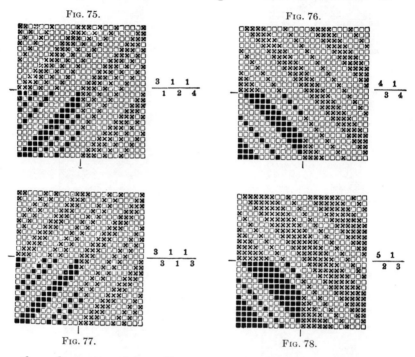

FIG. 75. FIG. 76.

FIG. 77. FIG. 78.

threads are necessarily uneven, and those with an even number may be made uneven. Regular balanced twills can be formed with only an even number of threads in the weave pattern.

The line of a twill can be run either to the right, Fig. 33, or to the left, Fig. 34. The directions of the twill and twist of the yarn have a great influence on the appearance of the cloth.

A twill to the right throws up and makes more prominent a left-twist warp; it throws down and makes less prominent a right-twist warp.

A twill to the left throws down and makes less prominent a left-twist warp; it throws up and makes more
prominent a right-twist warp.

A twill that runs to the right when the warp threads
are in a perpendicular position will be found to run to
the left when the cloth is turned one quarter around

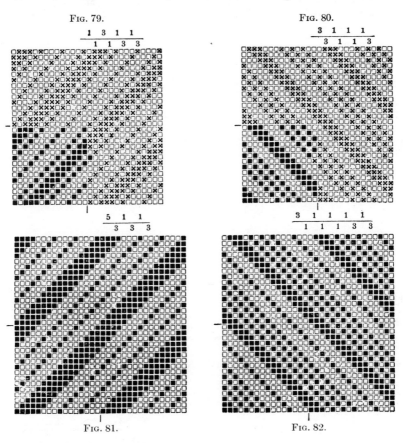

FIG. 79.   FIG. 80.

FIG. 81.   FIG. 82.

to bring the filling threads perpendicular. Thus a
twill runs in one direction in relation to the warp and
in the opposite direction in relation to the filling. It
is the custom, however, to designate the direction of
the twill as it runs when the warp is perpendicular.
In this sense of the term, a right twill will have the
opposite effect on the filling to that which it exerts on
the warp. Thus a twill to the right will throw a left-

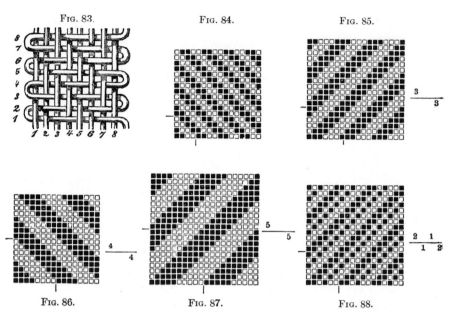

Fig. 83.   Fig. 84.   Fig. 85.

Fig. 86.   Fig. 87.   Fig. 88.

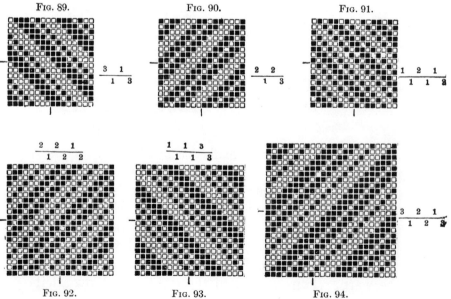

Fig. 89.   Fig. 90.   Fig. 91.

Fig. 92.   Fig. 93.   Fig. 94.

twist warp up and a left-twist filling down because the twill is in reality left hand in relation to the filling. The various combinations of twill and twist with their effects on the cloth are as follows:

	WARP TWILL	WARP TWIST	FILLING TWIST	EFFECT		
1.	Right	Left	Right	Warp thrown up	Filling thrown up	Twill not distinct
2.	Left	Left	Right	Warp thrown down	Filling thrown down	Twill not distinct
3.	Right	Right	Left	Warp thrown down	Filling thrown down	Twill not distinct
4.	Left	Right	Left	Warp thrown up	Filling thrown up	Twill not distinct
5.	Right	Left	Left	Warp thrown up	Filling thrown down	Warp twill distinct
6.	Left	Left	Left	Warp thrown down	Filling thrown up	Filling twill distinct
7.	Right	Right	Right	Warp thrown down	Filling thrown up	Filling twill distinct
8.	Left	Right	Right	Warp thrown up	Filling thrown down	Warp twill distinct

In practice these effects are greatly modified by the quality of the stock, amount of twist, size and character of the yarn, whether single or ply, set of the fabric and finish. As far as the mere direction of twill and twist is concerned, however, the effects are as indicated above.

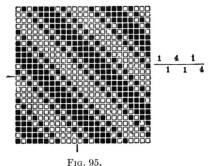

$$\frac{1 \quad 4 \quad 1}{1 \quad 1 \quad 4}$$

FIG. 95.

If the warp yarn is 2-ply, the two threads are ordinarily twisted to the left, Fig. 31. The twill should then run to the right, Fig. 33, to make the warp twill line more distinct.

If the twill in a pattern runs alternately to right and left and it is desired to have it equally distinct in both cases, right twist must be used for the warp yarn in the left twill; and left twist for the warp yarn in the right twill, Fig. 35.

The threads in a twill weave float farther than when a plain weave is used. The twilled cloth is more lustrous, softer, and more pliable than fabrics made with a plain weave.

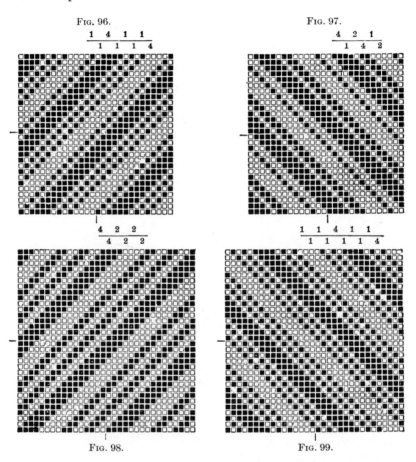

FIG. 96.

FIG. 97.

FIG. 98.

FIG. 99.

The number of shafts used for a twill is usually equal either to the number of threads in the twill weave or to a multiple of the latter number, making the drawing-in draft straight in either case.

Figs. 36 to 99 illustrate many of the different styles of twill weaves.

For wide twills the draft is often made out in the

following form: ^{4}—$_2$—^{1}—$_2$. This is equivalent to
4 up, 2 down, 1 up, 2 down, producing the 9-shaft
twill shown at Fig. 65. These illustrations, Figs. 36
to 99, give a good idea of the diversity of twill weaves
and the methods of combination. Thousands of similar twills can be drafted. With a large number of
shafts the number of twill weaves becomes practically
unlimited. Twills take the filling much more easily
than does the plain weave, and the set of twills can,
consequently, be closer, making the cloth thicker and
heavier.

THE SATIN WEAVE

The satin weave lacks the distinct diagonal line peculiar to the twill, and produces a smooth, lustrous face on the cloth. Adjacent threads in regular satin weaves must never be stitched on the same filling thread. The points or stitchers should be scattered as widely and as uniformly as possible. The farther they are removed from each other, the more indistinct do they become and the more attractive is the cloth.

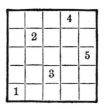

Fig. 100.

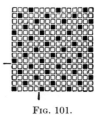

Fig. 101.

The particular draft to be used for a satin weave depends on the set of the fabric, the quality of the material and the size of the yarn. If the weave is too loose, the result will be a spongy fabric of poor appearance and handle and lacking durability. On the other hand if the weave is too tight for a closely set warp, it will be impossible to drive the required number of picks into the cloth, and the result will be a ribby appearance.

The satin weave requires at least five shafts and can be made on any number of shafts above five. Frequently the broken 4-leaf twill weave is called a satin, but strictly speaking it is a broken twill. The twill and satin weaves become merged on five shafts, the 5-shaft satin weave being sometimes called a satin

26

twill, because of the unavoidable twill line, as shown at Figs. 103 and 104. A twill effect is found in many satin weaves.

The following method is used for quickly determining the order of progression for the stitchers in satin weaves:

The number of threads in the pattern is divided into two unequal numbers, neither of which is divisible by the other (1 is not used). Beginning with

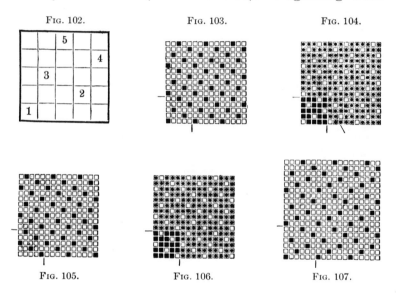

the first pick each filling thread is stitched a certain number of threads in advance of the stitcher on the preceding pick until every warp thread in the weave has been interlaced with the filling. This number of threads is called a rising number, being one of the two numbers into which the total number of threads was divided. It must be a number that will result in the stitching of every warp thread when used as a rising number.

For example, the number 5 is divisible into 2 and 3. Beginning with thread 1, Figs. 100 and 101, and progressing 2 warp threads to the right at each pick, the warp threads are stitched in the following order:

1, 3, 5, 2, 4. The first warp thread is stitched on the first pick; the third warp, on the second pick; the fifth warp, on the third pick; the second warp, on the fourth pick; and the fourth warp, on the fifth pick.

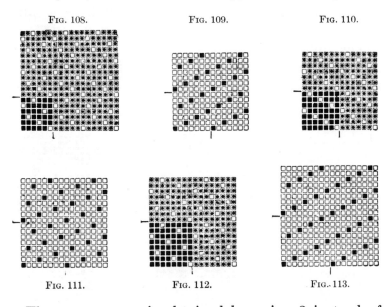

FIG. 108.　　　　　FIG. 109.　　　　　FIG. 110.

FIG. 111.　　　　　FIG. 112.　　　　　FIG. 113.

The same weave is obtained by using 3 instead of 2 as a rising number, the only difference being that the direction of the twill is reversed, Figs. 102 and 103. This is evident because the advance of 2 threads to

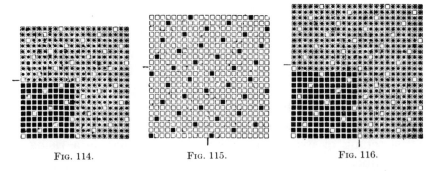

FIG. 114.　　　　　FIG. 115.　　　　　FIG. 116.

the right brings the stitcher 3 threads (the remaining number) to the left.

The order of progression can be carried upward instead of sideways. Thus in the 5-leaf satin weave,

Figs. 100 and 101, the first warp thread is stitched on the first pick; the second warp, on the fourth pick;

FIG. 117.　　　　　　　　　　　　FIG. 118.

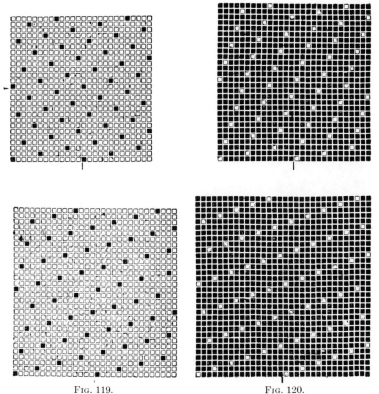

FIG. 119.　　　　　　　　　　　　FIG. 120.

the third warp, on the second pick; the fourth warp, on the fifth pick; the fifth warp, on the third pick, the rising number being 3. The first method, however, is the one generally used.

The 5-shaft satin is used for both warp and filling

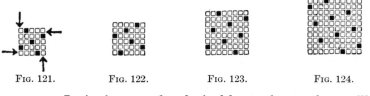

FIG. 121.　　　FIG. 122.　　　FIG. 123.　　　FIG. 124.

weaves. It is frequently desirable to have the twill line in a warp satin brought out distinctly. This can be done by regulating the direction of the twill in the cloth and of the twist in the yarn. For example, right-twist warp, with the weave at Fig. 104, will make a distinct twill running to the left, as indicated by the slanting line below the draft. If the cloth is woven with the back up, the weave draft should be as shown at Fig. 105.

If it is desired to have the face of the goods as smooth as possible; as in the case of doeskins, the weave shown at Fig. 106 should be used with right-twist warp in

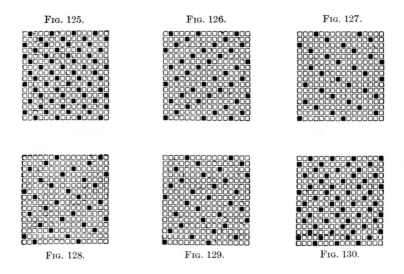

FIG. 125.   FIG. 126.   FIG. 127.

FIG. 128.   FIG. 129.   FIG. 130.

order to efface the twill effect as much as possible. If the cloth is woven face up with this weave, the weave draft, Fig. 101, should be used.

For the 6-shaft satin there is no regular order of progression, as 6 can be divided according to the rule only into 2 and 4, neither of which is suitable for a rising number. The following order is often used for the 6-shaft satin: 1, 3, 5, 2, 6, 4, Fig. 107; or 6, 4, 2, 5, 1, 3, Fig. 108.

For the 7-shaft satin there are two orders of interlacing available, as 7 can be divided into 2 and 5 or 3 and 4. With 2 for the riser the order is as follows: 1, 3, 5, 7, 2, 4, 6, Fig. 109. Fig. 110 shows a 7-shaft warp satin with weave reversed by using 5 as the rising number: 7, 5, 3, 1, 6, 4, 2.

For the 8-shaft satin there is but one order available, as 8 can be divided according to the rule only into 3 and 5. With 3 as a riser the order is as follows: 1, 4, 7, 2, 5, 8, 3, 6, Figs. 111 and 112.

For the 9-shaft satin the rising numbers are 2 and 7 or 4 and 5. With 2 as a rising number the order is 1, 3, 5, 7, 9, 2, 4, 6, 8, Fig. 113.

For the 10-shaft satin, the only division is into 3 and 7. With 3 the order is 1, 4, 7, 10, 3, 6, 9, 2, 5, 8, Fig. 114.

For the 11-shaft satin there are four divisions:

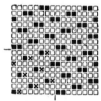
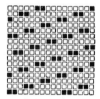
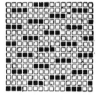

FIG. 131.   FIG. 132.   FIG. 133.

2 and 9, 3 and 8, 4 and 7, 5 and 6. With 4 the order is 1, 5, 9, 2, 6, 10, 3, 7, 11, 4, 8, Fig. 115.

For the 12-shaft satin there is one division only: 7 and 5. With 7 the order is 1, 8, 3, 10, 5, 12, 7, 2, 9, 4, 11, 6, Fig. 116.

For the 13-shaft satin there are five divisions: 2 and 11; 3 and 10; 4 and 9; 8 and 5; 7 and 6. With 5 the order is 1, 6, 11, 3, 8, 13, 5, 10, 2, 7, 12, 4, 9, Fig. 117.

For the 14-shaft satin there are two divisions: 3 and 11; 5 and 9. With 5 the order is 1, 6, 11, 2, 7, 12, 3, 8, 13, 4, 9, 14, 5, 10, Fig. 118.

For the 15-shaft satin there are three divisions: 2 and 13; 4 and 11; 7 and 8. With 4 the order is 1, 5, 9, 13, 2, 6, 10, 14, 3, 7, 11, 15, 4, 8, 12, Fig. 119.

For the 16-shaft satin there are three divisions: 3 and 13; 5 and 11; 7 and 9. With 3 the order is

1, 4, 7, 10, 13, 16, 3, 6, 9, 12, 15, 2, 5, 8, 11, 14, Fig. 120.

A satin weave with an even number of shafts can be drafted by using as the rising number one less than half the number of shafts if the half number is even, or two less if it is an odd number. For example, to draft an 8-shaft satin, 4 less 1, or 3, is used for the riser. For a 10-shaft satin, 5 less 2, or 3, is used for the riser. For a 12-shaft satin the riser is 6 less 1, or 5. There is no advantage gained by this method of finding the riser and the first one described is decidedly the better.

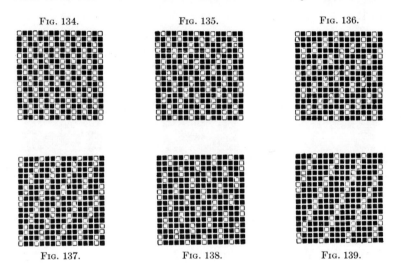

Fig. 134.   Fig. 135.   Fig. 136.

Fig. 137.   Fig. 138.   Fig. 139.

A third method of drafting satin weaves, which, however, is used but little, consists in writing the numbers of the shafts consecutively in columns. Following is the method applied to an 8-shaft satin, three numbers being placed in each column:

$$\frac{1 \quad 4 \quad 7 \quad 2 \quad 5 \quad 8 \quad 3 \quad 6}{\begin{array}{cccccccc} 2 & 5 & 8 & 3 & 6 & 1 & 4 & 7 \\ 3 & 6 & 1 & 4 & 7 & 2 & 5 & 8 \end{array}}$$

The upper horizontal row gives the order in which the stitchers are to be placed on successive filling threads. In the example given, the first warp thread is stitched by the first pick; the fourth warp by the second pick; the seventh warp by the third pick; the second warp by the fourth pick; and so on in progressive order until every warp thread in the pattern has been stitched, Fig. 111. The same order is given in each of the other two rows, the only difference being in the point of commencement. This method cannot be recommended in preference to the first one given, as it is necessary first to determine the order in which

FIG. 140.   FIG. 141.   FIG. 142.

FIG. 143.   FIG. 144.   FIG. 145.   FIG. 146.

the figures are to be placed under each other in a column.

The order of stitching satin weaves, already given, is shown in tabular form as follows:

ORDER OF STITCHING

Weave											
5-leaf	1	3	5	2	4						
6-leaf	1	3	5	2	6	4					
7-leaf	1	3	5	7	2	4	6				
8-leaf	1	4	7	2	5	8	3	6			
9-leaf	1	3	5	7	9	2	4	6	8		
10-leaf	1	4	7	10	3	6	9	2	5	8	
11-leaf	1	5	9	2	6	10	3	7	11	4	8
12-leaf	1	8	3	10	5	12	7	2	9	4	11	6

Weave

13-leaf	1	6 11	3	8 13	5 10	2	7 12	4 9	
14-leaf	1	6 11	2	7 12	3	8 13	4	9 14 5 10	
15-leaf	1	5	9 13	2	6 10 14	3	7 11 15 4	8 12	
16-leaf	1	4	7 10 13 16	3	6	9 12 15	2 5 8 11 14		

When goods are woven with warp and filling satin weaves combined to produce figured effects, the draft, to effect a good junction of the two weaves, must be arranged so that the last thread of the pattern is

FIG. 147.   FIG. 148. 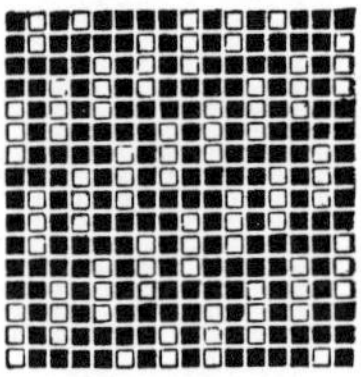   FIG. 149.

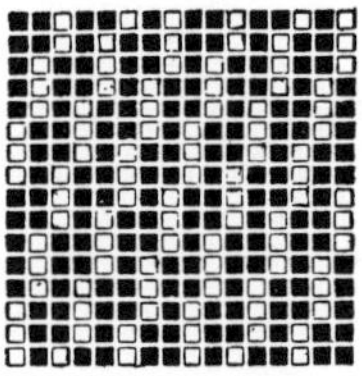

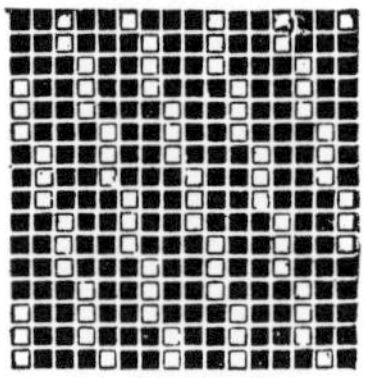

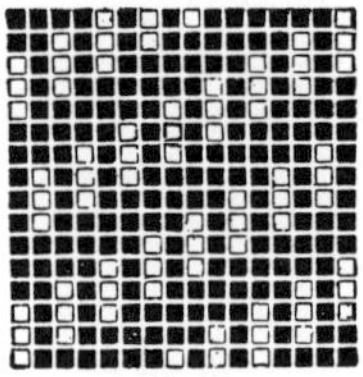

FIG. 150. 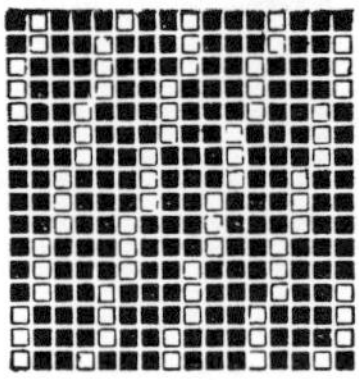   FIG. 151. 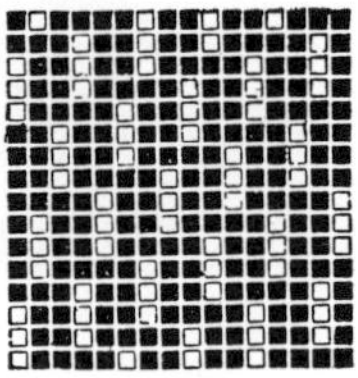   FIG. 152. 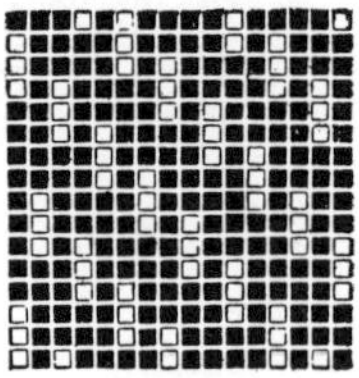   FIG. 153.

stitched in the reverse order from that of the first thread. Thus for a 5-shaft satin the order should be 4, 1, 3, 5, 2, Fig. 121; 6-shaft satin, 2, 6, 4, 1, 3, 5, Fig. 122; 8-shaft satin, 6, 1, 4, 7, 2, 5, 8, 3, Fig. 123; 10-shaft satin, 7, 10, 3, 6, 9, 2, 5, 8, 1, 4, Fig. 124.

With satin weaves either the warp or the filling color predominates on the face, the filling in warp satins and the warp in filling satins being hidden, providing the set of the fabric is close enough.

IRREGULAR SATINS

Satin weaves are often used in which the stitchers or risers are irregularly distributed, Figs. 125 to 130.

The weave pattern at Fig. 125 includes 4 warp threads and 12 picks; Fig. 126, 12 warp and 6 picks; Fig. 127, 8 warp and 16 picks; Figs. 128 and 129, 8 threads each way; Fig. 130, 13 threads each way.

DOUBLE-STITCHED SATINS

If two or more stitchers in a satin weave are brought together, one above the other, or side by side, or if stitchers are inserted regularly a short distance from the regular stitchers, the weave is called a double satin, and possesses certain characteristics and advantages.

In the single satin fabrics in which the warp lies on one side and the filling on the other, the stitchers are widely separated. This contributes to the smoothness and luster of the cloth, which is very desirable in

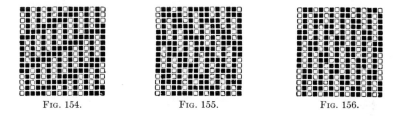

FIG. 154.   FIG. 155.   FIG. 156.

certain goods. It, however, lessens the durability of the fabric, and for this reason single satin weaves are better adapted for cloths in which luster and a smooth face are more desirable than wearing qualities. The durability of coatings and trouserings, which are subjected to hard wear, is increased by increasing the number of stitchers in the satin weave.

In double-filling satins 2, 3 or 4 risers are placed side by side on the same pick. In warp satins each warp thread is lowered below 2, 3 or 4 consecutive picks. In double-filling satins, stitchers are inserted at the right or left of each regular stitcher. In warp satins each warp thread is lowered below one or more picks before or after the single stitcher of the regular satin weave.

DOUBLE-STITCHED FILLING SATINS

Fig. 131 is an 8-shaft double-stitched filling satin. An extra stitcher, indicated by a cross in one repeat of the weave, is inserted at the right of each regular stitcher. Each pick floats over six warp threads, while the warp which floats on the back is woven 1—$_4$—1—$_2$. This weave is used for goods called "English leather."

Fig. 132 is a 10-shaft double-stitched filling satin.

Fig. 133 is an 11-shaft filling satin in which 2 risers have been placed at the side of the first one, bringing 3 risers together.

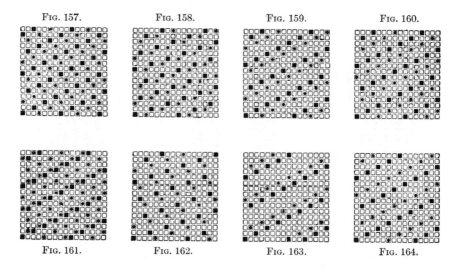

FIG. 157. FIG. 158. FIG. 159. FIG. 160.

FIG. 161. FIG. 162. FIG. 163. FIG. 164.

DOUBLE-STITCHED WARP SATINS

Figs. 134 to 145 are double-stitched warp satin weaves made by lowering each warp thread under two picks instead of one. The extra sinker is placed above the first, and stitches the filling thread, which floats on the back. These weaves are used chiefly for worsted cloths.

To reduce the number of shafts, a satin weave with half the number of shafts is sometimes woven with two picks in a shed. Fig. 146 shows a 5-shaft satin woven in this way, and serving as a substitute for the 10-shaft double satin, Fig. 141.

By lowering each warp thread for 3, 4 or 5 picks instead of 1 or 2, the filling, floating on the back, is stitched more closely and the twill is made more pronounced. In Figs. 147 to 153 each warp thread passes under 3 picks; in Figs. 154 and 155, under 4 picks in succession; in Fig. 156, under 5 picks.

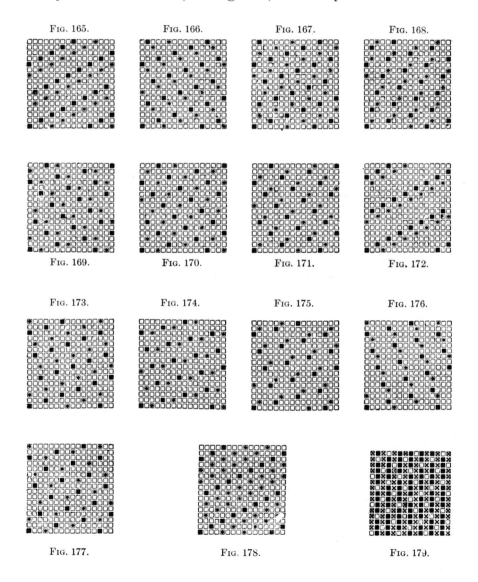

FIG. 165.   FIG. 166.   FIG. 167.   FIG. 168.

FIG. 169.   FIG. 170.   FIG. 171.   FIG. 172.

FIG. 173.   FIG. 174.   FIG. 175.   FIG. 176.

FIG. 177.   FIG. 178.   FIG. 179.

FILLING SATINS WITH EXTRA STITCHERS

Figs. 157 to 178 are satin weaves in which extra stitchers are placed regularly at short distances from the regular stitchers, and without regard to the tighter stitching of the warp threads floating on the back.

Attractive color effects can be produced with the satin weave. Fig. 179 shows a two-color diagonal obtained with a warp dressed 1 light, 1 dark and woven with a 5-leaf satin. Similar effects result from this warp pattern and a 7- or 9-leaf satin.

DERIVATIVE WEAVES

The great variety of elementary weaves has been shown by what has preceded. It will be readily understood that each elementary weave is capable of an almost endless number of modifications. An elementary weave becomes a modified or derivative weave when risers are added or removed. These alterations must, as a matter of course, be made uniformly throughout the weave pattern. Changes made in elementary weaves frequently necessitate alterations in the drawing-in draft.

There can be drawn on the same shaft only those threads that interlace the filling in exactly the same order from the start to the finish of the weave. The occurrence of but one place in the draft at which one warp thread is above a pick while another is below the same pick prevents the two threads from being drawn on the same shaft. Fig. 180 shows two threads which must be drawn on separate shafts owing to the variation in the order in which they interlace the two picks between the lines at the right, although in other respects they interlace the filling in the same way.

It is readily seen that in Fig. 181 thread 2 may be drawn on the same shaft with thread 1, thread 4 with 3, etc. In Fig. 182 threads 2 and 3 may be drawn on the same shaft with 1; threads 5 and 6 with 4, etc. In Fig. 183 threads 3, 5 and 7 may be drawn on the same shaft with 1; threads 4, 6 and 8 with 2; threads 11, 13 and 15 with 9; also threads 12, 14 and 16 with 10.

Figs. 181 and 182 each have but two different orders

of intersection of the warp with the filling, consequently either can be woven with two shafts. Fig. 183 has four different orders of intersection of warp with filling, and can, therefore, be woven on four shafts with the following drawing-in draft: 1, 2, 1, 2, 1, 2, 1, 2, 3, 4, 3, 4, 3, 4, 3, 4.

The drawing-in draft is placed either below the weave draft, as in Fig. 184, or above the weave draft, as in Fig. 516. On a line with the first warp thread a

FIG. 181.   FIG. 182.   FIG. 183.   FIG. 185.

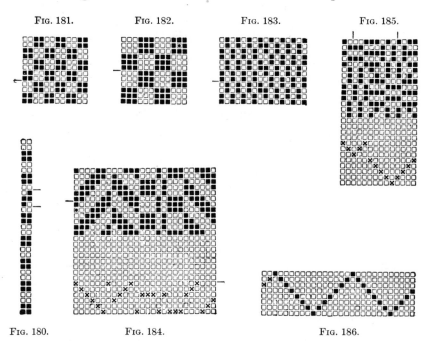

FIG. 180.   FIG. 184.   FIG. 186.

point is inserted in the first horizontal row of squares indicating that the first thread of the pattern is drawn on the first shaft. The second warp thread, if it interlaces the filling in a different order from the first, is then indicated by a point on the second horizontal row, which represents the second shaft. Each thread of the pattern is indicated successively, a new shaft being added when the thread intersects the filling in an order different from that of any of the preceding threads. If the intersection is the same as that of a preceding thread, a point is marked in the horizontal row already used for that thread.

When the entire weave pattern has thus been drafted, the drawing-in draft is complete, indicating the number of heddles on each shaft in one pattern. The 26 threads in the pattern at Fig. 184 are drawn on the shafts in the following order:

Thread 1 . . . . on shaft 1
Thread 2 . . . . on shaft 2
Thread 3 . . . . on shaft 3
Thread 4 . . . . on shaft 4
Thread 5 . . . . on shaft 5
Thread 6 . . . . on shaft 6
Thread 7 . . . . on shaft 1
Thread 8 . . . . on shaft 4
Thread 9 . . . . on shaft 3
Thread 10 . . . . on shaft 2
Thread 11 . . . . on shaft 1
Thread 12 . . . . on shaft 6
Thread 13 . . . . on shaft 3
Thread 14 . . . . on shaft 3
Thread 15 . . . . on shaft 3
Thread 16 . . . . on shaft 6
Thread 17 . . . . on shaft 3
Thread 18 . . . . on shaft 6
Thread 19 . . . . on shaft 6
Thread 20 . . . . on shaft 6
Thread 21 . . . . on shaft 3
Thread 22 . . . . on shaft 2
Thread 23 . . . . on shaft 1
Thread 24 . . . . on shaft 6
Thread 25 . . . . on shaft 5
Thread 26 . . . . on shaft 4

This pattern can be woven on six shafts. The drawing-in draft is clearly shown below the weave at Fig. 184.

The drawing-in draft should be arranged so as to be readily understood and to facilitate the work of drawing-in. For example, the weave at Fig. 185 can be drawn in as follows: 1, 2, 3, 2, 1, 4, 5, 6, 7, 8, 7, 6, 5, 4, as shown below the weave draft. The draft, however, is simpler and more easily followed by both drawer-in and weaver when the order of drawing-in on the first three shafts is reversed, making the drawing-in draft as shown at Fig. 186.

BASKET WEAVES

A basket weave is a plain weave in which two or more adjacent warp and filling threads are raised and lowered together as if they were a single thread. This produces a checkerboard effect, the size of the squares depending on the number of threads worked together.

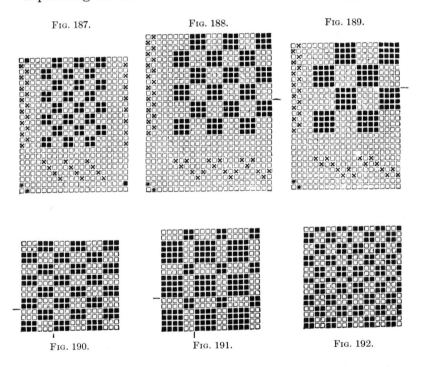

FIG. 187.   FIG. 188.   FIG. 189.

FIG. 190.   FIG. 191.   FIG. 192.

The warp threads working together side by side can be drawn on separate shafts or on the same shaft. It is sometimes found necessary when weaving coarse woolen goods to draw into one heddle the threads that work together side by side in order to prevent chafing of the warp yarn. It is also necessary at times to use a binding thread woven with a plain weave at each side of the cloth to prevent the filling from being drawn in when weaving.

Fig. 187 shows a 4-thread basket weave. A plain weave for the selvage is shown at the left. A plain shaft for an outside binding thread is shown at the right of the draft; the latter is used when the body of the selvage is woven with the basket weave used in the body of the cloth.

FIG. 193.   FIG. 194.   FIG. 195.

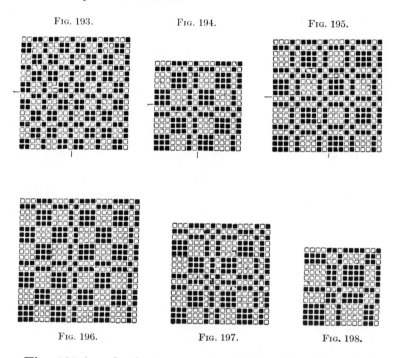

FIG. 196.   FIG. 197.   FIG. 198.

Fig. 188 is a basket weave in which three threads in warp and filling are woven together.

Fig. 189 is a basket weave in which four threads in warp and filling are woven together. Fig 187 is called a 4-leaf basket; Fig. 188, a 6-leaf; Fig. 189, an 8-leaf.

If the warp is set closer than the filling, a weave having more warp than filling threads working together is sometimes used in order to prevent the squares from becoming oblong. Fig. 190 shows such a weave having three threads woven together in the warp, and two threads in the filling. Squares of different sizes can be woven in the same pattern, as shown at Fig. 191, in which four threads working together alternate with two threads.

Pleasing effects can be produced by inserting single threads between the threads working together to form the basket, especially when the color of the single threads contrasts with the ground. Figs. 192 to 198 show various weaves of this kind.

RIB WEAVES

A rib weave is a modification of the plain weave. The simplest rib weave is made by weaving two, three or more threads together as one end next to several warp threads which are woven with a plain weave. The former, lying side by side and interlacing the filling like a single thread, rise above the surface of the adjoining threads that are woven plain, forming a ridge or rib running lengthways of the cloth.

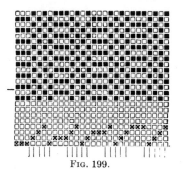

Fig. 199.

Fig. 200.

Fig. 203.

Fig. 205.

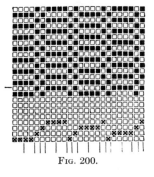

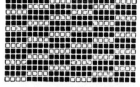

Fig. 201.

Fig. 202.

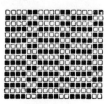

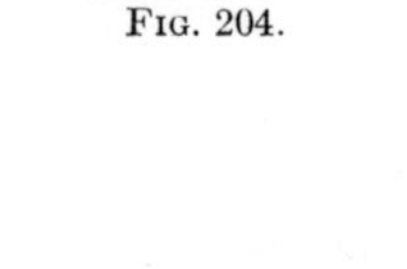

Fig. 204.

Fig. 206.   Fig. 207.   Fig. 208.

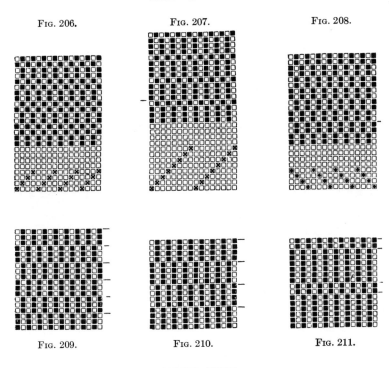

Fig. 209.   Fig. 210.   Fig. 211.

LONG RIBS

Ribs running lengthways of the cloth are called long ribs. Fig. 199 shows a pattern in which four warp threads woven plain alternate with three threads woven together as one end.

Fig. 214.

Generally the combined threads are drawn through the same dent in the reed, and can be drawn through the same heddle, if desired. If the combined threads are drawn through more than one dent in the reed, separate heddles must

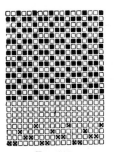

Fig. 212.

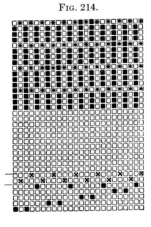

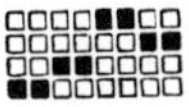

Fig. 213.

FIG. 216.

FIG. 215.

FIG. 218.

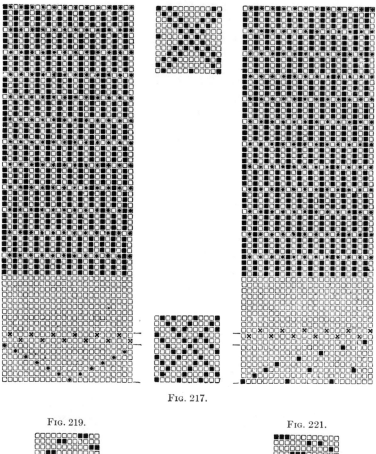

FIG. 217.

FIG. 219.

FIG. 221.

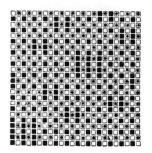

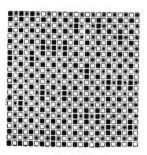

FIG. 220.

FIG. 222.

be used for the threads in each dent, otherwise the twisting of the threads in the heddle will result in their being broken by the reed. Fig. 200 shows four threads woven as one, alternating with two threads in a plain weave.

The lines below the drawing-in drafts at Figs. 199 and 200 indicate the order in which the warp is reeded.

Figs. 201 to 205 show weaves used for long ribs in fine worsted goods, in which, however, a very close

FIG. 223.

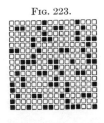

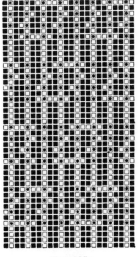

FIG. 224.

FIG. 225.

set is required in the filling. These are really plain weaves in which several warp threads are woven as one thread.

In the regular long-rib weaves, such as are shown at Figs. 201, 202 and 203, the warp is almost completely covered by the filling, hence the term "filling rib," applied to long-rib weaves.

CROSS RIBS

A second form of rib weave is found in the cross rib, which can be made by alternating a coarse filling thread with several fine threads in a plain weave.

In place of the coarse pick two or more single threads can be wound on a bobbin and woven as one. More or less twist is imparted to the threads in this way, however, giving an irregular appearance to the cloth. For this reason, when a very smooth face is desired, it is best

FIG. 227.

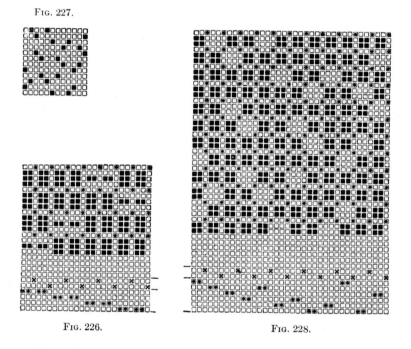

FIG. 226.   FIG. 228.

to have but one thread carried by the shuttle at each pick, inserting the desired number of picks in the same shed.

Fig. 206 shows two picks woven in every third shed; in Fig. 207 three picks are woven in every other shed.

A catch thread in the selvage is necessary with these weaves. The yarn forming the rib is sometimes made from cheaper material in order to reduce the cost of the goods.

Cross ribs are also made with the weaves shown at Figs. 208 to 211, in which two, three, four or six picks are woven in a shed. The lines of separation between the ribs are indicated by the lines at the side of draft.

In the regular cross-rib weaves, as shown at Figs. 207 to 211, the filling is almost completely covered

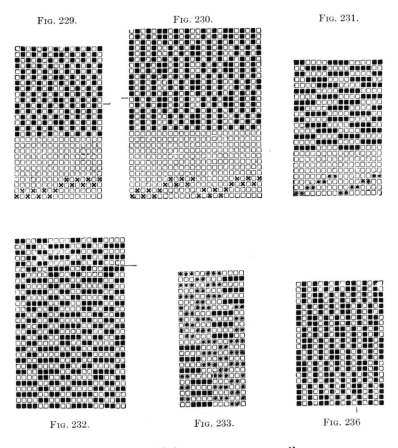

FIG. 229.   FIG. 230.   FIG. 231.

FIG. 232.   FIG. 233.   FIG. 236

by the warp, for which reason cross-rib weaves are sometimes called warp ribs.

The third class of rib weaves is the full rib for which fine and coarse yarn is used in both warp and filling. Goods woven with these weaves are used chiefly for upholstery, vestings, etc., and are frequently made of wool and cotton or silk and cotton. They are generally woven with 2 warp threads working together, al-

ternating with a single thread, Fig. 212. For a wool
and cotton fabric two threads of wool twist working
together alternate with one thread of fine cotton twist.
Two shafts only are required, but where the set is from
60 to 90 threads per inch four shafts are used.

The wool and silk warp should, if possible, be

FIG. 234.

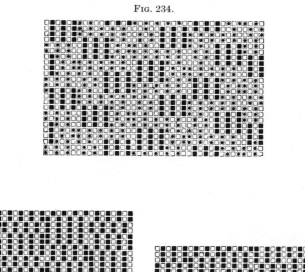

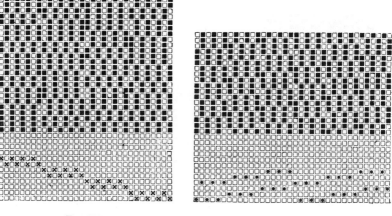

FIG. 235.   FIG. 237.

drawn on the front shafts to give a clear shed, the
cotton warp coming on the back shafts. When the
wool warp threads are raised, a coarse cotton pick is
inserted; the latter is thus covered by the wool
warp and is visible only on the back of the cloth.
When the cotton warp is raised, a single cotton pick of
the same kind of yarn is inserted. The fine filling is

woven when the wool warp is down, but is not prominent on the face, owing to its fineness.

In silk ribs the rib pick is also a coarse cotton thread, the other pick being a fine silk thread. The coarse cotton filling, which is hidden by the close-set warp, gives the cloth a better feel and reduces the cost.

The coarse rib warp and the fine warp must be woven from separate beams, as the former takes up

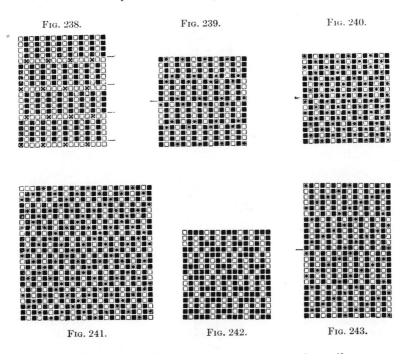

FIG. 238.   FIG. 239.   FIG. 240.

FIG. 241.   FIG. 242.   FIG. 243.

more rapidly in weaving. To make the rib more prominent, the fine division warp thread should be woven tight, and the coarse rib warp woven slack, the latter being weighted so that it will yield slightly when the lay beats in the coarse filling. On plain looms without the drop box these full ribs can be made by weaving two or more picks in a shed in place of the coarse rib pick, using but one kind of yarn in the filling. A weave for this method is shown at Fig. 207.

FIGURED RIBS

Figured effects are easily obtained on rib weaves by raising warp threads above the filling tie thread at certain places. This converts two warp floats into one, the warp thread being raised successively over a set of rib picks, a division pick and a second set of rib picks, as in threads 1 and 3, Fig. 214. In drafting figured ribs it is necessary first to select a motif for

FIG. 244.   FIG. 245.   FIG. 246.

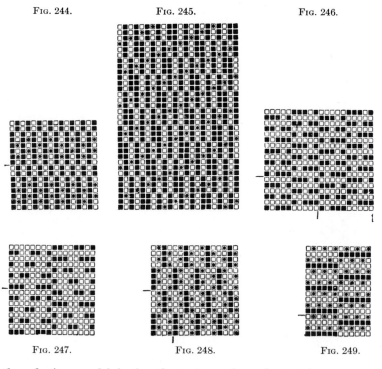

FIG. 247.   FIG. 248.   FIG. 249.

the design, which is then transferred to the weave draft. Figs. 213 to 225 are examples of figured ribs and motifs.

Fig. 213 . . . . motif for Fig. 214
Fig. 215 . . . . motif for Fig. 216
Fig. 217 . . . . motif for Fig. 218
Fig. 219 . . . . motif for Fig. 220
Fig. 221 . . . . motif for Fig. 222
Fig. 223 . . . . motif for Fig. 224

In Figs. 220, 222 and 224 the rib warp threads, drawn on one heddle, are, like the rib picks, represented as one thread, as is customary for this class of goods.

Another method of forming fancy ribs is to lower two or more adjacent rib warp threads to the back of the cloth under certain picks, each of which is thus brought to the face. This method is shown at Figs. 226 and 228. Fig. 213 is the motif for Fig. 226; Fig. 227, the motif for Fig. 228.

IRREGULAR RIBS

These are formed by offsetting the rib line at intervals. At the changing point the float forming the rib is raised slightly above the float of the preceding

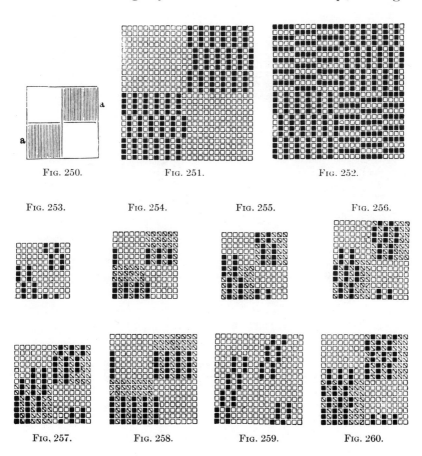

FIG. 250. FIG. 251. FIG. 252.

FIG. 253. FIG. 254. FIG. 255. FIG. 256.

FIG. 257. FIG. 258. FIG. 259. FIG. 260.

thread, and the rib is then continued on the new line until the pattern requires a change.

In Fig. 229 the rib is offset for one pick at the 1st and 9th warp threads. Each group with a regular rib includes eight warp threads.

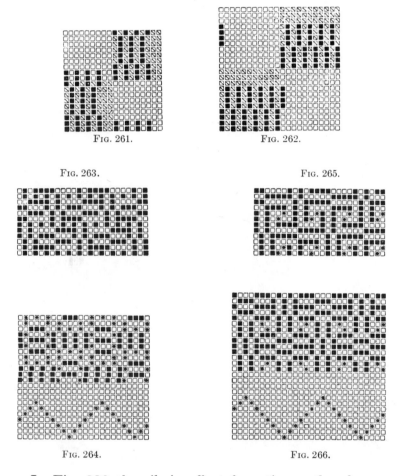

Fig. 261.

Fig. 262.

Fig. 263.

Fig. 265.

Fig. 264.

Fig. 266.

In Fig. 230 the rib is offset four times, the change being for three picks each time. Each group with a regular rib includes six threads.

Fig. 231 is a filling rib offset two threads every four picks.

Fig. 232 shows a ^{2}—$_2$ filling rib with ^{4}—$_4$ groups arranged in 5-leaf satin order. Pleasing effects are obtained by combining floats of different lengths in irregular ribs.

Fig. 233 shows the weave ^{4}—$_3$—^{2}—$_3$, in the filling; Fig. 234 shows the same order in the warp.

Fig. 235 shows ^{5}—$_5$ groups arranged in 4-leaf broken twill order. Fig. 236 shows a diagonal effect produced by offsetting the ribs.

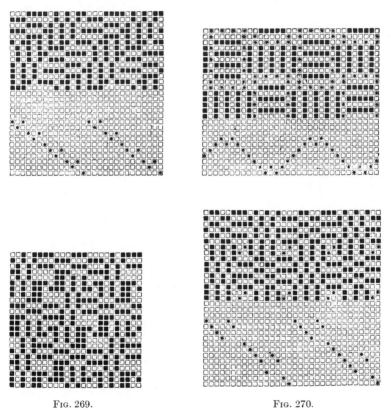

Fig. 267.　　　　　　　Fig. 268.

Fig. 269.　　　　　　　Fig. 270.

Fig. 237 shows a fancy rib weave in which the rib float is raised one pick at intervals of six warp threads; the pattern covers thirty-six warp and six filling threads.

In weaving cloth made of coarse carded woolen warp yarn with a rib weave it is often difficult to obtain a clear shed. Sometimes to facilitate the forming of a shed only one half of the shafts are changed at a time. This necessitates forming two sheds when the threads are changed. At the first of these two sheds half the warp threads that are to be raised are lifted and half of those to be lowered are dropped and no pick is inserted. At the next shed the remaining threads are lifted and dropped to complete the change and a pick is woven, as shown in Fig. 238. This requires a special attachment for the loom. A method of avoiding its use is by the weave shown at Fig. 239, in which half the threads to be raised are lifted on the preceding

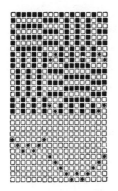

Fig. 271.

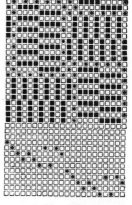

Fig. 272.

pick, and half of those to be lowered are raised for one pick more. This, however, causes the break in the rib to be less sharp than with the regular rib weave.

STITCHED RIBS

To increase the solidity and durability of rib fabrics the warp threads are often interlaced with the filling where the warp floats on the back. This makes the weave tighter and increases the solidity of the cloth.

Fig. 240 is a warp rib stitched with a plain weave. This style of weave is much used for ladies' dress goods.

Figs. 241 and 242 show 6-and-8-pick warp rib weaves stitched to produce a figured effect.

Fig. 243 is a 12-pick rib weave in which the threads floating on the back are stitched in the form of a broken twill, ^{1}—$_3$.

Fig. 244 is an 8-pick rib weave with the threads on the back stitched plain. This weave is often used for dress goods with the warp dressed 1 light, 1 dark.

Fig. 245 shows an irregular rib weave with the threads on the back stitched in diagonal form.

Stitched filling ribs are shown at Figs. 246 and 247.

FIG. 273.   FIG. 274.   FIG. 275.

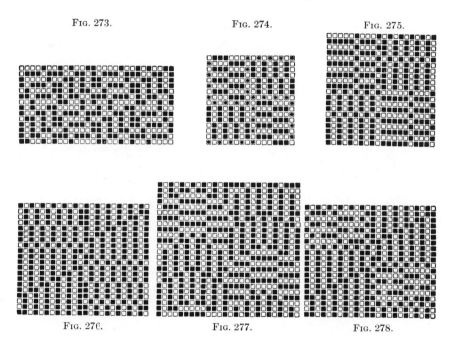

FIG. 276.   FIG. 277.   FIG. 278.

The filling of Fig. 246 is woven ^{5}—$_5$ and the floats on the back are stitched on each rib in a straight twill form. The filling at Fig. 247 is woven ^{8}—$_8$ and stitched in a reversed twill order.

Ribs are sometimes produced with special threads which are not to show on either side of the cloth, and which, therefore, must be very fine yarn. Fig. 248 shows a weave with special warp threads; Fig. 249, a weave with special filling threads. In both weaves the fine threads are woven with a plain weave.

COMBINATION RIBS

Under this head are included all rib weaves in which warp and filling ribs are combined to form a figure. The simplest order of combination is that of a plain weave. The space to be occupied by the pattern is divided into four equal parts, as shown at Fig. 250. The shaded parts are then filled in with the warp rib, Fig. 251, and the draft is completed by filling in the

FIG. 279.　　　　FIG. 280.　　　　FIG. 281.

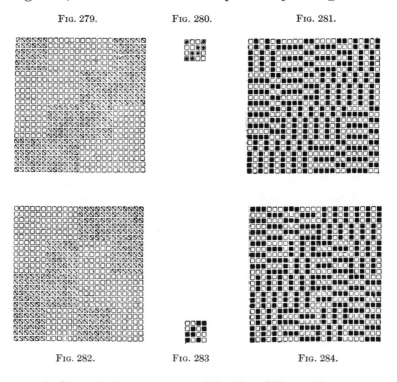

FIG. 282.　　　　FIG. 283　　　　FIG. 284.

remainder of the square with the filling rib weave, Fig. 252.

If the motif selected is larger than the allotted space, the figure must be extended into the adjoining space. Several cases of this kind are shown at Figs. 253 to 262.

These patterns, Figs. 253 to 262, are developed in Figs. 263 to 272, in which the relative position of the warp and filling ribs is readily seen. The threads in the spaces not covered by the motif are woven with a plain weave and serve to separate the warp and filling ribs.

Following are the motifs and corresponding weaves:

MOTIF	WEAVE
Fig. 253, 10 threads	Fig. 263, 10 shafts, 10 picks
Fig. 254, 12 threads	Fig. 264, 7 shafts, 12 picks
Fig. 255, 12 threads	Fig. 265, 12 shafts, 12 picks
Fig. 256, 14 threads	Fig. 266, 8 shafts, 14 picks
Fig. 257, 14 threads	Fig. 267, 10 shafts, 14 picks
Fig. 258, 16 threads	Fig. 268, 7 shafts, 16 picks
Fig. 259, 16 threads	Fig. 269, 16 shafts, 16 picks
Fig. 260, 16 threads	Fig. 270, 12 shafts, 16 picks
Fig. 261, 18 threads	Fig. 271, 8 shafts, 18 picks
Fig. 262, 22 threads	Fig. 272, 10 shafts, 22 picks

FIG. 286.

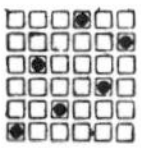

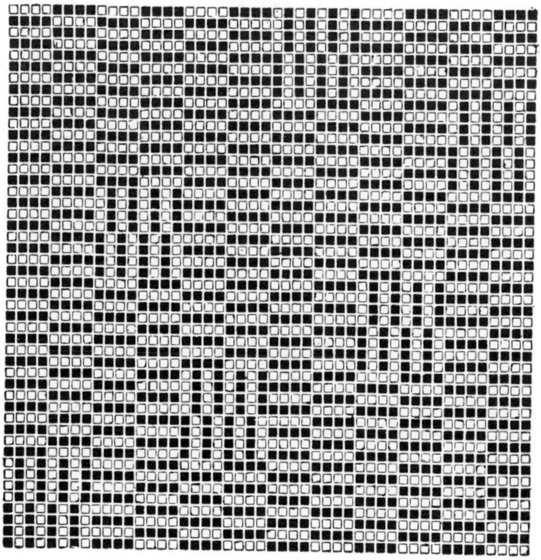

FIG. 285.

Several examples of irregular ribs with a plain weave for the motif are shown at Figs. 273 to 278.

If a 4-leaf twill is selected for the motif, the draft is first divided each way into four parts and shaded to develop the motif. Fig. 279 shows a 24 end pattern shaded in accordance with a balanced 4-leaf ^{2}—$_2$ twill, Fig. 280. The warp and filling rib weaves are next inserted, being transposed to conform to the

FIG. 287.   FIG. 288.   FIG. 289.

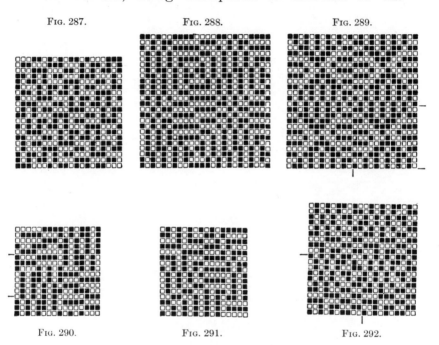

FIG. 290.   FIG. 291.   FIG. 292.

pattern. Fig. 281 shows the pattern at Fig. 279, developed by transposing ^{4}—$_2$ warp and filling rib weaves.

Figs. 282 and 284 are respectively outline and weave drafts derived from the 4-leaf broken ^{2}—$_2$ twill motif, Fig. 283. This motif is developed on 24 threads by transposing warp and filling rib ^{3}—$_3$ weaves. In this case the draft is divided into 4 parts to correspond with the 4-leaf twill motif.

Fig. 285 shows a weave draft of 48 threads on which has been developed the 6-leaf satin motif, Fig. 286,

Fig. 293.

Fig. 294

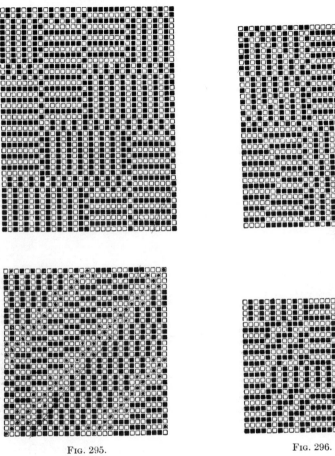

Fig. 295.

Fig. 296.

Fig. 297.

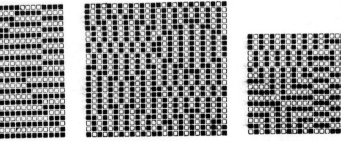

Fig. 298.

Fig. 299.

by transposing ^{4}—$_4$ warp and filling ribs. The draft is divided each way into six parts of 8 threads each.

From the examples already given it is evident that any desired motif can easily be developed with rib weaves. Additional examples are shown at Figs. 287 to 299.

Fig. 287 . . . . 20 × 20
Fig. 288 . . . . 14 × 14
Fig. 289 . . . . 12 × 12
Fig. 290 . . . . 16 × 16
Fig. 291 . . . . 16 × 16
Fig. 292 . . . . 10 × 10
Fig. 293 . . . . 32 × 40
Fig. 294 . . . . 24 × 40
Fig. 295 . . . . 30 × 30
Fig. 296 . . . . 24 × 24
Fig. 297 . . . . 24 × 16
Fig. 298 . . . . 26 × 16
Fig. 299 . . . . 18 × 18

STEEP TWILLS

A peculiar form of twill, known as a steep twill, is obtained when the warp float of each thread rises two or more picks instead of one pick above the float of the preceding thread. A steep twill can be made by drafting in succession the alternate threads of a regular twill. For example, Fig. 301 shows a steep twill

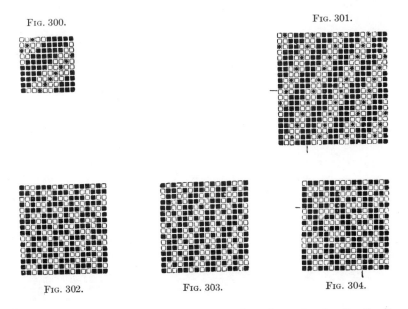

FIG. 300.

FIG. 301.

FIG. 302.

FIG. 303.

FIG. 304.

obtained by drafting successively threads 1, 3, 5, 7 and 9 of the 10-leaf twill, Fig. 300. This is equivalent to removing every other thread from the regular twill.

Raising the warp float two threads higher at each warp thread brings the twill line nearer the perpendicular. On the other hand, if the filling floats are set two or more threads to the right or left at each pick, the twill line is brought nearer to the horizontal, forming what is styled a flat twill. The steep twill is the more popular form.

The twill lines in steep twills are closer to each other,

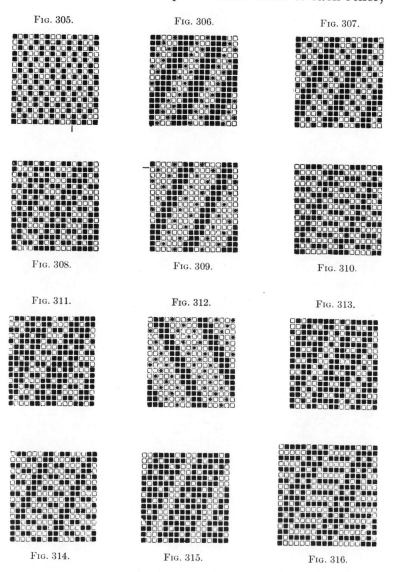

Fig. 305. Fig. 306. Fig. 307.

Fig. 308. Fig. 309. Fig. 310.

Fig. 311. Fig. 312. Fig. 313.

Fig. 314. Fig. 315. Fig. 316.

but frequently, owing to the filling floats on the back, are more prominent than in regular twill weaves.

If a regular twill having an even number of shafts, say 10, 12, 14, 16, etc., is selected for the construction of a steep twill, only one half of the threads are used, and consequently, only one half as many shafts are needed for the steep twill weave.

If, however, the regular twill has an uneven number of shafts, the resulting steep twill will have the same

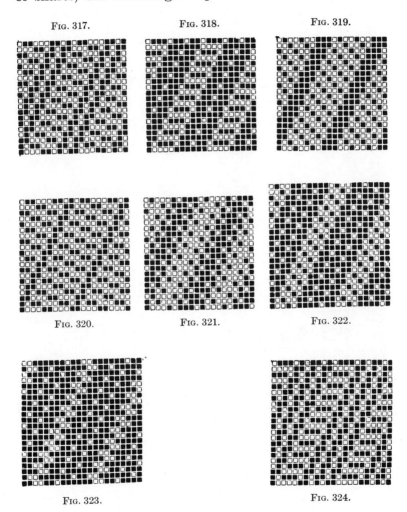

Fig. 317.   Fig. 318.   Fig. 319.

Fig. 320.   Fig. 321.   Fig. 322.

Fig. 323.   Fig. 324.

number of threads or shafts in the pattern as there are in the ground weave.

Figs. 302 to 353 show a number of different forms of steep twills in which the warp float rises two picks at each thread:

FIG. 325.　　　　FIG. 326.　　　　FIG. 327.　　　　FIG. 328.

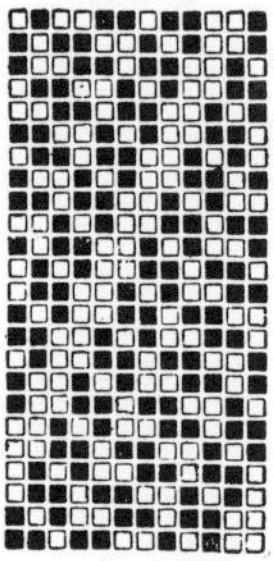

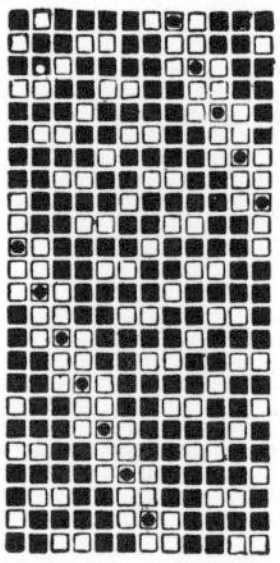

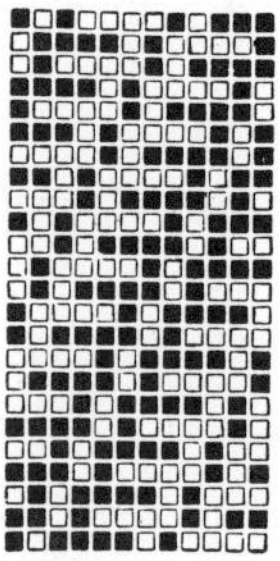

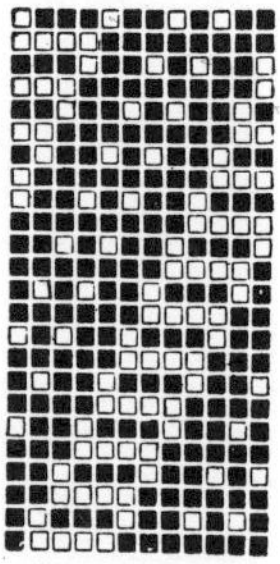

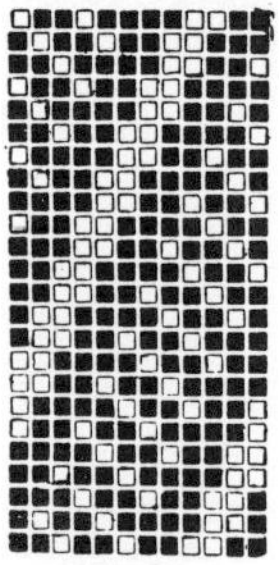

FIG. 329.　　　　FIG. 330.　　　　FIG. 331.　　　　FIG. 332.

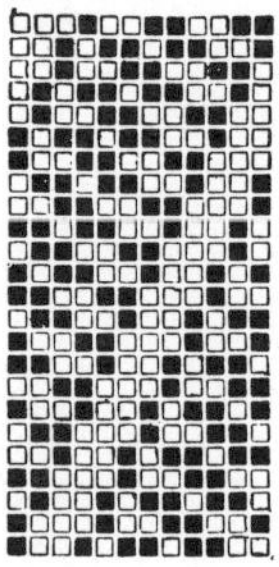

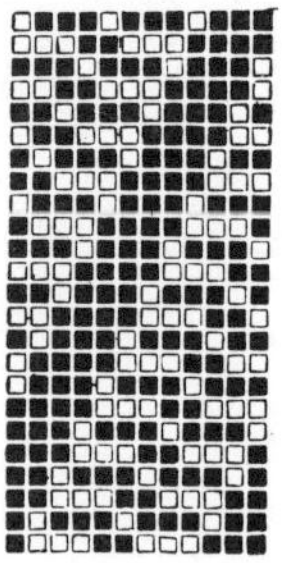

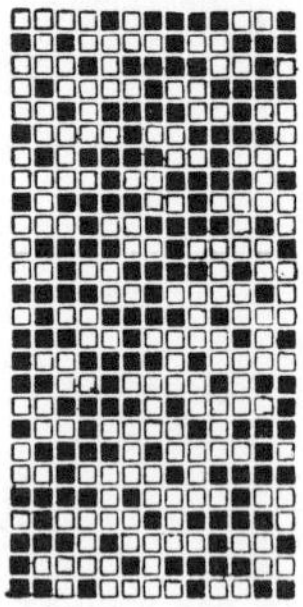

Fig. 319 . . . . 10 × 20
Fig. 320 . . . . 10 × 20
Fig. 321 . . . . 10 × 20
Fig. 322 . . . . 11 × 22
Fig. 323 . . . . 11 × 22
Fig. 324 . . . . 11 × 22

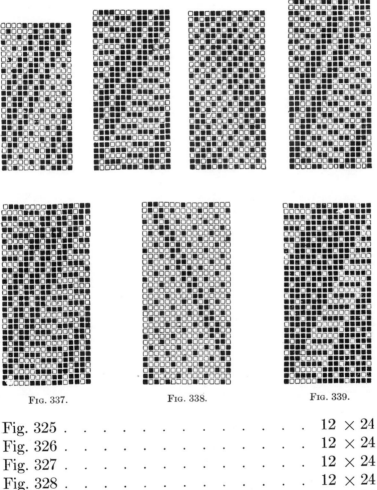

FIG. 333.
FIG. 334.
FIG. 335.
FIG. 336.

FIG. 337.

FIG. 338.

FIG. 339.

Fig. 325 . . . . 12 × 24
Fig. 326 . . . . 12 × 24
Fig. 327 . . . . 12 × 24
Fig. 328 . . . . 12 × 24
Fig. 329 . . . . 12 × 24
Fig. 330 . . . . 12 × 24
Fig. 331 . . . . 12 × 24
Fig. 332 . . . . 13 × 26

Fig. 333 . . . . 13 × 26
Fig. 334 . . . . 14 × 28
Fig. 335 . . . . 14 × 28
Fig. 336 . . . . 15 × 30
Fig. 337 . . . . 16 × 32

FIG. 340.

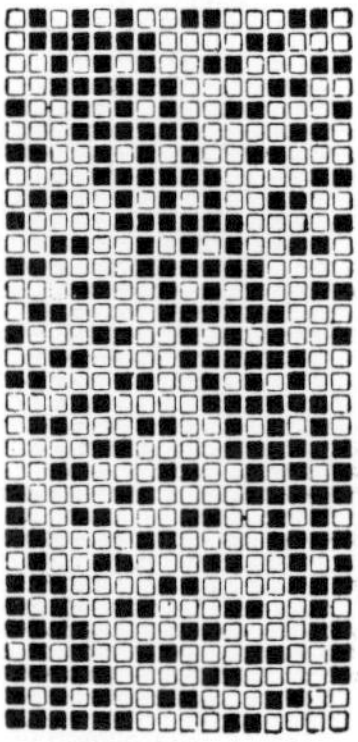

FIG. 341.

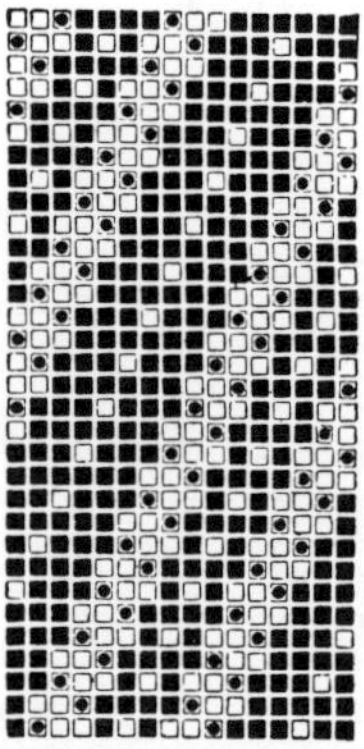

FIG. 342.

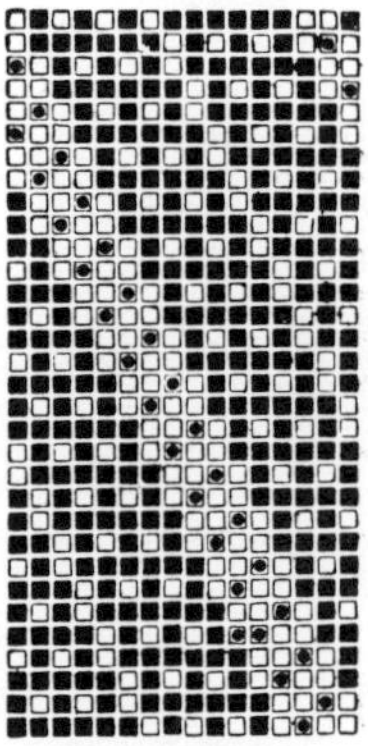

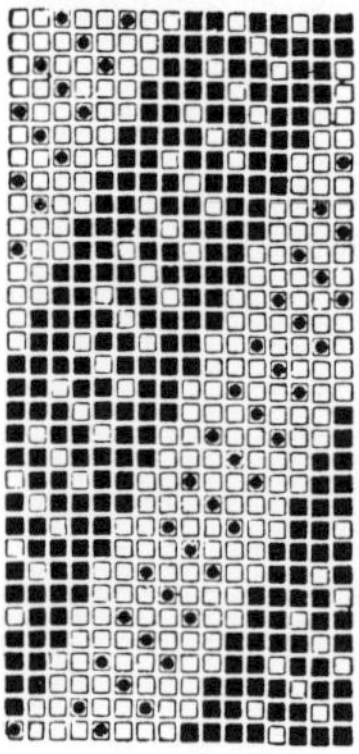

FIG. 343.

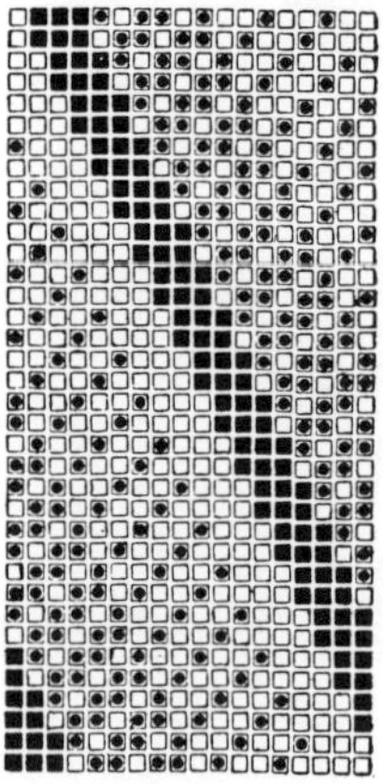

FIG. 344.

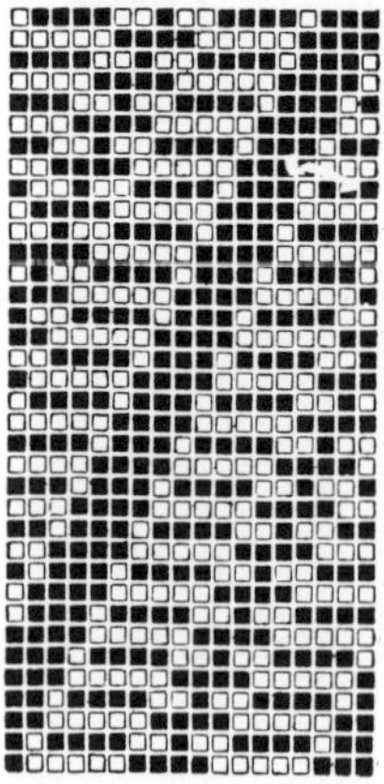

FIG. 345.

Fig. 338 . . . . 16 × 32
Fig. 339 . . . . 16 × 32
Fig. 340 . . . . 16 × 32
Fig. 341 . . . . 16 × 32
Fig. 342 . . . . 16 × 32
Fig. 343 . . . . 16 × 32

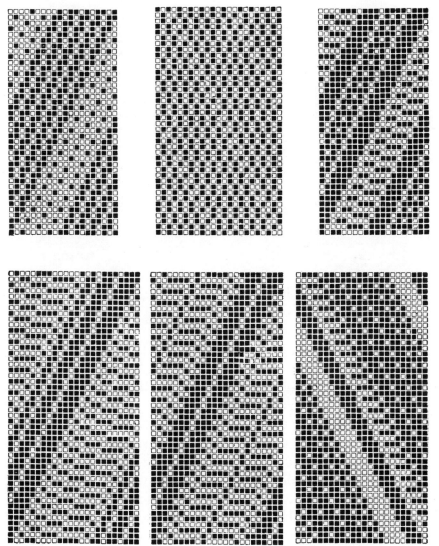

FIG. 346. FIG. 347. FIG. 348.

FIG. 349. FIG. 350. FIG. 351.

Figs. 302 to 353 show the effects obtained in steep twills made with different ground weaves. The

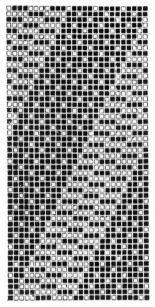

FIG. 352.

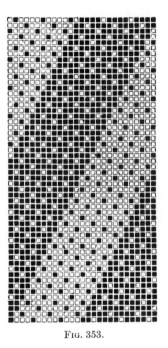

FIG. 353.

changes should be clearly understood when drafting new diagonals.

The examples given show that in drafting a steep twill with the float rising two picks:

1. Filling ribs are obtained when the warp in the ground twill is stitched plain, ^{1}—$_1$, several times in succession, Figs. 310, 316, 318, 324, 328, 339 and 345.

2. The filling ribs are offset when two risers or two sinkers are inserted after the plain stitchers, Figs. 334, 337, 348, 349, 350 and 352.

3. A 45° twill running in the opposite direction is obtained by interlacing the warp in ^{2}—$_1$ or ^{1}—$_2$ order,

Figs. 307, 312, 319, 322, 325, 329, 330, 332, 335, 343 and 344.

4. A ^{3}—$_1$ order gives a plain weave with a float on the back on alternate picks, Figs. 316, 328, 340, 342 and 348.

5. A ^{4}—$_1$ order results in a 5-shaft satin, Figs. 311, 315, 321, 322, 323, 338, 339, 352 and 353.

6. From a ^{3}—$_2$ order is obtained a 5-shaft double-warp satin, Figs. 317, 324 and 346.

7. From a ^{1}—$_1$—^{1}—$_2$ order is derived a 5-shaft double-filling satin, Figs. 314, 317, 320, 336 and 340.

8. A ^{5}—$_1$ order gives a 3-shaft twill on alternate picks, the intermediate threads floating on the back, Figs. 318 and 351.

FIG. 354.

FIG. 356.

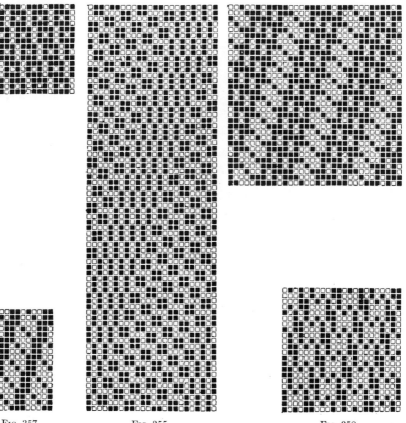

FIG. 357

FIG. 355.

FIG. 358.

In Figs. 354 to 362 the warp float rises either three or four picks at each thread.

Fig. 354 . . . . 4 × 12
Fig. 355 . . . . 24 × 72
Fig. 356 . . . . 32 × 32
Fig. 357 . . . . 6 × 18
Fig. 358 . . . . 11 × 22
Fig. 359 . . . . 15 × 45
Fig. 360 . . . . 13 × 39
Fig. 361 . . . . 8 × 32
Fig. 362 . . . . 16 × 48

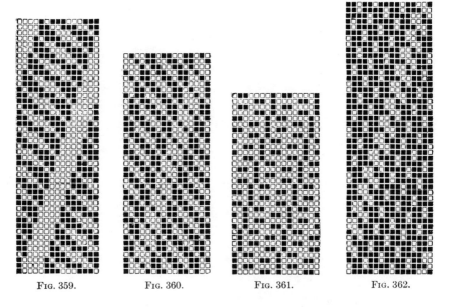

FIG. 359.　　　FIG. 360.　　　FIG. 361.　　　FIG. 362.

A steep twill with the warp floats rising three picks at each thread requires only one third as many shafts as are required for a base weave in which the number of shafts is divisible by 3.

Fig. 359, for example, shows a 15-shaft steep twill derived from one covering 45 threads; Fig. 360, a 13-shaft steep twill derived from a 39-shaft twill; Fig. 362, a 16-shaft steep twill derived from a 48-shaft twill.

If the original number of shafts is not divisible by 3, the resulting steep twill will require the same number of shafts as the base weave, as shown at Fig. 356, both base weave and steep twill being 32 shaft.

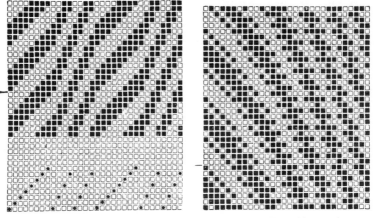

FIG. 363. FIG. 364.

FIG. 365.

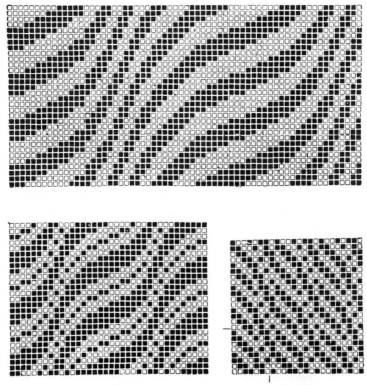

FIG. 366. FIG. 367.

UNDULATING TWILLS

Undulating twills are formed by an irregular off-setting of the warp and filling floats; for example, by moving the float 3 threads at one place and 4 threads at another, either vertically or horizontally.

The same effect can be obtained with a regular twill weave by combining groups of fine and coarse

FIG. 368.

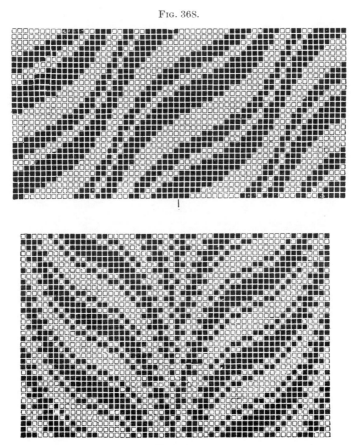

FIG. 369.

yarns, reeding them irregularly; for example, the fine threads 4 in a dent, the coarse threads 3 in a dent.

Figs. 363 to 379 are undulating effects produced by the weave.

Fig. 363 . . . . 16 ends, 8 picks
Fig. 364 . . . . 30 ends, 12 picks
Fig. 365 . . . . 40 ends, 8 picks

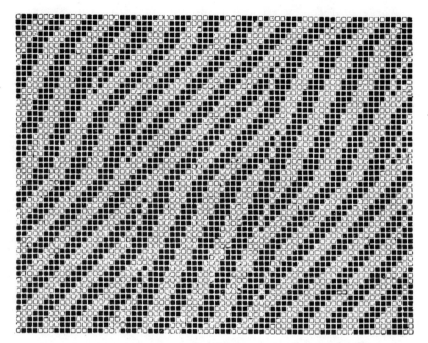

Fig. 370.

Fig. 366 . . . . 18 ends, 9 picks
Fig. 367 . . . . 8 ends, 8 picks
Fig. 368 . . . . 30 ends, 15 picks
Fig. 369 . . . . 56 ends, 12 picks
Fig. 370 . . . . 48 ends, 48 picks
Fig. 371 . . . . 16 ends, 16 picks
Fig. 372 . . . . 16 ends, 16 picks
Fig. 373 . . . . 16 ends, 16 picks
Fig. 374 . . . . 16 ends, 16 picks
Fig. 375 . . . . 24 ends, 48 picks

FIG. 371.

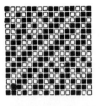

FIG. 372.

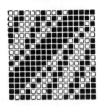

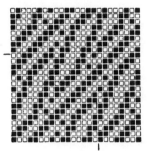

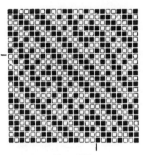

FIG. 373.

FIG. 374.

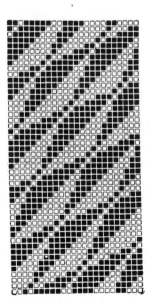

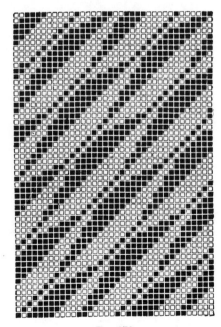

FIG. 375.

FIG. 376.

As the twill line is less distinct when the float is offset two threads instead of one, a twill with a longer float is often used in combination with a regular twill

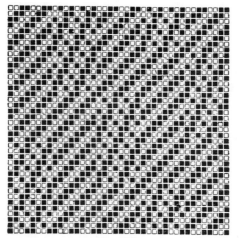

FIG. 377.

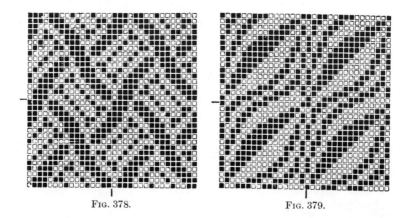

FIG. 378.　　　　　　　　FIG. 379.

for undulating twill effects. Thus, Fig. 367 is formed by a ^{2}—$_2$ twill offset one pick combined with a ^{3}—$_2$—^{1}—$_2$ twill offset two picks; the weave pattern covers eight shafts and eight picks.

Another example is shown at Fig. 370, in which are combined a ^{3}—$_3$ twill, offset one pick, and a ^{6}—$_6$ twill, offset two picks. Each twill covers 24 threads in each direction. The two twills are combined in plain weave order, the whole pattern covering 48 threads.

Attractive patterns can be obtained by using other motifs than the plain weave. Fig. 377 shows a weave pattern obtained by transposing two twills with a 5-shaft double satin as a motif.

BROKEN OR REVERSED TWILLS

Broken or reversed twills are formed by reversing the direction of the twill at intervals. The twill can be reversed in either the warp or filling. If the twill is broken in the warp, as shown at Fig. 382, a longitudinal stripe effect is obtained. The filling is stitched more closely and becomes less prominent. In Fig.

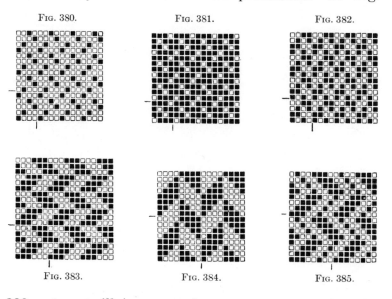

FIG. 380. FIG. 381. FIG. 382.

FIG. 383. FIG. 384. FIG. 385.

382 a ^{2}—$_2$ twill is reversed every two warp threads. The warp threads are still woven ^{2}—$_2$, but the reversing of the twill causes every alternate pick to interlace the warp in plain weave order.

If, on the other hand, the twill is reversed in the direction of the filling, as in Fig. 383, the filling becomes more prominent than the warp, which is then stitched more closely than the filling. These remarks apply to balanced twills, such as ^{2}—$_2$, ^{3}—$_3$, ^{4}—$_4$, etc.

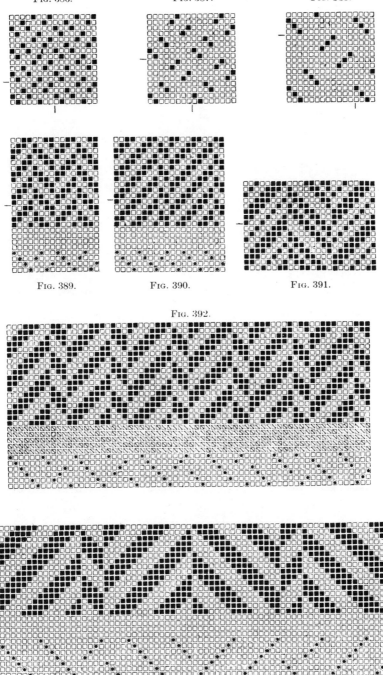

FIG. 386.   FIG. 387.   FIG. 388.

FIG. 389.   FIG. 390.   FIG. 391.

FIG. 392.

FIG. 393.

Among reversed or broken twills is classed the ^{1}—$_3$ weave stitched 1, 2, 4, 3, Fig. 380. This weave is sometimes styled a satin and frequently substituted for the regular satin. It is extensively used for a great variety of goods and is usually stitched in 1, 3, 2, 4, order. The same result is obtained in both cases, as well as with the order 1, 4, 2, 3.

FIG. 394.   FIG. 395.

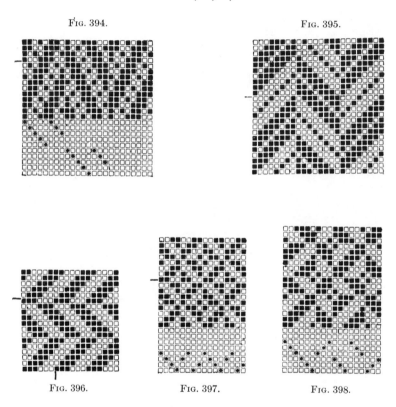

FIG. 396.   FIG. 397.   FIG. 398.

Fig. 381 is a ^{3}—$_1$ reversed or broken twill, stitched in 1, 3, 2, 4 order.

Fig. 382 is a ^{2}—$_2$ twill, reversed warp ways and often called *croisé*. Fig. 382 is well suited for woolen frieze fabrics, as it shows no twill.

Fig. 383 is a ^{3}—$_3$ twill reversed filling ways.

Fig. 384 is a ^{4}—$_4$ twill reversed warp ways.

Fig. 385 shows an 8-leaf twill, ^{3}—$_2$—^{1}—$_2$, reversed filling ways.

Motifs for attractive designs can be obtained by rearranging the parts of a twill so that two groups of threads with the twill running in the same direction alternate with two groups having the twill running in

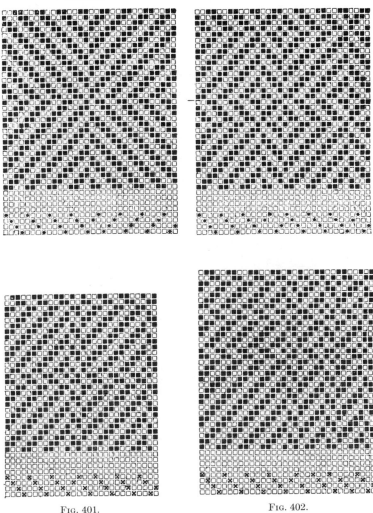

FIG. 399.

FIG. 400.

FIG. 401.

FIG. 402.

the opposite direction, Figs. 386, 387 and 388. The twill in either direction may include more than half the weave, making the two groups of unequal size. Care must be taken to have a sharp break at the junction of the right and left twills, the risers of one twill coming opposite the sinkers of the other.

Figs. 389 to 419 are weave patterns with the twill reversed, some warp ways, some filling ways, and others in both warp and filling.

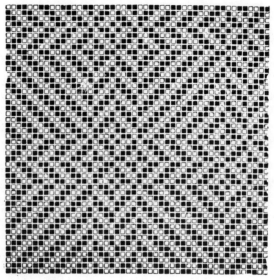

Fig. 403.

The following are reversed warp ways, forming longitudinal stripes:

Fig. 389, twill ^{2}—$_2$ divided 4 and 4.
Fig. 390, twill ^{2}—$_2$ divided 8 and 2.
Fig. 392, twill ^{3}—$_3$ divided 8 and 3.
Fig. 393, twill ^{4}—$_4$ divided 16, 4, 16, 16, 4 and 16.
Fig. 394, steep twill ^{5}—$_2$—^{1}—$_2$ divided 8 and 8.
Fig. 395, twill ^{3}—$_1$—^{3}—$_3$—^{1}—$_3$ divided 8 and 8.

If a twill weave does not permit of a sharp break at the point of reversal, another twill is formed by substituting risers for the sinkers, and sinkers for the risers of the first twill, Fig. 391. One is then used for the right twill; the other for the left. This method, however, necessitates an increase in the number of shafts.

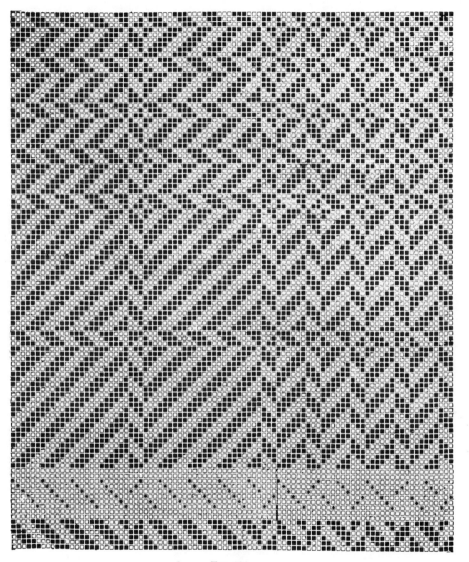

Fig. 404.

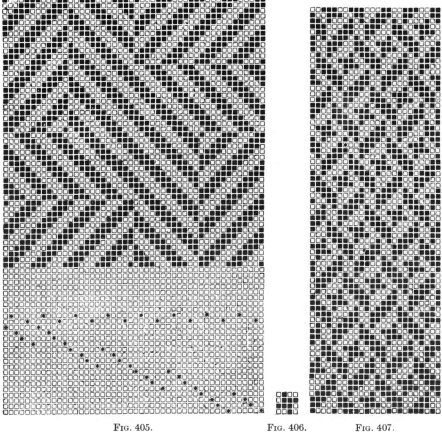

FIG. 405.

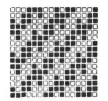

FIG. 406.

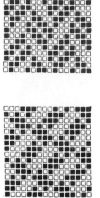

FIG. 407.

FIG. 408.

FIG. 409.

FIG. 410.

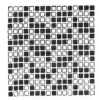

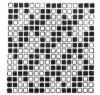

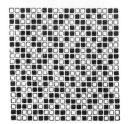

FIG. 411.

FIG. 412.

FIG. 413.

Fig. 396 shows a ^{3}—$_3$ twill reversed filling ways.

In Figs. 397 to 404 the twill is reversed in both warp and filling.

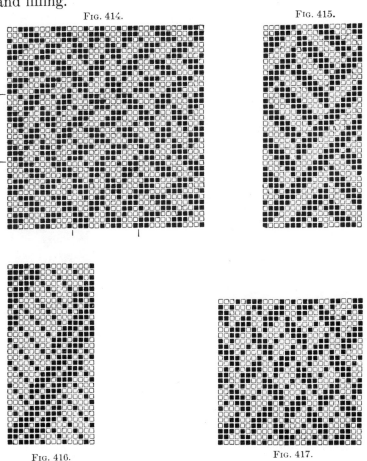

FIG. 414.

FIG. 415.

FIG. 416.

FIG. 417.

This arrangement is used for the production of a great variety of designs.

Fig. 397, twill ^{2}—$_2$ divided 4 and 4 each way.

Fig. 398, twill ^{3}—$_3$ divided 6 and 3 each way.

Fig. 399, twill ^{2}—$_2$ divided 16 and 16 each way.

Fig. 400, twill ^{2}—$_2$ divided 12 and 4 each way.

Fig. 401, twill ^{2}—$_2$ divided 12 and 2 each way.

Fig. 402, twill ^{2}—$_2$ divided 16, 2, 5, 2, 5, 2 each way.

Fig. 403, twill ^{2}—$_2$ divided 16, 4, 4, 16, 4, 4 each way.

Fig. 404, twill ^{3}—$_3$ divided 24, 3, 24, 3, 6, 3, 6, 3, 6, 3, 6, 3 each way.

Very attractive patterns are made by reversing the twill in accordance with previously selected motifs.

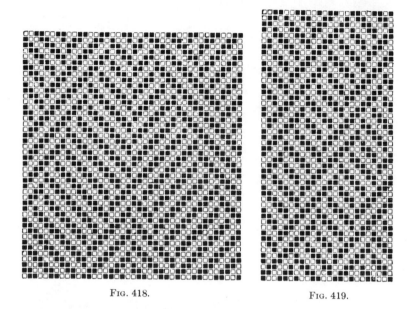

FIG. 418.   FIG. 419.

An example is shown at Fig. 405, which is developed from the motif, Fig. 406, with a ^{3}—$_3$ twill.

Another design is shown at Fig. 414, in which isolated squares of 12 threads each are formed by reversing the twill alternately in warp and filling. In this particular pattern the twill is reversed every 3 threads.

Figs. 407 to 419 show several variations of this class of weave effects, of which the number is unlimited:

Fig. 407, pattern 24 warp, 72 filling threads.

Fig. 408, pattern 8 warp, 4 filling threads.

Fig. 409, pattern 12 warp, 6 filling threads.

Fig. 410, pattern 8 warp, 8 filling threads.

Fig. 411, pattern 6 warp, 12 filling threads.

Fig. 412, pattern 20 warp, 20 filling threads.
Fig. 413, pattern 16 warp, 8 filling threads.
Fig. 414, pattern 24 warp, 24 filling threads.
Fig. 415, pattern 18 warp, 36 filling threads.
Fig. 416, pattern 16 warp, 32 filling threads.
Fig. 417, pattern 26 warp, 26 filling threads.
Fig. 418, pattern 40 warp, 44 filling threads.
Fig. 419, pattern 24 warp, 48 filling threads.

OFFSET TWILLS

Twills may be broken without reversing the direction. In balanced twills the risers of the first thread of a group are usually, but not necessarily, brought opposite the sinkers of the last thread of the preceding group.

The intermittent drawing-in draft, No. 5, Fig. 16, is required for these effects. The break may be in either or both directions (warp and filling). The direction of the twill may be reversed at intervals, if desired, in which case the intermittent drawing-in draft, No. 5, Fig. 17, is required. Examples of offset twills are shown at Figs. 420 to 454.

The following are broken in the warp:

Fig. 420, twill ^{1}—$_3$ divided 2 and 2.

Fig. 421, twill ^{2}—$_2$ divided 2 and 2.

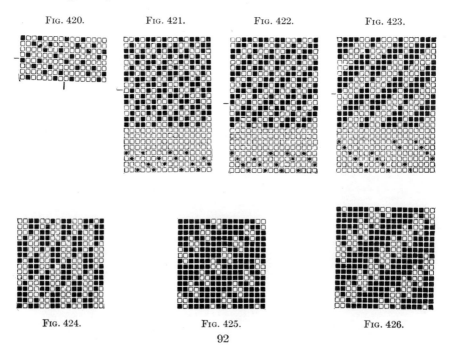

FIG. 420.   FIG. 421.   FIG. 422.   FIG. 423.

FIG. 424.   FIG. 425.   FIG. 426.

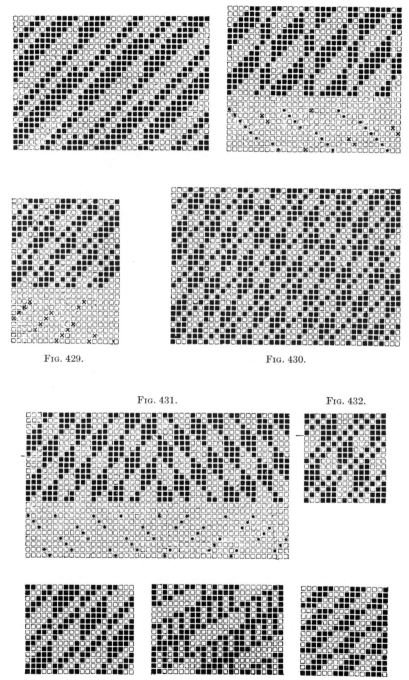

FIG. 427.

FIG. 428.

FIG. 429.

FIG. 430.

FIG. 431.

FIG. 432.

FIG. 433.

FIG. 434.

FIG. 435.

Fig. 422, twill ^{2}—$_2$ divided 4 and 4.

Fig. 423, twill ^{3}—$_3$ divided 6 and 6.

Fig. 424, twill ^{4}—$_4$ divided 2 and 2.

Fig. 425, twill ^{6}—$_2$ divided 2 and 2.

Fig. 426, twill ^{6}—$_3$ divided 2 and 2.

Fig. 427, twill ^{4}—$_2$—^{2}—$_4$ divided 12 and 12.

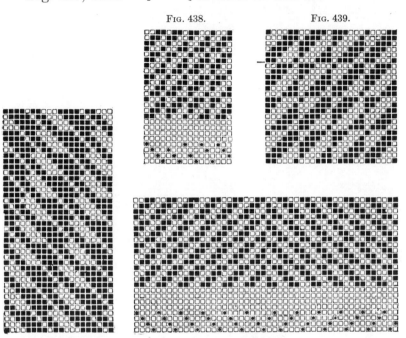

FIG. 438.   FIG. 439.

FIG. 436.   FIG. 437.

Fig. 428, twill ^{4}—$_4$ divided 6 and 2.

Fig. 429, twill ^{3}—$_1$—^{1}—$_3$ divided 4 and 4.

Fig. 430, twill ^{3}—$_1$—^{3}—$_3$—^{1}—$_3$ divided 3 and 3.

Fig. 431, twill ^{4}—$_4$ divided 3 and 3; twill reversed every 24 threads.

Fig. 432, twill ^{1}—$_4$—^{1}—$_1$—^{4}—$_1$ divided 3 and 3.

Fig. 433, twill ^{4}—$_2$—^{2}—$_4$—^{2}—$_2$ divided 5 and 5.

Fig. 434, twill ^{5}—$_3$—^{1}—$_3$ divided 1 and 1.

The following are broken in the filling:

Fig. 435, twill ^{3}—$_3$ divided 4 and 4.

Fig. 436, twill ^{4}—$_1$—^{2}—$_3$ divided 4 and 4.

Fig. 437, twill ^{2}—$_2$ divided 4 and 4; twill reversed every 24 threads.

FIG. 440.

FIG. 441.

FIG. 442.

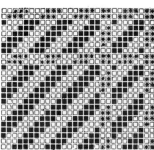

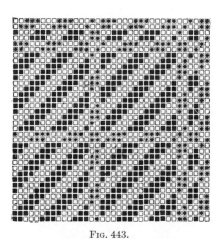

FIG. 443.

FIG. 444.

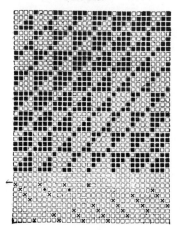

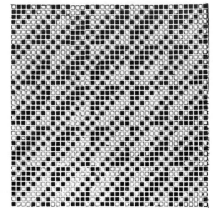

FIG. 445.

FIG. 446.

By the arrangement shown at Fig. 435 the twill is started at the same place at the beginning of each group of 4 picks. This produces a longitudinal groove effect which is very attractive in fine worsted fabrics.

The following twills are broken in both warp and filling:

Fig. 438, twill ^{2}—$_2$ divided 4 and 4.
Fig. 439, twill ^{3}—$_3$ divided 6 and 6.

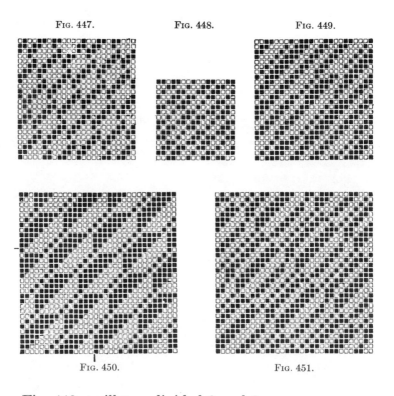

FIG. 447.   FIG. 448.   FIG. 449.

FIG. 450.   FIG. 451.

Fig. 440, twill ^{3}—$_3$ divided 9 and 2.
Fig. 441, twill ^{2}—$_2$ divided 6 and 2.
Fig. 442, twill ^{3}—$_3$ divided 18, 2, 6, 2.
Fig. 443, twill ^{3}—$_3$ divided 14, 2, 14, 2, 2, 2.
Fig. 444, twill ^{2}—$_2$ divided 4 and 4; twill reversed in both warp and filling every 16 threads.
Fig. 445, twill ^{4}—$_4$ divided 4 and 4.
Fig. 446, twill ^{1}—$_1$—^{3}—$_1$—^{1}—$_3$ divided 8 and 8.

Various patterns made by breaking the twill in both warp and filling are shown in Figs. 447 to 454.

Fig. 447 . . . . 24 × 24
Fig. 448 . . . . 14 × 14
Fig. 449 . . . . 16 × 24
Fig. 450 . . . . 15 × 20
Fig. 451 . . . . 32 × 32
Fig. 452 . . . . 32 × 16
Fig. 453 . . . . 40 × 40
Fig. 454 . . . . 80 × 16

FIG. 452.   FIG. 453.

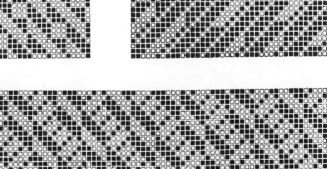

FIG. 454.

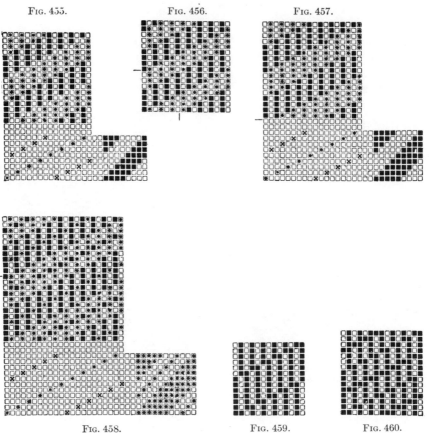

FIG. 455.   FIG. 456.   FIG. 457.

FIG. 458.   FIG. 459.   FIG. 460.

FIG. 462.

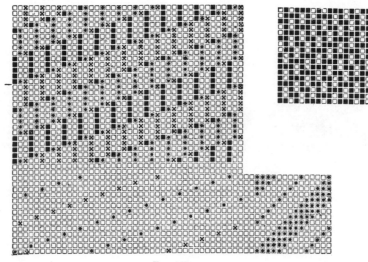

FIG. 461.

CORKSCREW TWILLS

These weaves, also called diagonal ribs, require the manifold drawing-in draft, No. 6, Figs. 20, 21 and 22. The peculiar feature of corkscrew weaves is the combination of two or more distinct twill lines, which may be of different colors.

Corkscrew fabrics, which are usually made of fine worsted, should be set close in the warp, otherwise the twill will look thin and ragged. Examples of corkscrew weaves are given at Figs. 455 to 509.

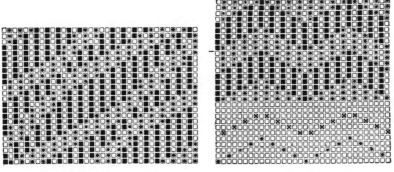

Fig. 463.   Fig. 464.

Fig. 455, 8-shaft, 2 twills.
Fig. 456, 7-shaft, 2 twills.
Fig. 457, 9-shaft, 2 twills.
Fig. 458, 11-shaft, ^{6}—$_2$—^{1}—$_2$, 2 twills.
Fig. 459, 13-shaft, 2 twills.
Fig. 460, 15-shaft, 2 twills.
Fig. 461, 14-shaft, ^{5}—$_4$—^{1}—$_4$, 3 twills.
Fig. 462, 17-shaft, 2 twills.

The single risers which are separated from the warp floats in Figs. 458, 460, 461 and 462 are introduced to stitch the floats on the back of the cloth. Corkscrew twills can be reversed, deflected or made in

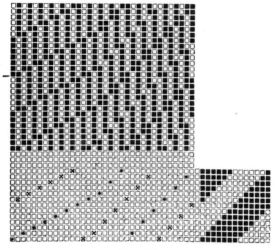

FIG. 465.

wavelike or undulating form, as shown by Figs. 463, 464 and 465.

FIG. 466. FIG. 467. FIG. 468.

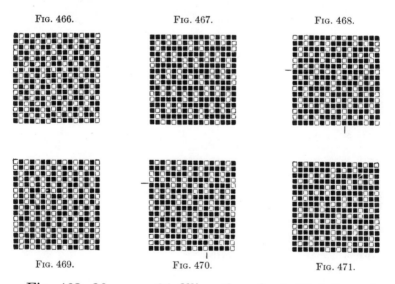

FIG. 469. FIG. 470. FIG. 471.

Fig. 463, 36 warp, 24 filling threads, twill deflected.
Fig. 464, 9 shafts, twill ^{5}—$_4$, reversed.
Fig. 465, 13 shafts, twill ^{7}—$_6$, deflected.
Other variations are shown at Figs. 466 to 478.

Fig. 466	7-shaft
Fig. 467	8-shaft
Fig. 468	9-shaft
Fig. 469	11-shaft
Fig. 470	11-shaft
Fig. 471	11-shaft
Fig. 472	13-shaft
Fig. 473	13-shaft
Fig. 474	15-shaft
Fig. 475	17-shaft
Fig. 476	13-shaft
Fig. 477	19-shaft
Fig. 478	23-shaft

FIG. 472.

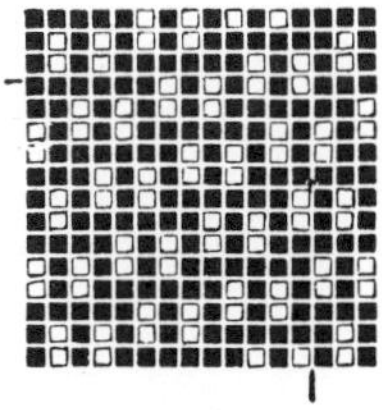

FIG. 473.

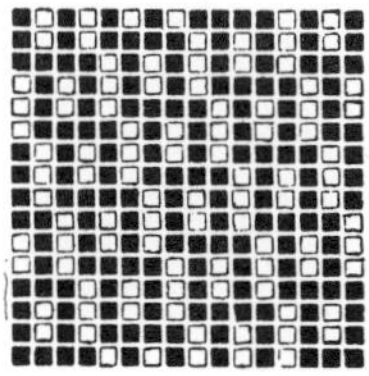

FIG. 474.

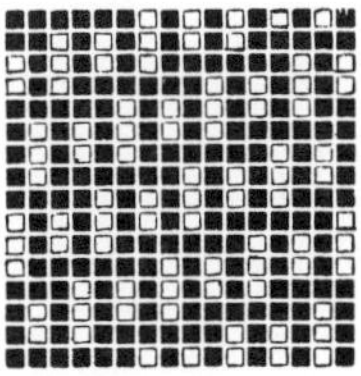

FIG. 475.

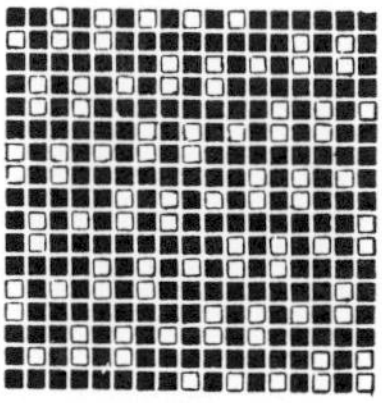

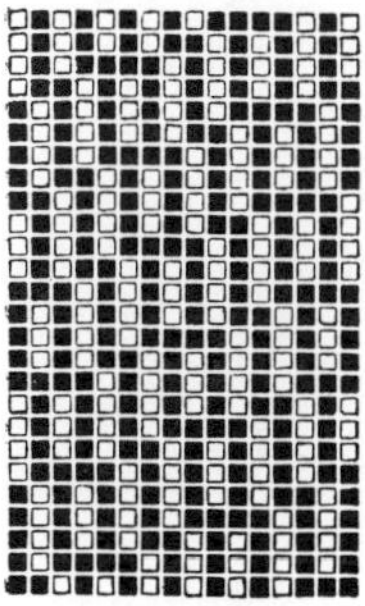

FIG. 476.

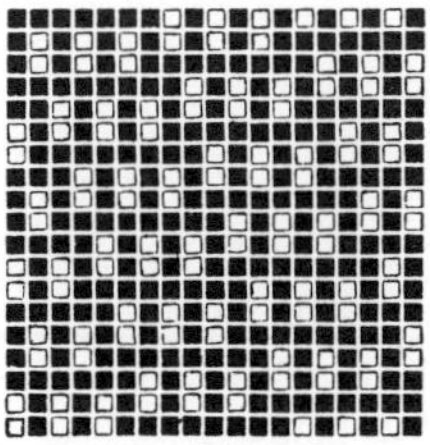

FIG. 477.

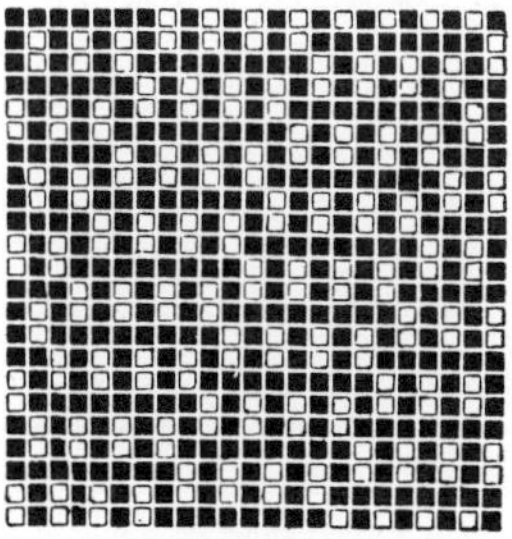

FIG. 478.

Corkscrew twills may be developed with filling as well as with warp floats. Two-filling corkscrews are shown at Figs. 479 and 480. Woven 1 light, 1 dark, the cloth shows two distinct filling twills, one of which is light, the other dark.

At Fig. 481 is shown a filling corkscrew in which the

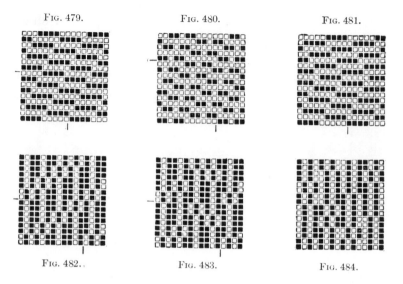

FIG. 479.   FIG. 480.   FIG. 481.

FIG. 482.   FIG. 483.   FIG. 484.

twill is run alternately to right and left, to give an undulating effect suitable for stripes in worsted goods.
Corkscrews, particularly the warp variety, are fre-

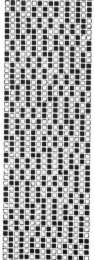

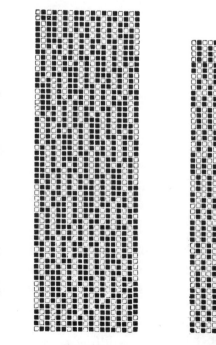

FIG. 485.   FIG. 486.   FIG. 487.

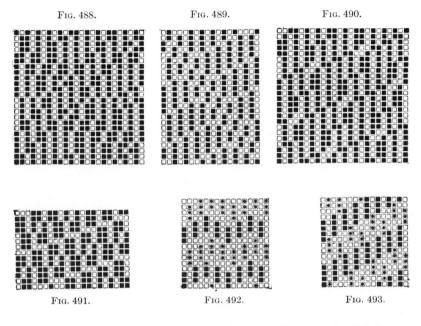

FIG. 488.   FIG. 489.   FIG. 490.

FIG. 491.   FIG. 492.   FIG. 493.

quently arranged to produce fancy effects, of which a few examples are given at Figs. 482 to 509.

Fig. 482 . . . . 12 warp, 8 filling
Fig. 483 . . . . 12 warp, 8 filling

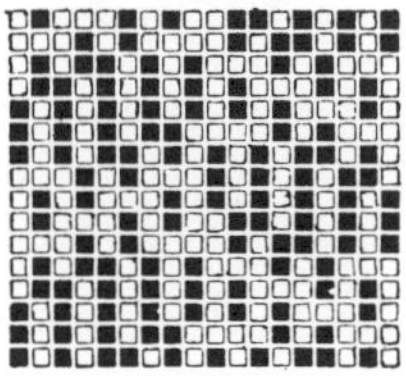

FIG. 494. 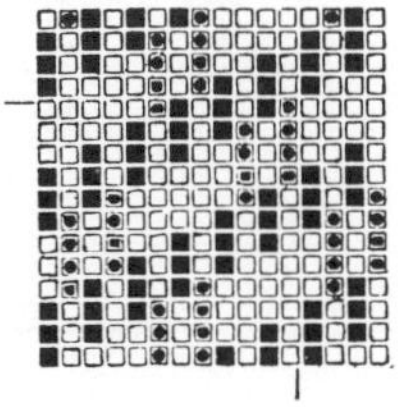   FIG. 495. 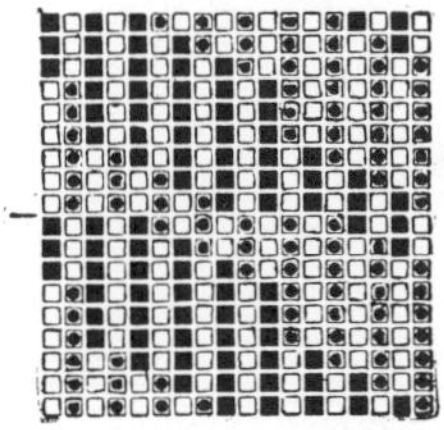   FIG. 496.

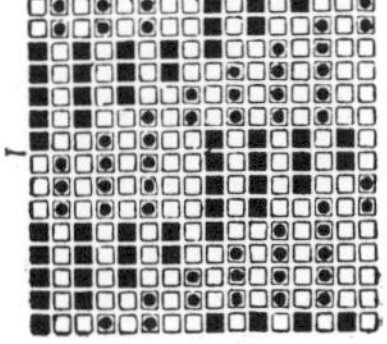

FIG. 497. 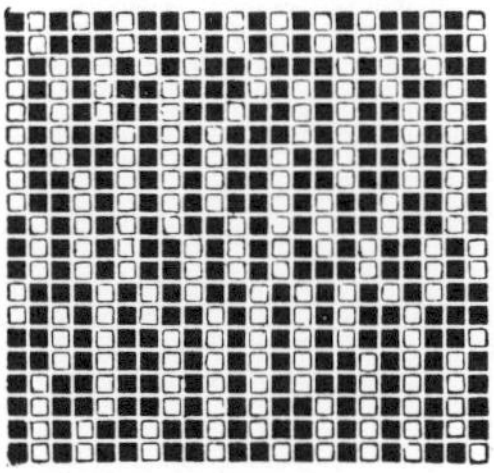   FIG. 498. 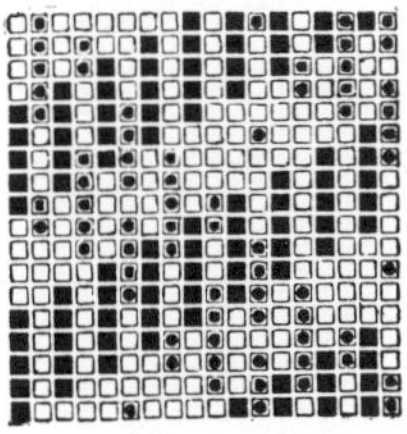   FIG. 499.

FIG. 500.　　　　　　　　　　　　FIG. 501.

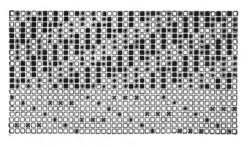

FIG. 502.　　　　FIG. 503.　　　　FIG. 504.

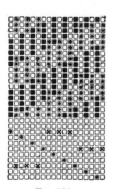

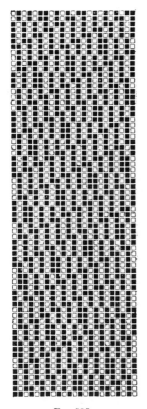

FIG. 505.　　　　　FIG. 506.

Fig. 500	. . . .	42 warp, 7 filling
Fig. 501	. . . .	20 warp, 20 filling
Fig. 502	. . . .	18 warp, 9 filling
Fig. 503	. . . .	12 warp, 6 filling
Fig. 504	. . . .	32 warp, 24 filling

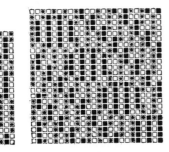

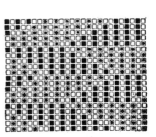

FIG. 507.　　　　FIG. 508.　　　　FIG. 509.

Fig. 505	23 warp, 69 filling
Fig. 506	20 warp, 70 filling
Fig. 507	20 warp, 20 filling
Fig. 508	24 warp, 24 filling
Fig. 509	26 warp, 10 filling

INTERLOCKING TWILLS

These twills are formed in two ways:

1. By interlocking a twill with itself, one draft of this twill coming on the even-numbered threads, and

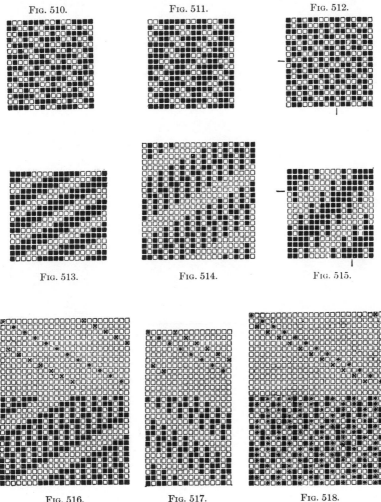

FIG. 510. FIG. 511. FIG. 512.

FIG. 513. FIG. 514. FIG. 515.

FIG. 516. FIG. 517. FIG. 518.

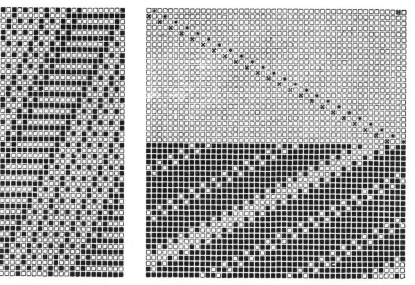

FIG. 519.   FIG. 520.

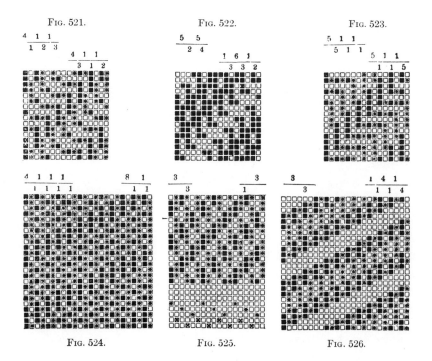

FIG. 521.   FIG. 522.   FIG. 523.

FIG. 524.   FIG. 525.   FIG. 526.

the other draft of the same weave coming on the odd-numbered threads, Figs. 510 to 520.

2. By interlocking two twills, bringing one of the weaves on the even-numbered threads, and the other on the odd-numbered threads, Figs. 521 to 539.

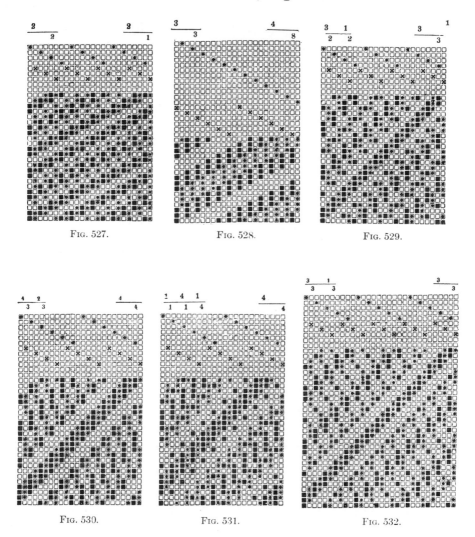

Fig. 527. Fig. 528. Fig. 529.

Fig. 530. Fig. 531. Fig. 532.

The objects of interlocking twills may be summarized as follows:

1. To obtain wide diagonals with a small number of shafts.

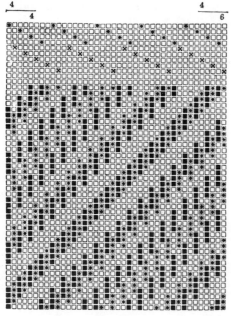

FIG. 533.

2. To produce new weave designs.

3. To obtain a weave structure in which a ground weave is brought on alternate picks and the pattern is developed on the other picks, Fig. 519.

4. To increase the filling-absorbing capacity of the weave, Figs. 510 and 511.

An unlimited number of new patterns can be obtained by interlocking weaves in warp and filling. Like the kaleidoscope, a change of position results in an entirely new effect.

Examples are shown at Figs. 510 to 520, in each of which a weave is interlocked with itself.

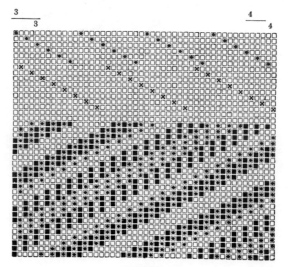

FIG. 534.

Figs. 521 to 539 show interlocking twill weaves each obtained from two twills, the threads being taken alternately from each.

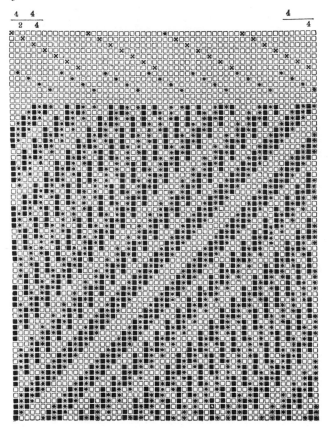

Fig. 535.

Fig. 521, twill ^{4}—$_1$—^{1}—$_2$—^{1}—$_3$, twill ^{4}—$_3$—^{1}—$_1$—^{1}—$_2$.

Fig. 522, twill ^{5}—$_2$—^{5}—$_4$, twill ^{1}—$_3$—^{6}—$_3$—^{1}—$_2$.

Fig. 523, twill ^{5}—$_5$—^{1}—$_1$—^{1}—$_1$, twill ^{5}—$_1$—^{1}—$_1$—^{1}—$_5$.

Fig. 524, twill ^{4}—$_1$—^{1}—$_1$—^{1}—$_1$—^{1}—$_1$, twill ^{8}—$_1$—^{1}—$_1$

Fig. 525, twill ^{3}—$_3$, twill $_1$—^{3}, 5 shafts, 12 picks.

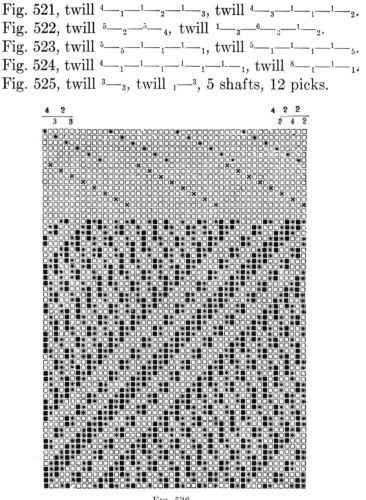

Fig. 536.

Fig. 526, twill ^{3}—$_3$, twill ^{1}—$_1$—^{4}—$_1$—^{1}—$_4$, 18 shafts, 12 picks.

Fig. 527, twill ^{2}—$_2$, twill ^{2}—$_1$, 7 shafts, 12 picks.

Fig. 528, twill ^{3}—$_3$, twill ^{4}—$_8$, 18 shafts, 12 picks.

Fig. 529, twill ^{3}—$_2$—^{1}—$_2$, twill ^{3}—$_3$, 17 shafts, 24 picks.

Fig. 530, twill ^{4}—$_3$—^{2}—$_3$, twill ^{4}—$_4$, 10 shafts, 24 picks.

Fig. 531, twill ^{1}—$_1$—^{4}—$_1$—^{1}—$_4$, twill ^{4}—$_4$, 10 shafts, 24 picks.

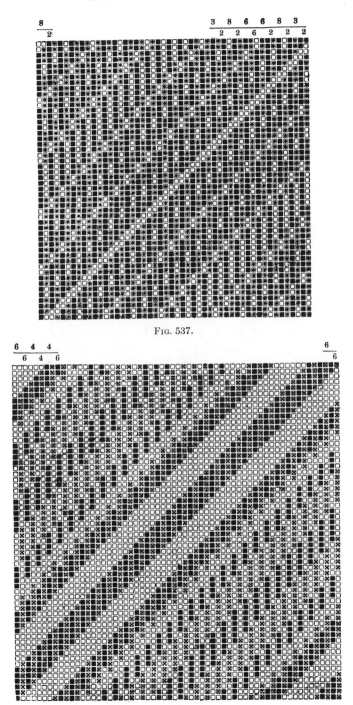

FIG. 537.

FIG. 538.

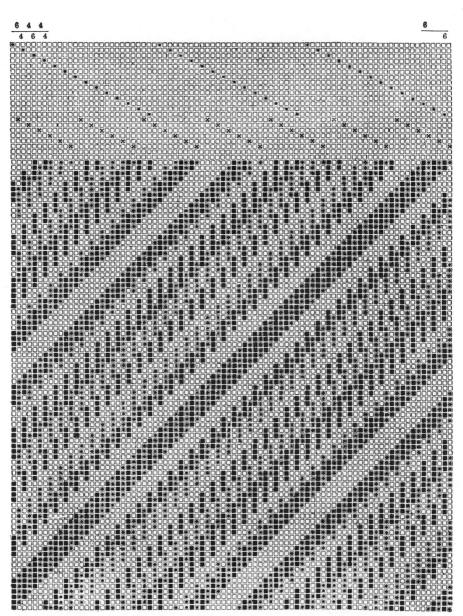

FIG. 539.

Fig. 532, twill ^{3}—$_3$—^{1}—$_3$, twill ^{3}—$_3$, 8 shafts, 30 picks.

Fig. 533, twill ^{4}—$_4$, twill ^{4}—$_6$, 9 shafts, 40 picks.

Fig. 534, twill ^{3}—$_3$, twill ^{4}—$_4$, 14 shafts, 24 picks.

Fig. 535, twill ^{4}—$_2$—^{4}—$_4$, twill ^{4}—$_4$, 11 shafts, 56 picks.

Fig. 536, twill ^{4}—$_3$—^{2}—$_3$, twill ^{4}—$_2$—^{2}—$_4$—^{2}—$_2$, 14 shafts, 48 picks.

Fig. 537, twill ^{8}—$_2$, twill ^{3}—$_2$—^{8}—$_2$—^{6}—$_6$—^{6}—$_2$—^{8}—$_2$—^{3}—$_2$, 30 shafts, 50 picks.

Fig. 538, twill ^{6}—$_6$—^{4}—$_4$—^{4}—$_6$, twill ^{6}—$_6$, 21 shafts, 60 picks.

Fig. 539, twill ^{6}—$_4$—^{4}—$_6$—^{4}—$_4$, twill ^{6}—$_6$, 20 shafts, 84 picks.

In drafting interlocking twills, two steep twills with the warp floats rising two picks at each thread are generally combined, the object being to obtain a 45° twill in the interlocked weave, Figs. 521 to 523, 525, 529 to 533 and 535 to 539.

Fig. 540.   Fig. 541.   Fig. 542.   Fig. 543.

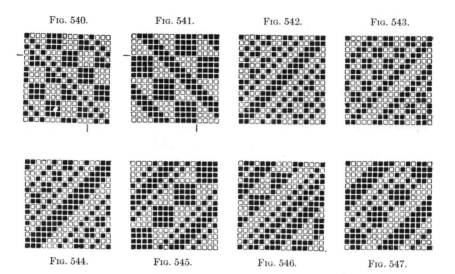

Fig. 544.   Fig. 545.   Fig. 546.   Fig. 547.

Fig. 548.

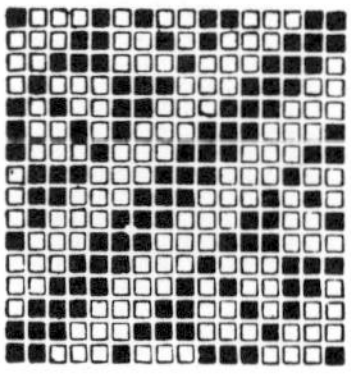

Fig. 549.

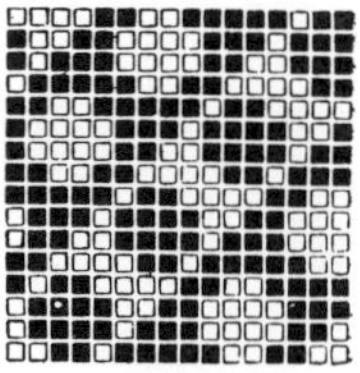

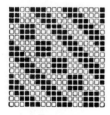

Fig. 550. 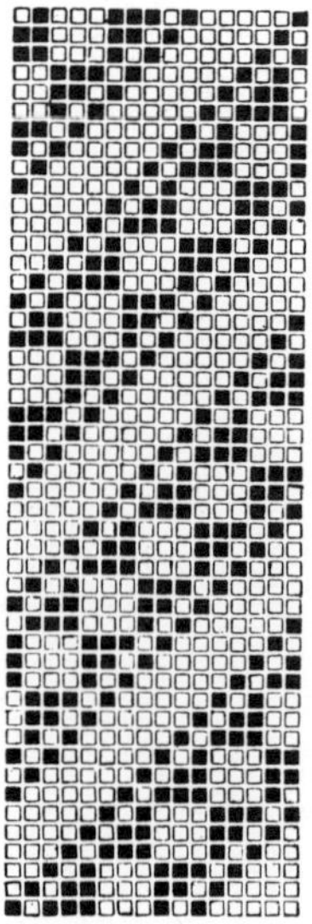   Fig. 551.

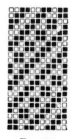

Fig. 552.

FANCY TWILLS

An endless variety of attractive twill effects can be obtained by combining basket, rib and other weaves to form a twill line, or by arranging a twill to form braided effects. Such patterns, however, require a large number of shafts, and frequently can be made only with a jacquard attachment. The weaves are drafted by first inserting the twill which is to form the main feature of the pattern and then filling the re-

FIG. 553.

FIG. 554.

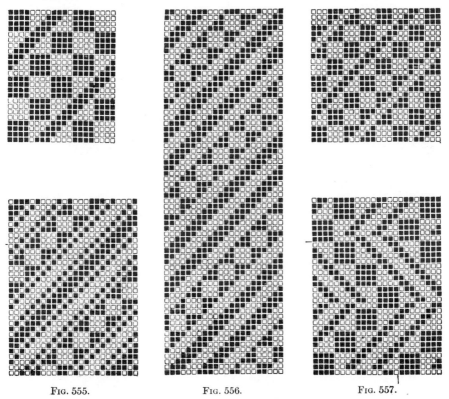

FIG. 555.

FIG. 556.

FIG. 557.

117

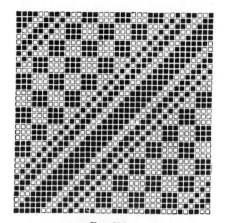

FIG. 558.

FIG. 559.

FIG. 560.

FIG. 561.

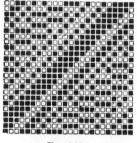

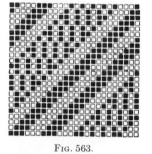

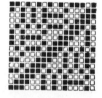

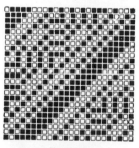

FIG. 562.

FIG. 563.

FIG. 564.

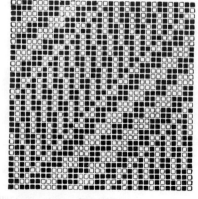

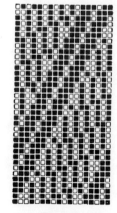

FIG. 565.

FIG. 566.

maining space with the basket, rib or other weave as
desired. Examples are shown at Figs. 540 to 623.

The following are twills combined with basket
weaves:

Fig. 540 . . . . 12 warp, 12 filling
Fig. 541 . . . . 12 warp, 12 filling
Fig. 542 . . . . 16 warp, 16 filling

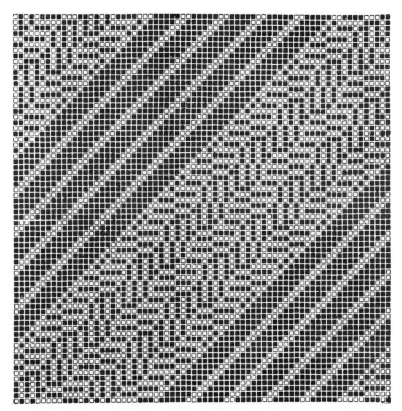

FIG. 567.

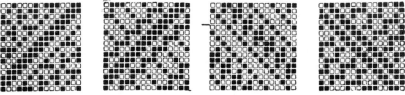

FIG. 568.   FIG. 569.   FIG. 570.   FIG. 571.

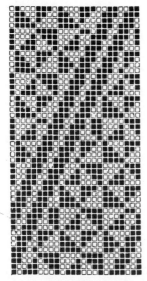

FIG. 572.

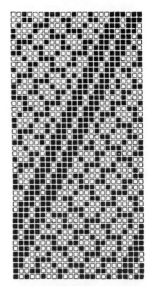

FIG. 573.

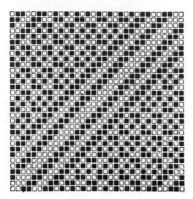

FIG. 574.

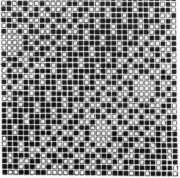

FIG. 575.

Fig. 576.

Fig. 577.

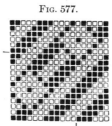

Fig. 578.

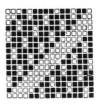

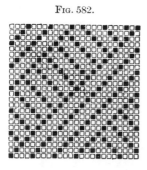

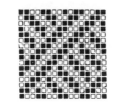

Fig. 579.

Fig. 580.

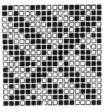

Fig. 581.

Fig. 582.

Fig. 583.

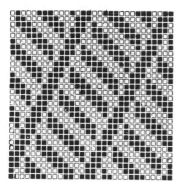

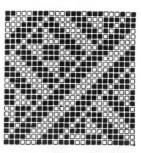

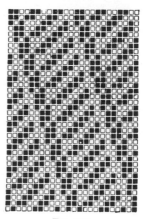

Fig. 584.

Fig. 585.

FIG. 586. FIG. 587. FIG. 588.

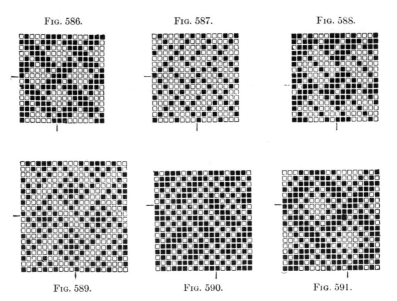

FIG. 589. FIG. 590. FIG. 591.

FIG. 592. FIG. 593.

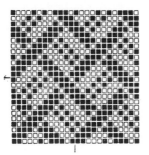

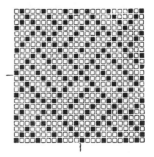

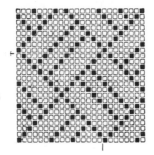

FIG. 594.

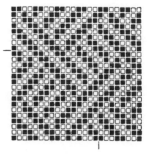

FIG. 595.

Fig. 553 . . . . 20 warp, 20 filling
Fig. 554 . . . . 24 warp, 24 filling
Fig. 555 . . . . 24 warp, 24 filling
Fig. 556 . . . . 22 warp, 66 filling
Fig. 557 . . . . 16 warp, 24 filling
Fig. 558 . . . . 36 warp, 36 filling

The following are twills combined with rib weaves:

Fig. 559 . . . . 14 warp, 14 filling
Fig. 560 . . . . 12 warp, 12 filling
Fig. 561 . . . . 16 warp, 16 filling
Fig. 562 . . . . 24 warp, 24 filling
Fig. 563 . . . . 24 warp, 24 filling
Fig. 564 . . . . 24 warp, 24 filling
Fig. 565 . . . . 34 warp, 34 filling

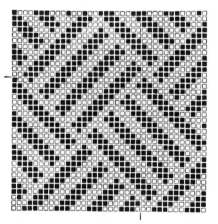

Fig. 596.

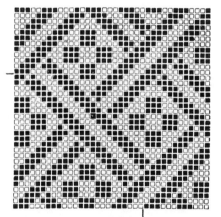

Fig. 597.

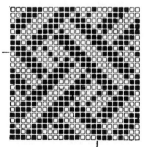

Fig. 598.

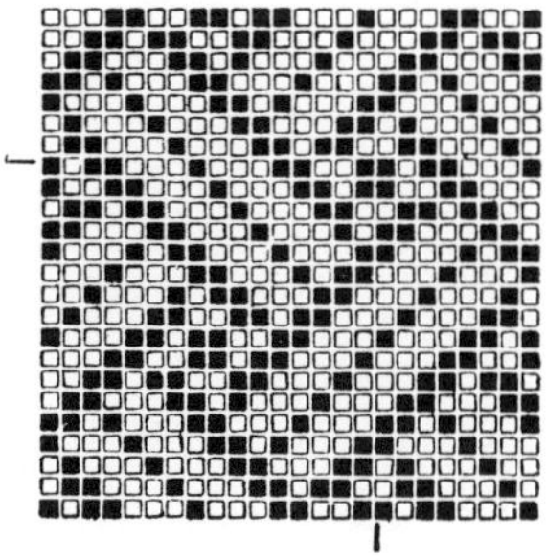

Fig. 599.

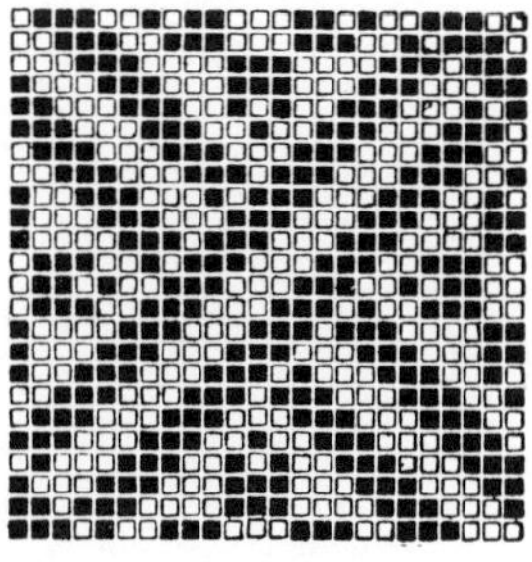

Fig. 600.

Fig. 566 . . . . 18 warp, 36 filling
Fig. 567 . . . . 70 warp, 70 filling

The following are twills combined with crêpe weaves:

Fig. 568 . . . . 16 warp, 16 filling
Fig. 569 . . . . 16 warp, 16 filling

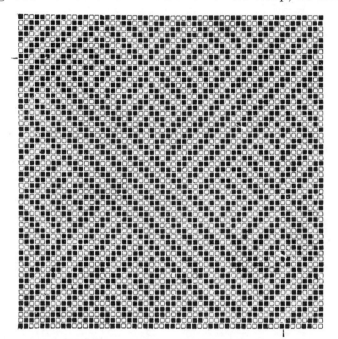

FIG. 601.

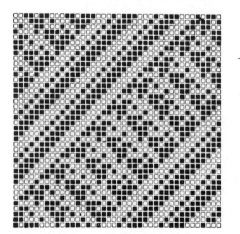

FIG. 602.

FIG. 603.

Fig. 570 . . . . 12 warp, 12 filling
Fig. 571 . . . . 16 warp, 16 filling
Fig. 572 . . . . 24 warp, 48 filling
Fig. 573 . . . . 24 warp, 48 filling
Fig. 574 . . . . 32 warp, 32 filling
Fig. 575 . . . . 32 warp, 32 filling

The following effects are produced by twills running in opposite directions:

Fig. 576 . . . . 12 warp, 12 filling
Fig. 577 . . . . 18 warp, 18 filling
Fig. 578 . . . . 16 warp, 16 filling
Fig. 579 . . . . 12 warp, 12 filling
Fig. 580 . . . . 16 warp, 16 filling
Fig. 581 . . . . 18 warp, 18 filling
Fig. 582 . . . . 24 warp, 24 filling
Fig. 583 . . . . 24 warp, 24 filling
Fig. 584 . . . . 30 warp, 30 filling
Fig. 585 . . . . 12 warp, 36 filling

Fig. 604.

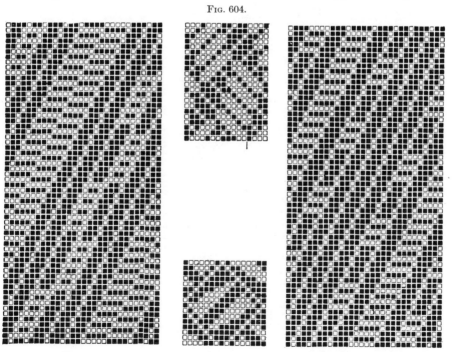

Fig. 605.   Fig. 606.   Fig. 607.

The following weaves show twills arranged to produce basket or braided effects:

Fig. 586 . . . . 8 warp, 8 filling
Fig. 587 . . . . 8 warp, 8 filling

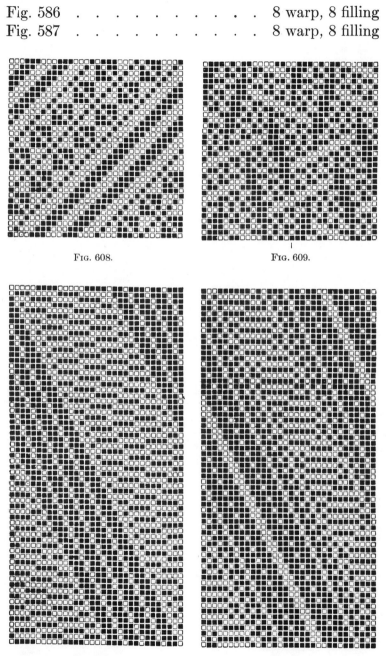

FIG. 608.

FIG. 609.

FIG. 610.

FIG. 611.

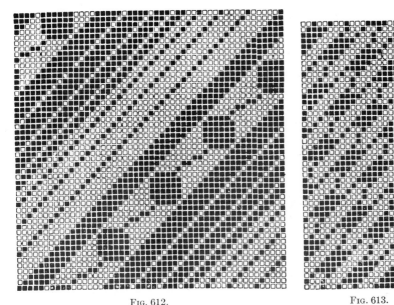

FIG. 612.

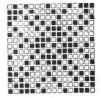

FIG. 613.

FIG. 614.

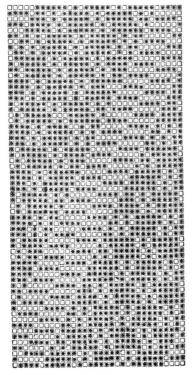

FIG. 615.

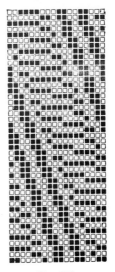

FIG. 616.

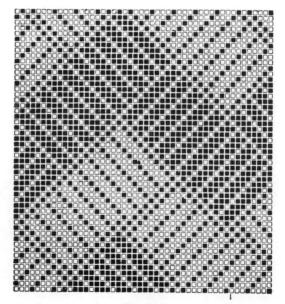

FIG. 617.　　　　FIG. 618.　　　　　　FIG. 619.

Fig. 588 . . . . 8 warp, 8 filling
Fig. 589 . . . . 10 warp, 10 filling
Fig. 590 . . . . 12 warp, 12 filling
Fig. 591 . . . . 12 warp, 12 filling
Fig. 592 . . . . 12 warp, 12 filling
Fig. 593 . . . . 12 warp, 12 filling
Fig. 594 . . . . 16 warp, 16 filling

FIG. 620.

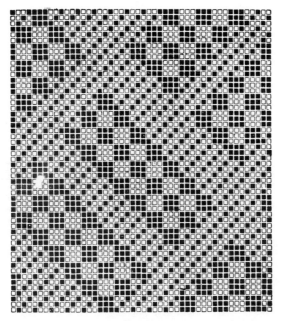

Fig. 621.

Fig. 622.

Fig. 595	16 warp, 16 filling
Fig. 596	24 warp, 16 filling
Fig. 597	24 warp, 24 filling
Fig. 598	16 warp, 16 filling
Fig. 599	16 warp, 16 filling
Fig. 600	24 warp, 24 filling
Fig. 601	48 warp, 48 filling

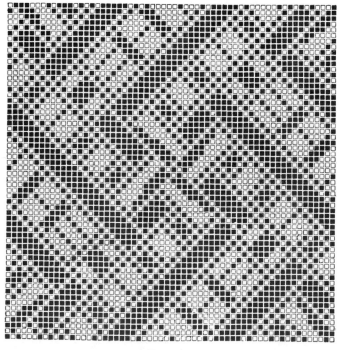

Fig. 623.

Figs. 602 to 623 show fancy twills formed by combinations of twill lines with various other weaves:

Fig. 602	40 warp, 40 filling
Fig. 603	30 warp, 30 filling
Fig. 604	12 warp, 22 filling
Fig. 605	30 warp, 60 filling
Fig. 606	16 warp, 16 filling
Fig. 607	30 warp, 60 filling
Fig. 608	32 warp, 32 filling

Fig. 624.

Fig. 625.

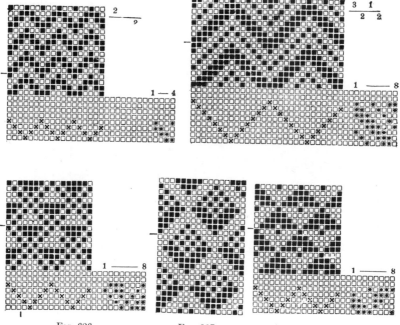

Fig. 626.   Fig. 627.   Fig. 628.

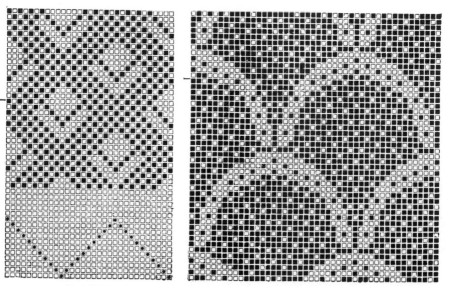

Fig. 629.   Fig. 630.

HERRINGBONE OR POINTED TWILLS

The true herringbone or pointed twill is one in which the twill at certain points slants in opposite directions from the float of one thread, as shown at Fig. 624.

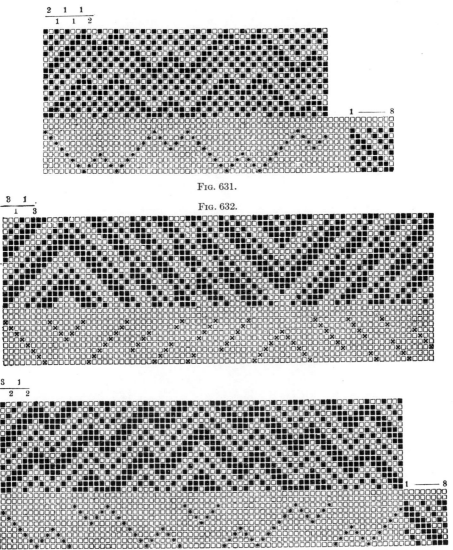

FIG. 631.

FIG. 632.

FIG. 633.

The twill runs to the right up to and including the fourth thread, which is common to both right and left twills.   The float of the fifth thread forms a twill to the left with that of the fourth thread, and this twill

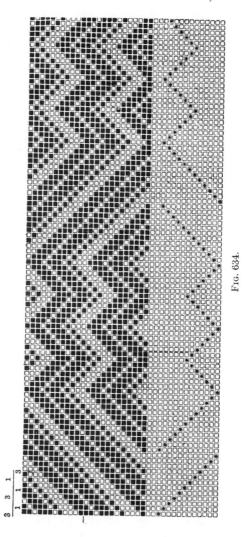

Fig. 634.

is continued until the next point of reversal at the seventh thread, which is common to both right and left twills.

The term herringbone is also applied to reversed twills in which a sharp break occurs when the twill is

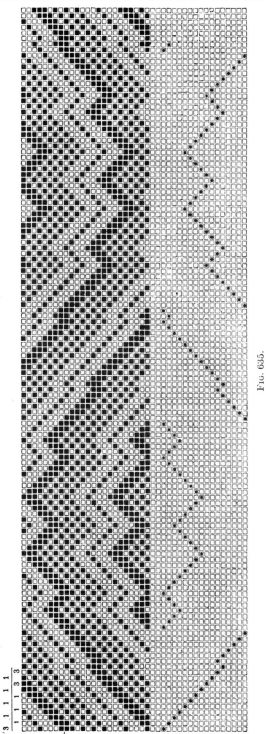

Fig. 635.

reversed, especially when the twill runs for a considerable distance before being reversed, Figs. 380 to 396.

The pointed herringbone effect is obtained with a twill chain and a pointed drawing-in draft, No. 3,

FIG. 636.

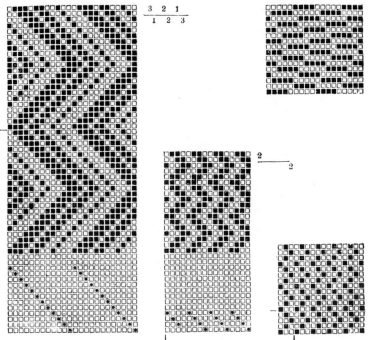

FIG. 637.

FIG. 638.

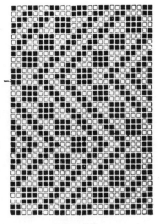

FIG. 639.

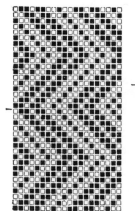

FIG. 640.

FIG. 641.

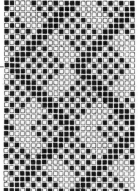

FIG. 642.

FIG. 643.   FIG. 644.   FIG. 645.

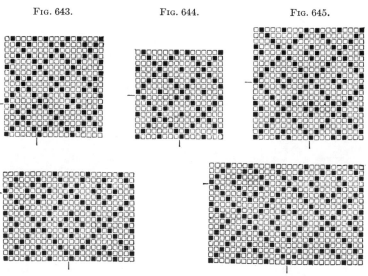

FIG. 646.   FIG. 647.

FIG. 648.   FIG. 649.

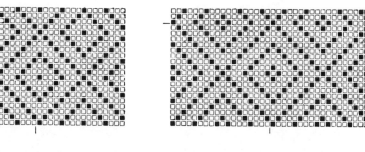

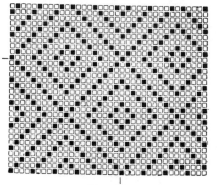

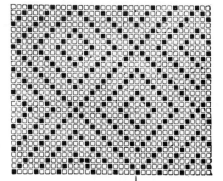

FIG. 650.   FIG. 651.

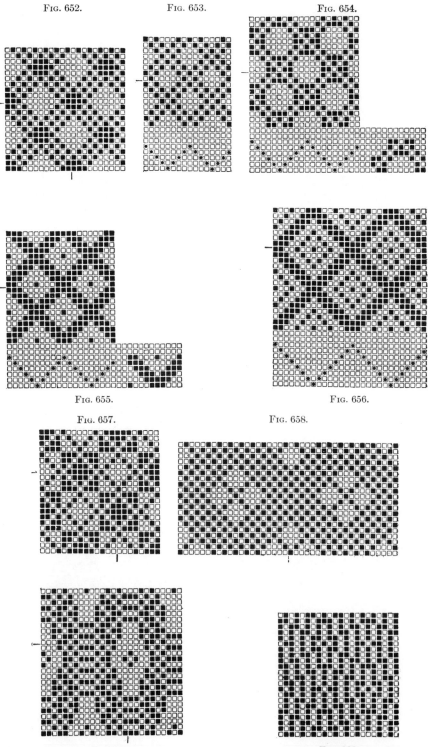

Fig. 652.   Fig. 653.   Fig. 654.

Fig. 655.   Fig. 656.

Fig. 657.   Fig. 658.

Fig. 659.   Fig. 660.

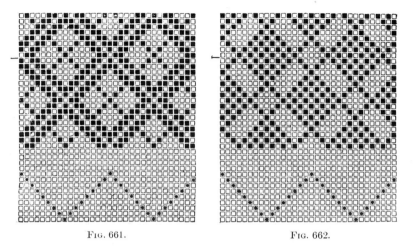

FIG. 661.   FIG. 662.

Figs. 9 and 10.   The simplest form of this draft consists in drawing in straight from the first to the last
shaft, then reversing and drawing in straight back to
the first shaft, as shown at Fig. 624.   This brings but
half as many threads on the first and last shafts as
on the others.   Figs. 624 to 630 and Fig. 642 are
examples of pointed or herringbone twills with this
method of drawing-in.

FIG. 663.

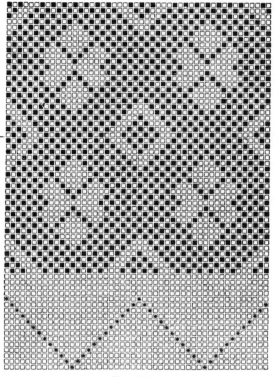

Fig. 664.

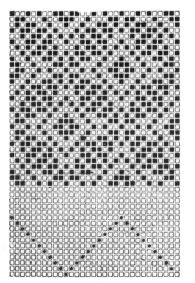

Fig. 665.

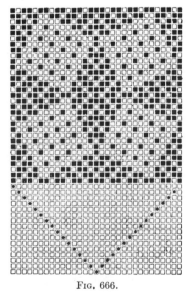

Fig. 666.

Fig. 624, twill ^{2}—$_2$, 4-leaf.

Fig. 625, twill ^{3}—$_2$—^{1}—$_2$, 8-leaf.

Fig. 626, 5-leaf twill.

Fig. 627, 6-leaf twill.

Fig. 628, 5-leaf twill.

Fig. 629, pattern 16 warp, 16 filling.

Fig. 630, pattern 30 warp, 36 filling.

Fig. 642, pattern 13 warp, 13 filling.

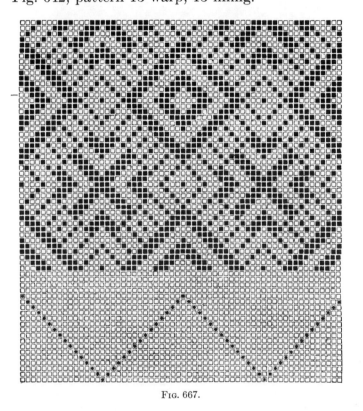

Fig. 667.

In the foregoing pointed-twill drafts the twill runs for the same distance each time before the direction is changed. A great variety of zigzag effects can be obtained by varying the distance over which the twill is carried continuously in the same direction. Several such patterns are shown at Figs. 631 to 635, the arrangement of the twill being shown in each case by the drawing-in draft.

Fig. 631, twill $2-_1-^1-_1-^1-_2$.

Fig. 632, twill $3-_1-^1-_3$.

Fig. 633, twill $3-_2-^1-_2$.

Fig. 634, twill $3-_1-^3-_1-^1-_3$.

Fig. 635, twill $3-_1-^1-_1-^1-_1-^1-_3-^1-_3$.

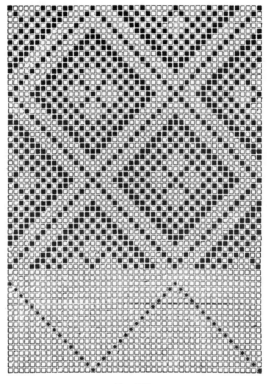

FIG. 668.

The twill in a herringbone weave can be arranged to bring the points at the side of the pattern, as shown at Fig. 638. For such weaves a straight drawing-in draft is used, the twill being reversed after a certain number of picks, as shown at Figs. 636 to 641.

Fig. 636, 9 warp, 16 filling.

Fig. 637, twill $3-_1-^2-_2-^1-_3$.

Fig. 638, twill $2-_2$.

Fig. 639, twill $1-_2$.

Fig. 640, twill ^{2}—$_1$—^{2}—$_2$—^{1}—$_2$.

Fig. 641, 12 warp, 22 filling.

In Fig. 639 each third warp thread is woven plain, while the two intermediate threads are woven ^{1}—$_3$. This makes the weave well suited for lightweight

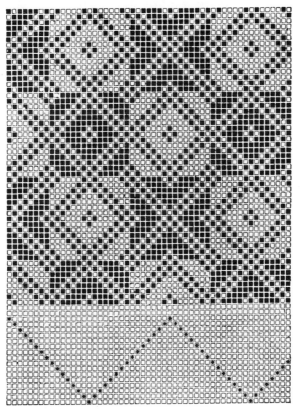

Fig. 669.

fancy cotton warp suitings. The pattern is arranged to bring all the fancy threads on the plain shafts. The cotton threads come on the ^{1}—$_3$ shafts and also on the plain shafts when the pattern requires it. The filling, which is wool, floats on the face in ^{3}—$_1$ order, covering the cotton warp.

TWILLS POINTED IN BOTH WARP AND FILLING

By reversing the twill at intervals in both warp and filling the lines intersect at four points, forming squares. The effects are most satisfactory when the diagonally opposite points are formed in the same way.

The patterns can be readily modified by increasing the number of threads from point to point in both

FIG. 670.

warp and filling. This is illustrated by Figs. 643 to 651. The twill, ^{1}—$_3$, is the same in all of these patterns, but each has one thread more from point to point than is found in the preceding one: Fig. 643, 4 threads; Fig. 644, 5 threads; Fig. 645, 6 threads; Fig. 646, 7 threads; Fig. 647, 8 threads; Fig. 648, 9 threads; Fig. 649, 10 threads; Fig. 650, 11 threads; Fig. 651, 12 threads.

The drawing-in drafts for these weaves are as follows:

Fig. 643,   1, 2, 3, 4, 3, 2.
Fig. 644,   1, 2, 3, 4, 1, 4, 3, 2.
Fig. 645,   1, 2, 3, 4, 1, 2, 1, 4, 3, 2.
Fig. 646,   1, 2, 3, 4, 1, 2, 3, 2, 1, 4, 3, 2.
Fig. 647,   1, 2, 3, 4, 1, 2, 3, 4, 3, 2, 1, 4, 3, 2.
Fig. 648,   1, 2, 3, 4, 1, 2, 3, 4, 1, 4, 3, 2, 1, 4, 3, 2.
Fig. 649,   1, 2, 3, 4, 1, 2, 3, 4, 1, 2, 1, 4, 3, 2, 1, 4, 3, 2.
Fig. 650,   1, 2, 3, 4, 1, 2, 3, 4, 1, 2, 3, 2, 1, 4, 3, 2, 1, 4, 3, 2.
Fig. 651,   1, 2, 3, 4, 1, 2, 3, 4, 1, 2, 3, 4, 3, 2, 1, 4, 3, 2, 1, 4, 3, 2.

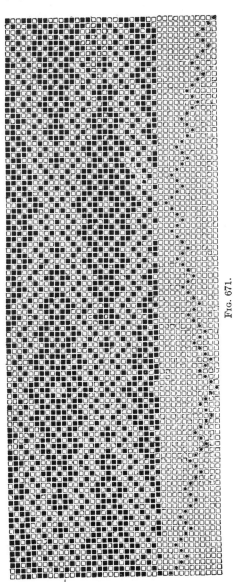

Fig. 671.

The weave in each case is arranged in the filling to correspond with the drawing-in draft.

Figs. 652 to 671 show other examples of this style of twill patterns. The limits of the pattern are indicated on most of these figures by a short line at the side and bottom of the draft.

The pattern is developed by reversing the weave in the filling to correspond with the drawing-in draft. Thus in Fig. 670 the picks should be arranged as follows to correspond with the warp pattern: 1 to 8, reverse to 4, forward to 8, reverse to 1, forward to 5, reverse to 2, total 30 picks.

Fig. 671 is another pattern of this kind, requiring 10 shafts. The ground weave and drawing-in draft show the method of construction. The weave draft is made by arranging the filling to correspond with the pattern.

Pointed-twill patterns have the general defect that the float at the apex is nearly double that of the other floats. When it is important to have the size of the floats practically uniform, the longer floats at the points are broken up by the insertion or removal of risers. This is illustrated at Figs. 672

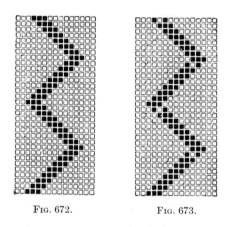

FIG. 672.   FIG. 673.

and 673. Fig. 672 is a pointed twill reversed filling ways. At the point is found a float of five risers, while the regular float of the twill is but three risers. Fig. 673 shows the same draft in which the float of five at the point has been broken up by the removal of one riser. This causes an increase in the number of shafts required for the weave.

DIVERSIFIED WEAVES

Very attractive patterns can be obtained by adding or removing risers from a ground weave. These alterations are made according to a previously selected motif. Examples are shown at Figs. 674 to 740.

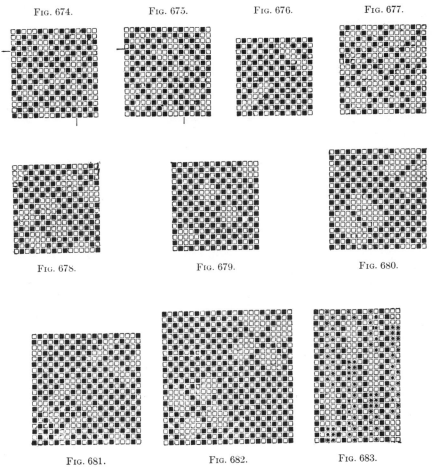

FIG. 674. FIG. 675. FIG. 676. FIG. 677.

FIG. 678. FIG. 679. FIG. 680.

FIG. 681. FIG. 682. FIG. 683.

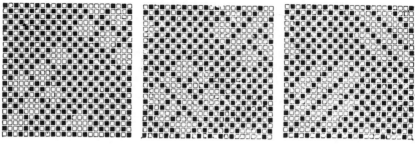

FIG. 684.　　　　FIG. 685.　　　　FIG. 686.

FIG. 687.　　　　FIG. 688.　　　　FIG. 689.

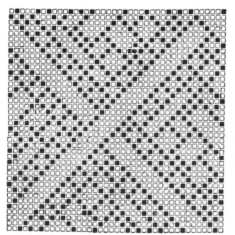

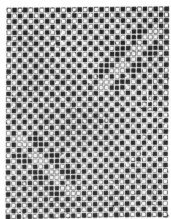

FIG. 690.　　　　FIG. 691.

DIVERSIFIED PLAIN WEAVES

In Figs. 674 to 693 the ground is a plain weave. Fig. 683 is adapted for a cloth dressed 2 worsted, 2 silk.

In Figs. 683, 691 and 693 points are both added and removed to develop the design. In drafting these

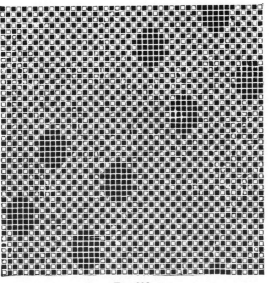

Fig. 692.

weaves the motif is first painted on the draft and the ground weave and floats are then inserted to correspond.

DIVERSIFIED TWILLS

Figs. 694 to 722 show effects obtained on twill weaves by adding or removing risers. Fig. 710 is the motif for Fig. 709, the black squares in this draft representing sinkers, the white squares risers; Fig. 712, the motif for Figs. 714 and 715; Fig. 716, the motif for Fig. 718.

The spotting in several of the other designs is arranged as follows: Figs. 708, 711, 713, 8-leaf satin; Figs. 717, 719 and 722, 5-leaf satin.

DIVERSIFIED SATIN WEAVES

Weave designs formed on a satin ground are shown at Figs. 723 to 729.

Fig. 694 . . . . 15 × 15
Fig. 695 . . . . 12 × 12
Fig. 696 . . . . 15 × 15
Fig. 697 . . . . 18 × 18
Fig. 698 . . . . 18 × 18
Fig. 699 . . . . 24 × 24

FIG. 693.

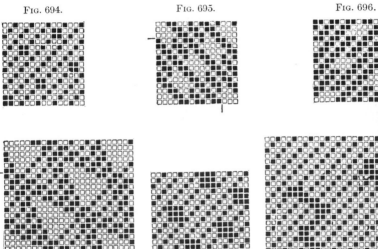

FIG. 694.   FIG. 695.   FIG. 696.

FIG. 697.   FIG. 698.   FIG. 699.

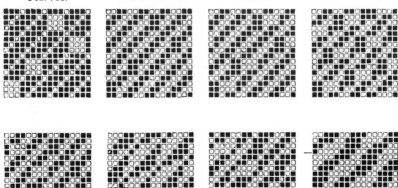

FIG. 700.   FIG. 701.   FIG. 702.   FIG. 703.

FIG. 704.   FIG. 705.   FIG. 706.   FIG. 707.

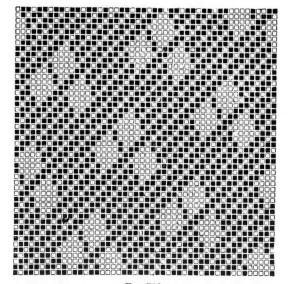

Fig. 708.

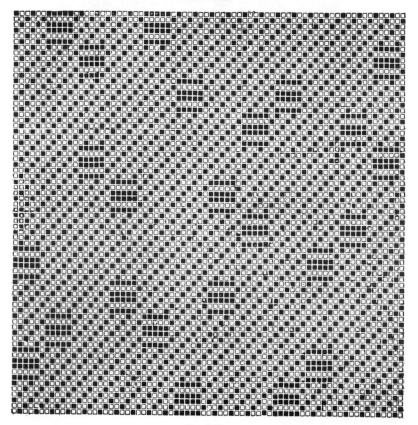

Fig. 709.

FIG. 710.

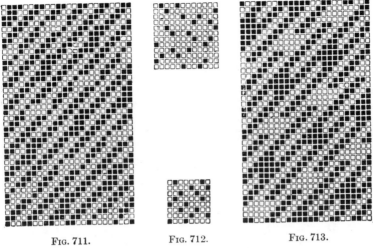

FIG. 711. FIG. 712. FIG. 713.

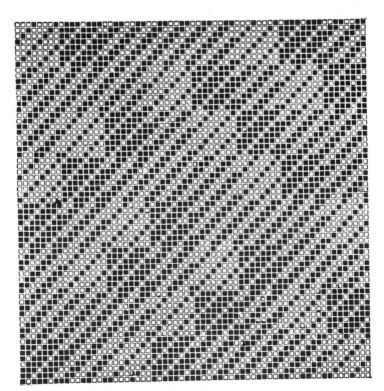

FIG. 714.

Fig. 706	16 × 16
Fig. 707	12 × 12
Fig. 708	48 × 48
Fig. 709	72 × 72
Fig. 711	24 × 40

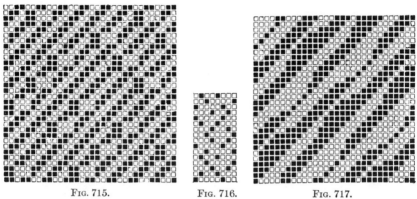

Fig. 715.

Fig. 716.

Fig. 717.

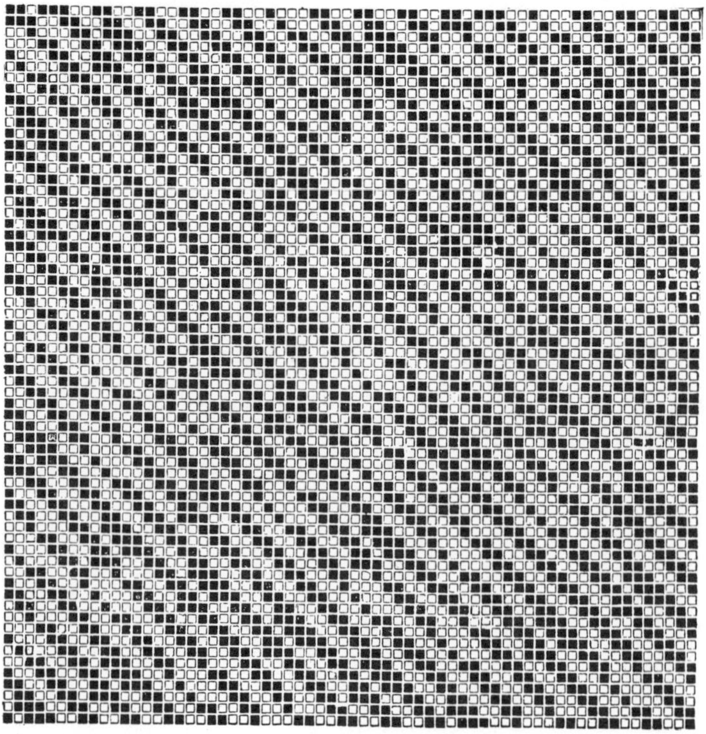

Fig. 718.

Fig. 713 . . . . 24 × 40
Fig. 714 . . . . 64 × 64
Fig. 715 . . . . 32 × 32
Fig. 717 . . . . 30 × 30
Fig. 718 . . . . 64 × 64
Fig. 719 . . . . 30 × 30

FIG. 719.

FIG. 721.

FIG. 720.

Fig. 720 . . . . 24 × 72
Fig. 721 . . . . 24 × 24
Fig. 722 . . . . 60 × 60
Fig. 723 . . . . 16 × 80
Fig. 724 . . . . 16 × 16
Fig. 725 . . . . 20 × 20
Fig. 726 . . . . 12 × 12

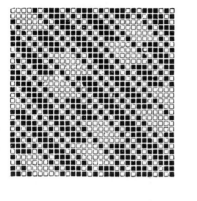

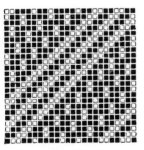

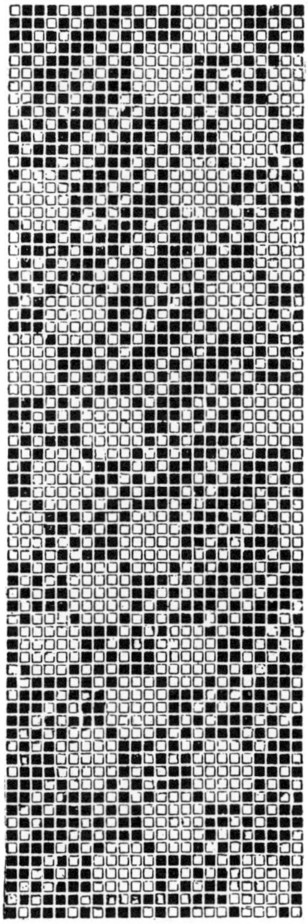

DIVERSIFIED RIB WEAVES

Very pleasing effects can be obtained by grouping floats on a diagonal rib weave, Figs. 730 to 740. Particularly suitable for such a groundwork is the 9-leaf weave shown at Fig. 731, from which are derived Figs. 734, 735, 737 and 738.

FIG. 722.

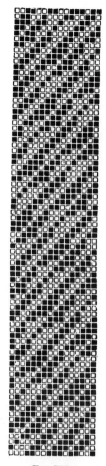

Fig. 723.

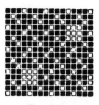

Fig. 724.

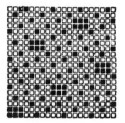

Fig. 725.

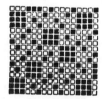

Fig. 726.

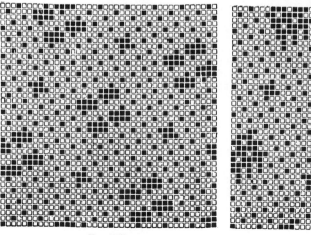

Fig. 727.

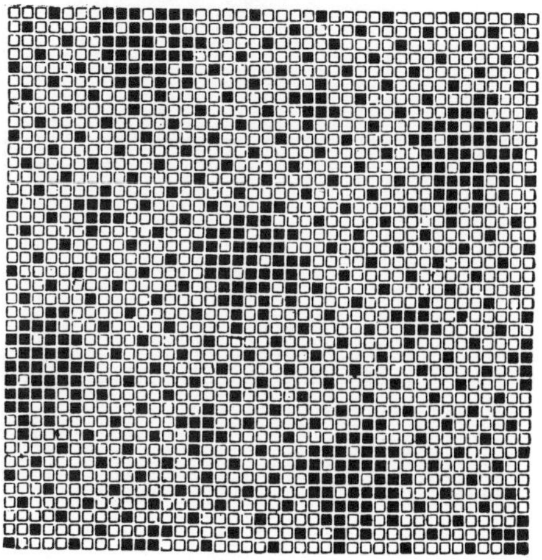

Fig. 728.

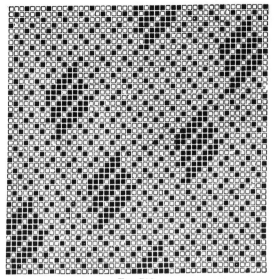

Fig. 729.

Fig. 730.   Fig. 731.   Fig. 732.

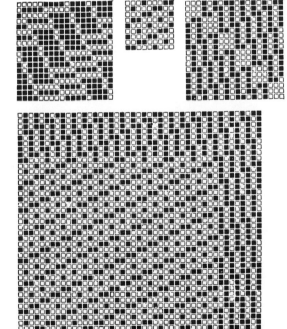

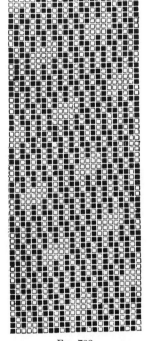

Fig. 734.

Fig. 733.

Fig. 735.

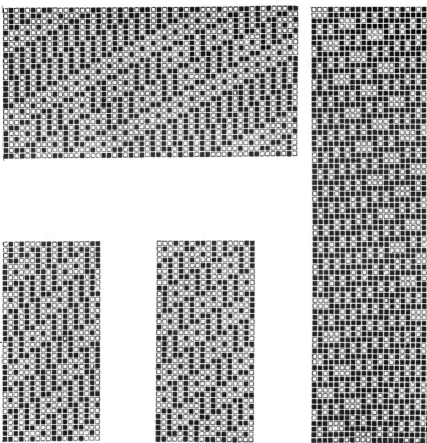

Fig. 736.   Fig. 737.   Fig. 738.

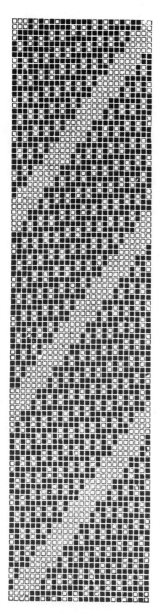

Fig. 739.

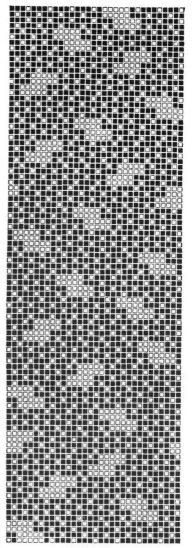

Fig. 740.

HONEYCOMB WEAVES

Attractive effects are obtained by arranging groups of warp and filling floats with a plain weave to form raised and sunken squares, the face of the cloth resembling a honeycomb. The honeycomb effect is especially pronounced when coarse cotton or zephyr yarn is used.

The ordinary honeycomb weaves are 4, 5, 6 or 7 harness pointed designs, Figs. 741 to 745. Modified forms are shown at Figs. 746 to 749, in which the honeycomb square is developed by two threads in each direction. Similar effects are obtained by throwing pronounced warp and filling floats on a plain weave, as shown at Figs. 750 to 755.

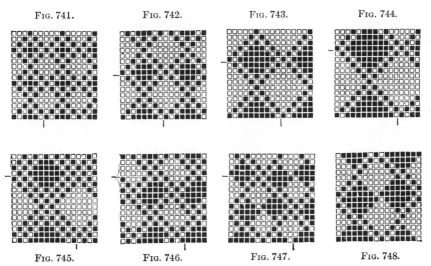

Fig. 741.   Fig. 742.   Fig. 743.   Fig. 744.

Fig. 745.   Fig. 746.   Fig. 747.   Fig. 748.

Fig. **741**	6 × 6
Fig. 742	8 × 8
Fig. 743	10 × 10
Fig. 744	12 × 12
Fig. 745	12 × 12
Fig. 746	12 × 12
Fig. 747	12 × 12

Fig. 749.

Fig. 750.

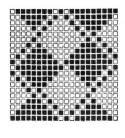

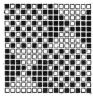

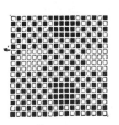

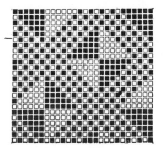

Fig. 751.

Fig. 752.

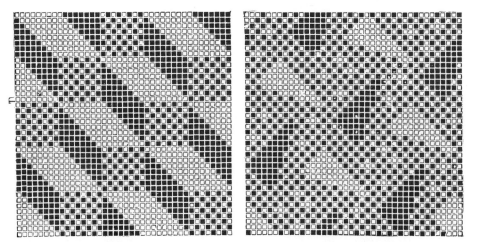

Fig. 753.

Fig. 754.

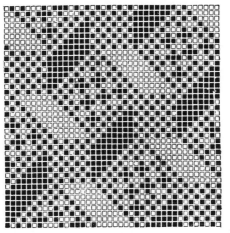

Fig. 755.

BREAKS OR RECESSES IN THE CLOTH

Under this head are included the weaves in which perpendicular and horizontal breaks or recesses occur at intervals where adjacent warp and filling threads are stitched in opposite order. The effect is most pronounced where the break is formed by two adjacent threads stitched with a plain weave, which separates

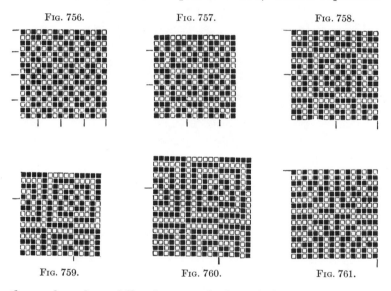

Fig. 756.　　　　Fig. 757.　　　　Fig. 758.

Fig. 759.　　　　Fig. 760.　　　　Fig. 761.

them sharply, while the remainder of the weave allows the other threads to approach each other easily.

The general character of these weaves is shown by Figs. 756 to 761. The breaks are indicated by short lines at the side and bottom. Examples on a somewhat larger scale are shown at Figs. 762 and 763.

Fig. 756 . . . . 4 × 4
Fig. 757 . . . . 6 × 6
Fig. 758 . . . . 8 × 8

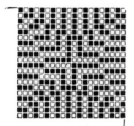

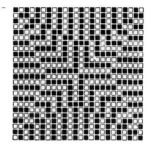

Fig. 762.   Fig. 763.

LACE OR MOCK LENO WEAVES

These weaves are designed to cause apertures or open spaces in the cloth, and are called lace or mock leno weaves from the resemblance to lace and leno fabrics.

The mock leno weave is used chiefly for ladies' dress goods. The open or lace effect is often height-

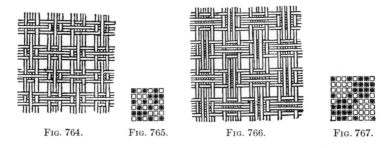

FIG. 764.   FIG. 765.   FIG. 766.   FIG. 767.

ened by making the goods with a plain back of a contrasting color, which shows through the openings in the face weave.

Groups of three or more warp or filling threads are interlaced in such a way that the threads of each group can come together easily in one bunch, while they are separated from the adjacent groups by reason of the last thread of one group and the first thread of the next group being interlaced in directly opposite order. Such an intersection prevents the two threads from coming together and causes an opening at this point.

A 6-leaf mock leno weave is shown at Fig. 765. The interlacing of the threads is shown at Fig. 764. As pick 2 floats under threads 1, 2 and 3, and over threads 4, 5 and 6, picks 1 and 3, which interlace the

166

warp in the same order, are left free to approach each
other so that picks 1, 2 and 3 are brought together in
a bunch.   Picks 4, 5 and 6 are likewise brought together because pick 5 floats over and under each successive group of 3 warp threads, allowing picks 4 and
6 to come together and form a group with pick 5.
The two groups of three picks each are separated by
the breaks in the weave between picks 3 and 4, and

FIG. 768.

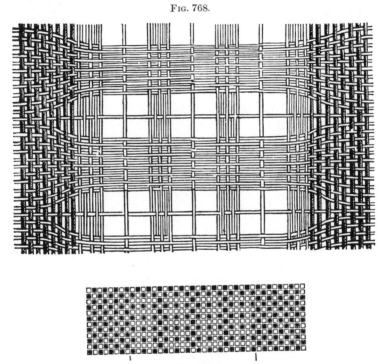

FIG. 769.

between picks 6 and 1, causing an open space in the
cloth at each of these points.

The floating of warp threads 2 and 5 alternately
under and over successive groups of three picks, together with the breaks between threads 3 and 4 and
between threads 6 and 1, causes in like manner a slit
or open space in the warp between threads 3 and 4 and
between threads 6 and 1.

These slits in the warp can be enlarged by reeding 3 threads in a dent and bringing a wire of the reed between threads 3 and 4 and also between threads 6 and 1. Skipping a dent at each of these points makes the slit still wider.

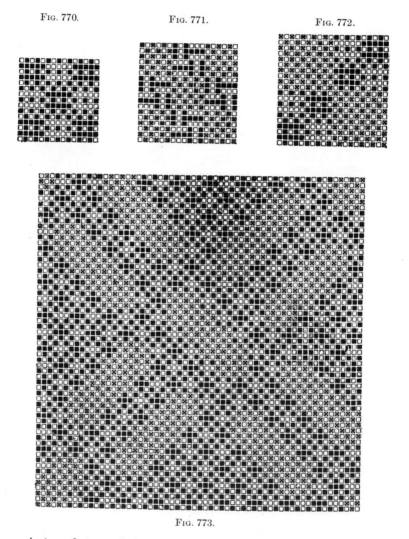

Fig. 770.   Fig. 771.   Fig. 772.

Fig. 773.

A 4 and 4 mock leno weave is shown at Figs. 766 and 767. From what has been said regarding the 3 and 3 weave, Fig. 765, it is evident that the best effect will be obtained at Figs. 766 and 767 by reeding 4 threads in a dent and bringing a reed wire or empty dent between threads 4 and 5 and between threads 8 and 1.

A 5 and 5 mock leno weave is shown at Fig. 770.

Fig. 769 shows a weave for the mock leno stripe effect, Fig. 768.

Very attractive patterns are obtained by combining these lace weaves with a plain ground weave, Figs. 771 to 773.

Fig. 765	6 × 6
Fig. 767	8 × 8
Fig. 769	40 × 12
Fig. 770	10 × 10
Fig. 771	12 × 12
Fig. 772	20 × 20
Fig. 773	60 × 60

Lace effects may also be obtained by weaving alternate groups of cotton and woolen threads in warp and filling, and afterward carbonizing the goods to remove the cotton.

WEAVES THAT DEFLECT CERTAIN THREADS

A peculiar effect is given to the cloth by the weaves shown at Figs. 774 to 794. It arises from the fact that the effect threads in the cloth do not retain the position indicated on the draft. Owing to the method of interlacing the effect picks, these threads are drawn in a slanting direction in the cloth.

Fig. 774.   Fig. 775.   Fig. 776.

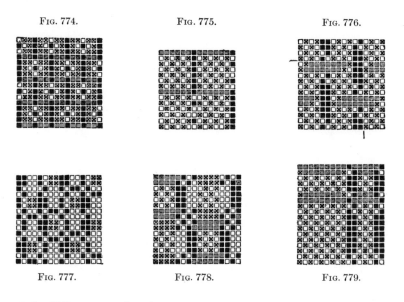

Fig. 777.   Fig. 778.   Fig. 779.

A different color is usually selected for the deflected threads. Mohair and loosely twisted two-color twist heighten the effect.

In Figs. 774 to 794 the effect threads in warp and filling are indicated by the black squares. The warp color pattern begins with the first thread at the left. The filling color pattern begins with the first thread at the bottom of the draft.

170

Unfortunately the changed position of the threads is not shown in the drafts. In Figs. 774, 775 and 794, the threads assume a curved or undulating form.

Figs. 786, 789, 791 and 793 are of special interest because the warp and filling threads separate, taking the position shown at Fig. 785. When the cloth is stretched, the threads are forced back into the position shown in the weave drafts, forming a rib effect.

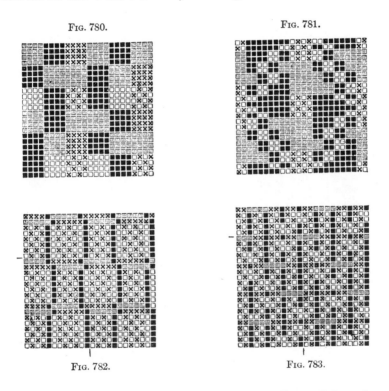

FIG. 780.

FIG. 781.

FIG. 782.

FIG. 783.

The filling floating on the face is indicated by the shaded squares. To increase the undulating effect of the filling, a weave that will facilitate the approach of the effect threads to each other is used. This is well illustrated by the twill in Fig. 794.

If Fig. 787 is woven with the warp and filling pattern, 4 red, 2 black, the part (a) will show a black and red checked effect, while in the part (b) the red will be completely covered.

In the following color patterns the words "light" and "dark" are used to indicate the contrasting colors in the pattern, such as light shade and dark shade, fine and coarse, worsted and mohair, etc. Usually the effect thread is ply yarn and coarser than the ground yarn.

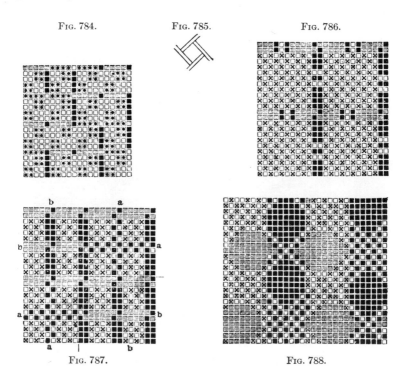

FIG. 784. FIG. 785. FIG. 786.

FIG. 787. FIG. 788.

FIG.	WEAVE	
774	6 × 8	Warp, 1 dark, 2 light; filling, 1 dark, 3 light
775	14 × 4	Warp, 6 light, 1 dark; filling, 6 light, 1 dark
776	12 × 12	Warp, 4 light, 2 dark; filling, 4 light, 2 dark
777	16 × 16	Warp, 2 dark, 2 light; filling, 2 dark, 2 light
778	16 × 16	Warp, 4 light, 4 dark; filling, 2 dark, 2 light, 2 dark

Fig.	Weave	
779	16 × 18	Warp, 9 light, 2 dark, 3 light, 2 dark; filling, 11 light, 2 dark, 3 light, 2 dark
780	24 × 24	Warp, 8 dark, 4 light; filling, 4 light, 8 dark
781	24 × 24	Warp, 2 light, 8 dark, 2 light; filling, 2 light, 8 dark, 2 light
782	12 × 16	Warp, 4 light, 2 dark; filling, 6 light, 2 dark
783	12 × 20	Warp, 2 light, 1 dark; filling, 4 light, 1 dark
784	20 × 20	Warp, 4 light, 1 dark; filling, 4 light, 1 dark

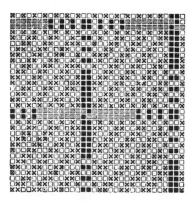

Fig. 789.

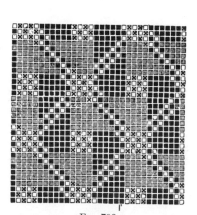

Fig. 790.

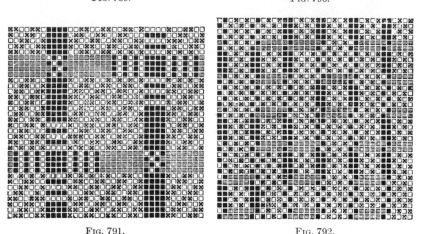

Fig. 791.

Fig. 792.

Fig.	Weave	
786	24 × 24	Warp, 10 light, 2 dark; filling, 10 light, 2 dark
787	24 × 24	Warp, 4 light, 2 dark; filling, 4 light, 2 dark
788	30 × 26	Warp, 8 light, 7 dark; filling, 7 dark, 6 light
789	32 × 32	Warp, 13 light, 2 dark, 14 light, 2 dark, 1 light; filling, same as warp
790	20 × 20	Warp, 1 dark, 4 light, 5 dark; filling, 3 light, 6 dark, 1 light
791	36 × 34	Warp, 7 light, 4 dark, 14 light, 4 dark, 7 light; filling, 8 light, 4 dark, 13 light, 4 dark, 5 light
792	36 × 36	Warp, 2 dark, 4 light; filling, 2 dark, 4 light
793	12 × 14	Warp, 8 light, 4 dark; filling, 10 light, 4 dark
794	52 × 22	Warp, 9 light, 1 dark, 6 light, 1 dark, 9 light; filling, 10 light, 1 dark

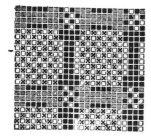

Fig. 793.

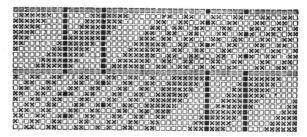

Fig. 794.

CREPE WEAVES

These are weaves in which the warp and filling are interlaced so as to give the cloth a mixed or uniformly mottled appearance. The more uniform this mixed effect is, the better is the crêpe effect considered to be. In constructing crêpe fabrics great care must be taken to avoid stripe effects and to have each thread stitched with floats of practically the same length. Crêpe weaves are used for all varieties of fabrics.

No general rules for the construction of these weaves can be laid down, as each weave is peculiar to itself, but examples will be given to show how they are drafted. A number of the most frequently used crêpe weaves are shown at Figs. 795 to 919. The limits of the pattern are indicated by the lines at the left side and the bottom of the respective drafts.

The crêpe weaves, Figs. 795 to 919, are drafted as follows:

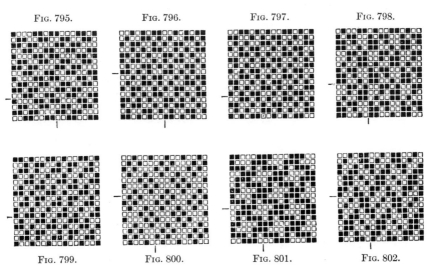

Fig. 795.   Fig. 796.   Fig. 797.   Fig. 798.

Fig. 799.   Fig. 800.   Fig. 801.   Fig. 802.

Fig. 795	8 × 4
Fig. 796	8 × 8
Fig. 797	8 × 4
Fig. 798	6 × 6
Fig. 799	6 × 6
Fig. 800	6 × 6
Fig. 801	6 × 6
Fig. 802	6 × 8

Fig. 803.

Fig. 804.

Fig. 805.

Fig. 806.

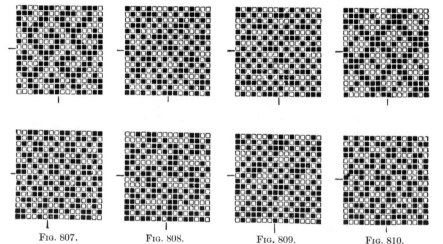

Fig. 807.

Fig. 808.

Fig. 809.

Fig. 810.

Fig. 811.

Fig. 812.

Fig. 813.

Fig. 814.

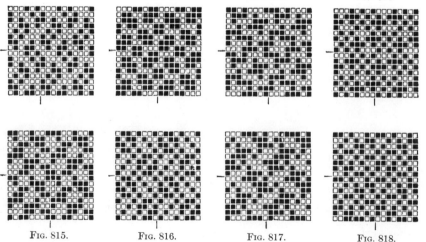

Fig. 815.

Fig. 816.

Fig. 817.

Fig. 818.

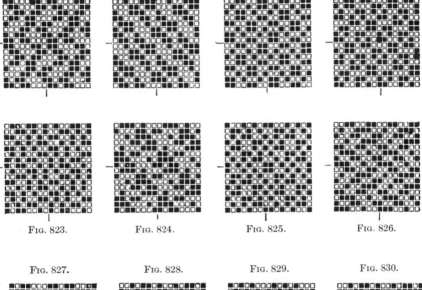

FIG. 819.   FIG. 820.   FIG. 821.   FIG. 822.

FIG. 823.   FIG. 824.   FIG. 825.   FIG. 826.

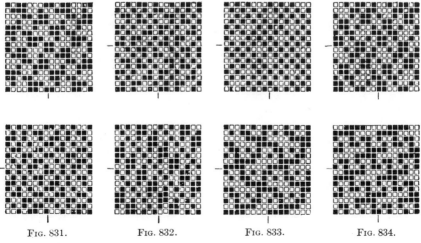

FIG. 827.   FIG. 828.   FIG. 829.   FIG. 830.

FIG. 831.   FIG. 832.   FIG. 833.   FIG. 834.

N

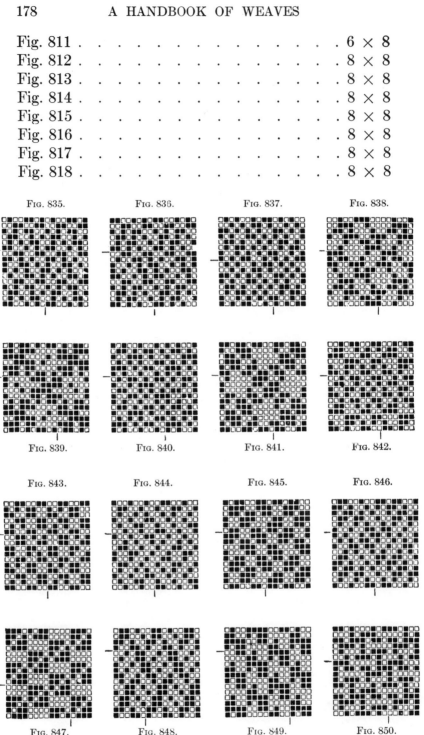

FIG. 835.　　FIG. 836.　　FIG. 837.　　FIG. 838.

FIG. 839.　　FIG. 840.　　FIG. 841.　　FIG. 842.

FIG. 843.　　FIG. 844.　　FIG. 845.　　FIG. 846.

FIG. 847.　　FIG. 848.　　FIG. 849.　　FIG. 850.

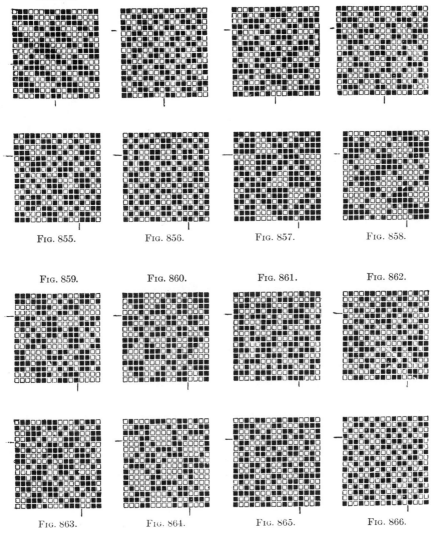

FIG. 851.   FIG. 852.   FIG. 853.   FIG. 854.

FIG. 855.   FIG. 856.   FIG. 857.   FIG. 858.

FIG. 859.   FIG. 860.   FIG. 861.   FIG. 862.

FIG. 863.   FIG. 864.   FIG. 865.   FIG. 866.

Fig. 827	8 × 8
Fig. 828	8 × 8
Fig. 829	8 × 8
Fig. 830	8 × 8
Fig. 831	8 × 8
Fig. 832	8 × 8
Fig. 833	8 × 8
Fig. 834	8 × 8
Fig. 835	8 × 10
Fig. 836	8 × 10
Fig. 837	8 × 10
Fig. 838	10 × 10
Fig. 839	10 × 10
Fig. 840	10 × 10
Fig. 841	10 × 10
Fig. 842	10 × 10
Fig. 843	8 × 10
Fig. 844	10 × 10
Fig. 845	10 × 10
Fig. 846	10 × 10
Fig. 847	12 × 6
Fig. 848	6 × 12
Fig. 849	12 × 6

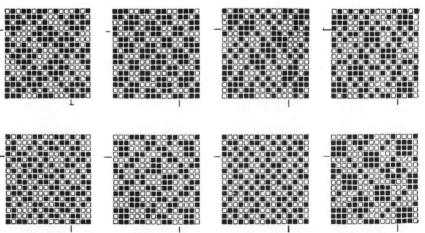

Fig. 867.

Fig. 868.

Fig. 869.

Fig. 870.

Fig. 871.

Fig. 872.

Fig. 873.

Fig. 874.

Fig. 850	10 × 10
Fig. 851	8 × 12
Fig. 852	8 × 12
Fig. 853	10 × 12
Fig. 854	10 × 12
Fig. 855	12 × 12
Fig. 856	12 × 12
Fig. 857	12 × 12
Fig. 858	12 × 12
Fig. 859	12 × 12
Fig. 860	12 × 12
Fig. 861	12 × 12
Fig. 862	12 × 12
Fig. 863	12 × 12
Fig. 864	12 × 12
Fig. 865	12 × 12
Fig. 866	12 × 12
Fig. 867	12 × 12
Fig. 868	12 × 12
Fig. 869	12 × 12
Fig. 870	12 × 12
Fig. 871	12 × 12
Fig. 872	12 × 12

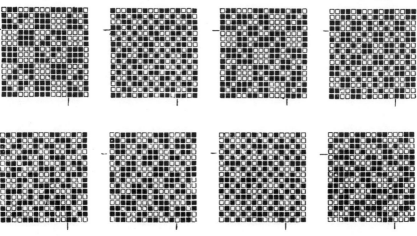

Fig. 875.

Fig. 876.

Fig. 877.

Fig. 878.

Fig. 879.

Fig. 880.

Fig. 881.

Fig. 882.

Fig. 873 . . . . 12 × 12
Fig. 874 . . . . 12 × 12
Fig. 875 . . . . 12 × 12
Fig. 876 . . . . 12 × 12
Fig. 877 . . . . 12 × 12
Fig. 878 . . . . 12 × 12
Fig. 879 . . . . 12 × 12
Fig. 880 . . . . 12 × 12
Fig. 881 . . . . 12 × 12
Fig. 882 . . . . 12 × 12
Fig. 883 . . . . 12 × 12
Fig. 884 . . . . 12 × 12
Fig. 885 . . . . 12 × 12
Fig. 886 . . . . 12 × 12
Fig. 887 . . . . 12 × 12
Fig. 888 . . . . 12 × 14
Fig. 889 . . . . 12 × 16
Fig. 890 . . . . 16 × 12
Fig. 891 . . . . 16 × 16
Fig. 892 . . . . 16 × 16
Fig. 893 . . . . 16 × 16
Fig. 894 . . . . 16 × 16
Fig. 895 . . . . 16 × 16

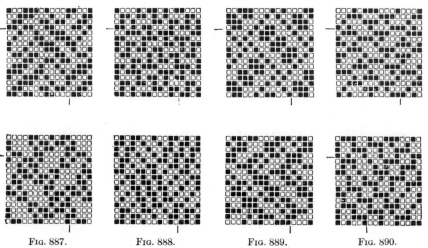

Fig. 883.

Fig. 884.

Fig. 885.

Fig. 886.

Fig. 887.

Fig. 888.

Fig. 889.

Fig. 890.

FIG. 891.　　　　FIG. 892.　　　　FIG. 893.　　　　FIG. 894.

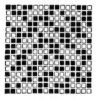

FIG. 895.　　　　FIG. 896.　　　　FIG. 897.　　　　FIG. 898.

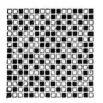

FIG. 899.　　　　FIG. 900.　　　　FIG. 901.　　　　FIG. 902.

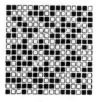

FIG. 903.　　　　FIG. 904.　　　　FIG. 905.　　　　FIG. 906.

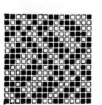
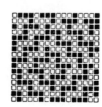
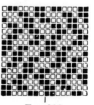

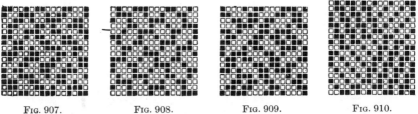

FIG. 907.   FIG. 908.   FIG. 909.   FIG. 910.

FIG. 911.   FIG. 912.   FIG. 913.

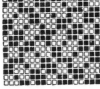

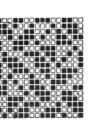
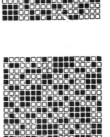
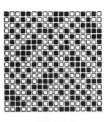

FIG. 914.   FIG. 915.   FIG. 916.

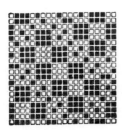
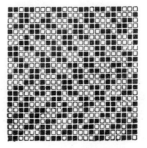
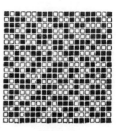

FIG. 917.   FIG. 918.   FIG. 919.

Fig. 909	16 × 16
Fig. 910	16 × 18
Fig. 911	18 × 18
Fig. 912	18 × 18
Fig. 913	18 × 18
Fig. 914	18 × 18
Fig. 915	18 × 18
Fig. 916	18 × 18
Fig. 917	20 × 20
Fig. 918	24 × 24
Fig. 919	20 × 20

CRÊPE WEAVES DERIVED FROM SATIN WEAVES

The satin weave is first drafted and then one or more stitching points are added, either above, below or at one side of the satin points, the number depending on the distance between the latter. Other weaves may be drafted in the space between the satin points, the size of the weave pattern depending on the number of threads in the satin weave. Several examples are shown at Figs. 920 to 931. The points or risers of the original satin weave are indicated by different type in a part of each draft.

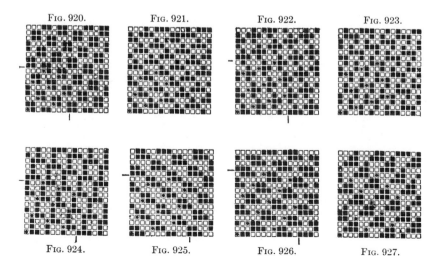

Fig. 920.

Fig. 921.

Fig. 922.

Fig. 923.

Fig. 924.

Fig. 925.

Fig. 926.

Fig. 927.

Fig. 920	8 × 8
Fig. 921	8 × 8
Fig. 922	10 × 10
Fig. 923	10 × 10
Fig. 924	10 × 10
Fig. 925	11 × 11
Fig. 926	12 × 12
Fig. 927	12 × 12
Fig. 928	13 × 13
Fig. 929	13 × 13
Fig. 930	15 × 15
Fig. 931	16 × 16

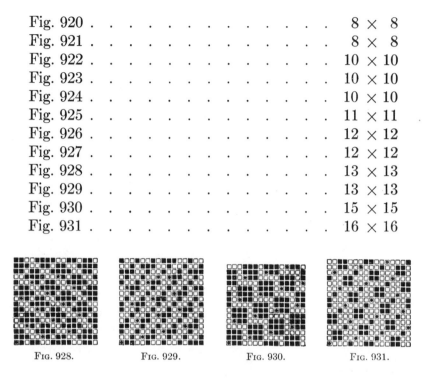

Fig. 928.   Fig. 929.   Fig. 930.   Fig. 931.

CRÊPE EFFECTS BY ARRANGING FLOATS IN SATIN ORDER

A great variety of crêpe effects can be obtained by forming a group of risers and then arranging it in satin order with any desired number of threads in the pattern. The resulting weave may have warp and filling threads floating too far; these must be stitched down in some regular order to connect the groups. Examples are shown at Figs. 932 to 996.

Above each of the first nine drafts, Figs. 932 to 940,

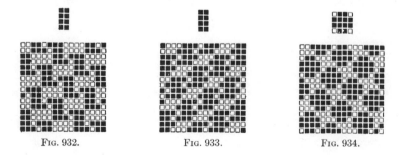

Fig. 932.   Fig. 933.   Fig. 934.

is placed the group of floats that is arranged in crêpe weave order.

Fig. 932 . . . . 10 × 10 5-leaf satin, 1, 4, 2, 5, 3
Fig. 933 . . . . 10 × 10 5-leaf satin, 1, 3, 5, 2, 4
Fig. 934 . . . . 10 × 10 5-leaf satin, 1, 4, 2, 5, 3
Fig. 935 . . . . 10 × 10 5-leaf satin, 1, 4, 2, 5, 3

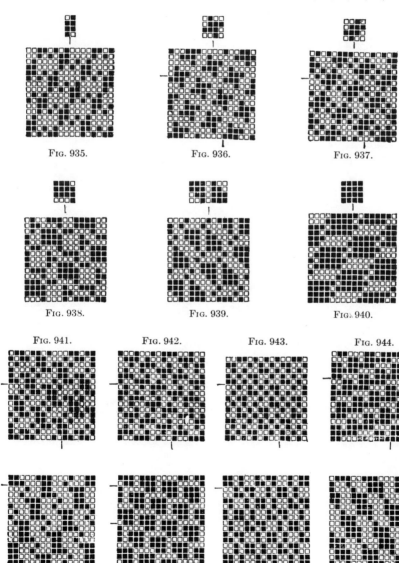

FIG. 935.   FIG. 936.   FIG. 937.

FIG. 938.   FIG. 939.   FIG. 940.

FIG. 941.   FIG. 942.   FIG. 943.   FIG. 944.

FIG. 945.   FIG. 946.   FIG. 947.   FIG. 948.

Fig. 936 . . . . 10 × 10 5-leaf satin, 1, 4, 2, 5, 3
Fig. 937 . . . . 10 × 10 5-leaf satin, 2, 5, 3, 4, 1
Fig. 938 . . . . 15 × 15 5-leaf satin, 1, 3, 5, 2, 4
Fig. 939 . . . . 15 × 15 5-leaf satin, 1, 3, 5, 2, 4
Fig. 940 . . 16 × 16 8-leaf satin, 1, 4, 7, 2, 5, 8, 3, 6
Fig. 941 . . . . 10 × 10 5-leaf satin
Fig. 942 . . . . 10 × 10 5-leaf satin
Fig. 943 . . . . 10 × 10 5-leaf satin
Fig. 944 . . . . 11 × 11 11-leaf satin
Fig. 945 . . . . 14 × 14 7-leaf satin
Fig. 946 . . . . 14 × 7 7-leaf satin

Fig. 949.
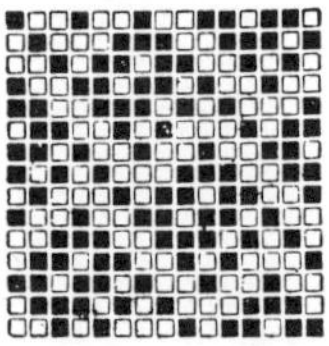
Fig. 950.
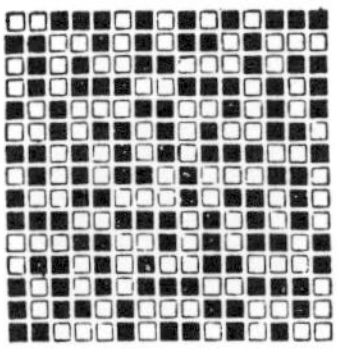
Fig. 951.
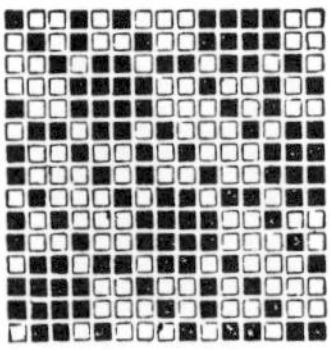
Fig. 952.
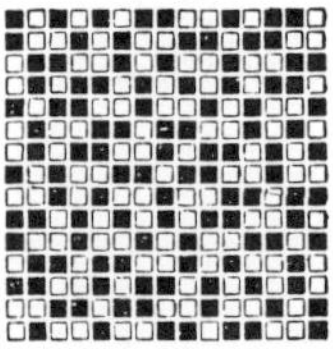

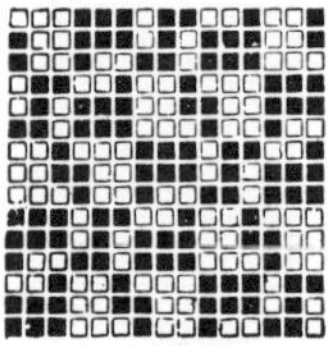
Fig. 953.
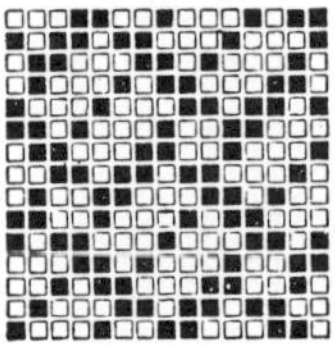
Fig. 954.
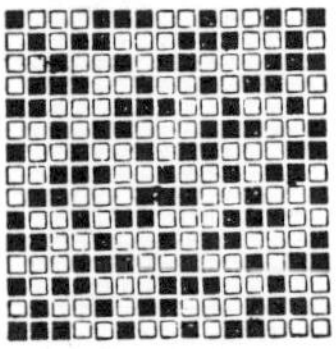
Fig. 955.
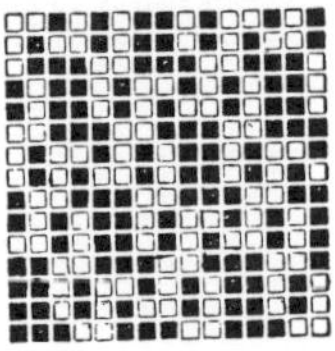
Fig. 956.

Fig. 957.
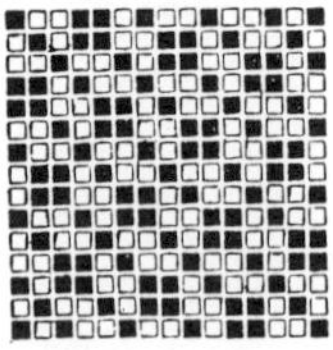
Fig. 958.
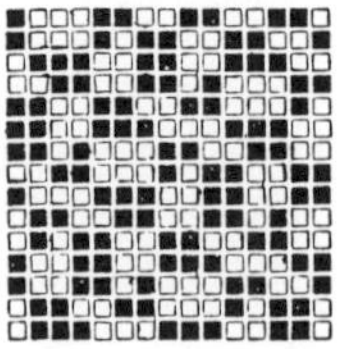
Fig. 959.
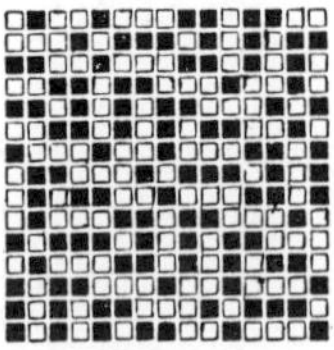
Fig. 960.
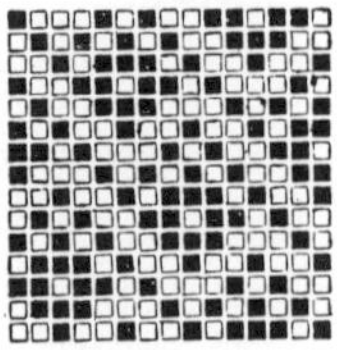

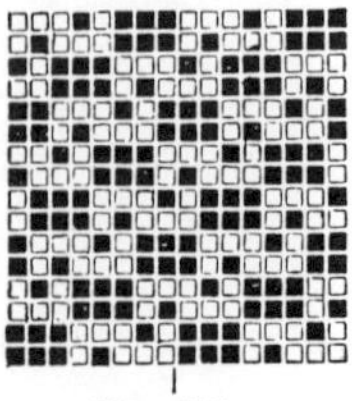
Fig. 961.
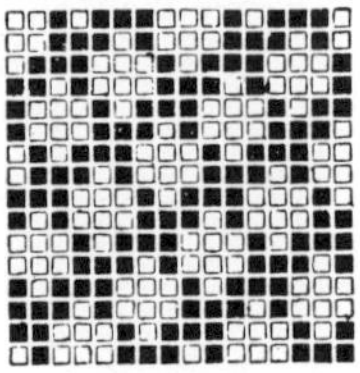
Fig. 962.
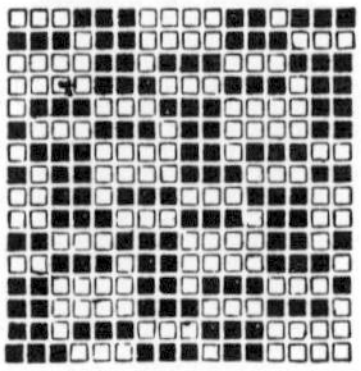
Fig. 963.
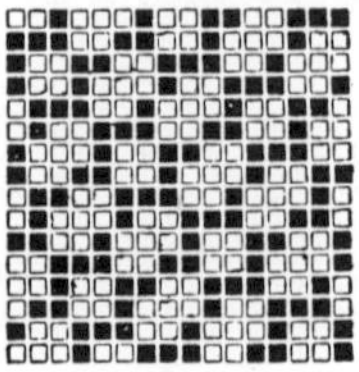
Fig. 964.

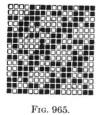

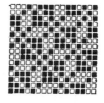

FIG. 965.   FIG. 966.   FIG. 967.   FIG. 968.

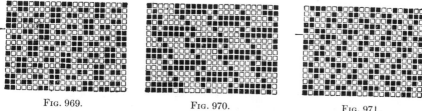

FIG. 969.   FIG. 970.   FIG. 971.

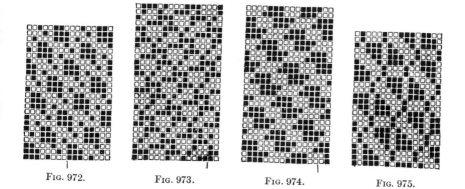

FIG. 972.   FIG. 973.   FIG. 974.   FIG. 975.

Fig. 959	15 × 15	5-leaf satin
Fig. 960	15 × 15	5-leaf satin
Fig. 961	8 × 16	8-leaf satin
Fig. 962	16 × 16	16-leaf satin
Fig. 963	16 × 16	8-leaf satin

Fig. 976.

Fig. 977.

Fig. 978.

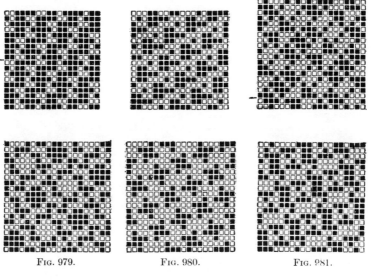

Fig. 979.

Fig. 980.

Fig. 981.

Fig. 982.

Fig. 983.

Fig. 984.

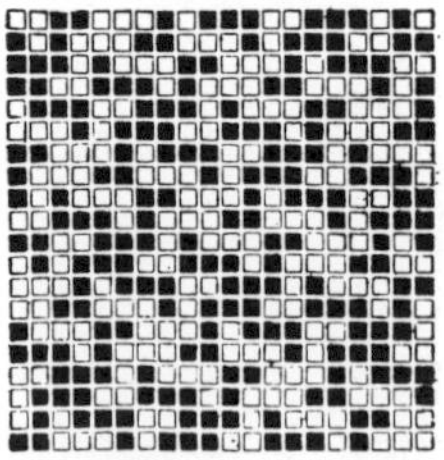

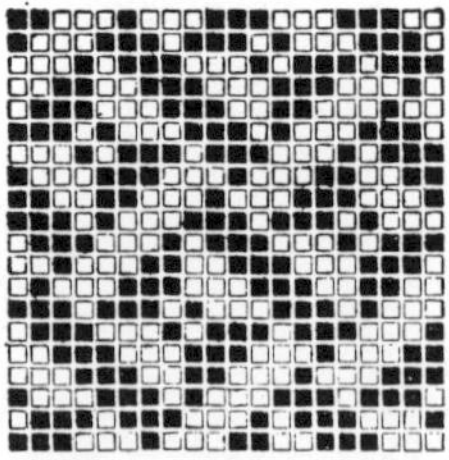

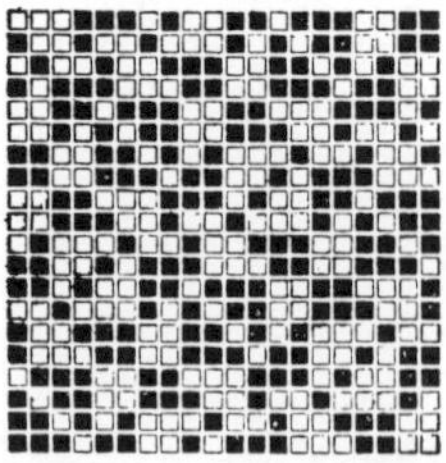

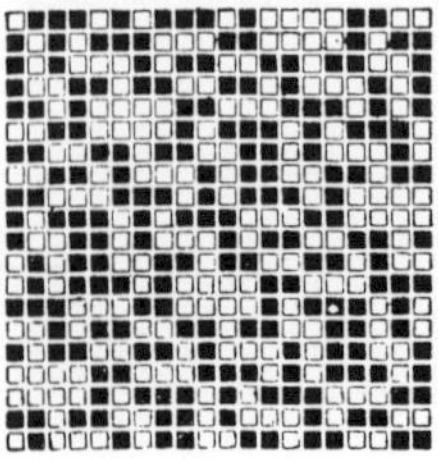

Fig. 985.

Fig. 986.

Fig. 987.

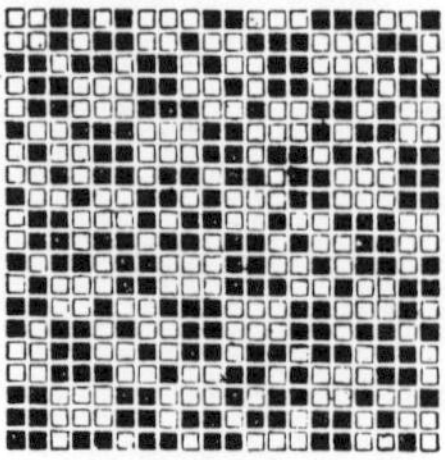

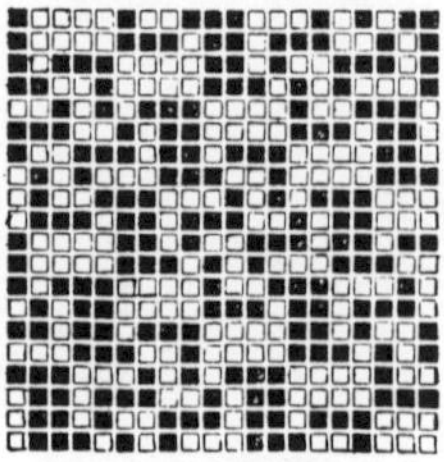

Fig. 964	16 × 16	8-leaf satin
Fig. 965	16 × 16	8-leaf satin
Fig. 966	16 × 16	8-leaf satin
Fig. 967	16 × 16	8-leaf satin

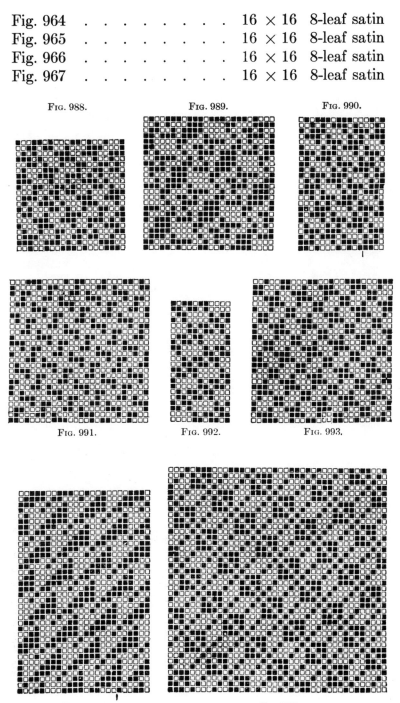

FIG. 988.   FIG. 989.   FIG. 990.

FIG. 991.   FIG. 992.   FIG. 993.

FIG. 994.   FIG. 995.

FIG. 996.

Fig. 968 . . .	16 × 16	8-leaf satin
Fig. 969 . . .	22 × 11	11-leaf satin
Fig. 970 . . .	16 × 16	8-leaf satin
Fig. 971 . . .	22 × 11	11-leaf satin
Fig. 972 . . .	8 × 24	8-leaf satin
Fig. 973 . . .	14 × 28	14-leaf satin
Fig. 974 . . .	14 × 28	14-leaf satin
Fig. 975 . . .	16 × 24	8-leaf satin
Fig. 976 . . .	18 × 9	9-leaf satin
Fig. 977 . . .	18 × 18	18-leaf satin
Fig. 978 . . .	20 × 20	5-leaf satin
Fig. 979 . . .	20 × 20	5-leaf satin
Fig. 980 . . .	20 × 20	10-leaf satin
Fig. 981 . . .	20 × 20	10-leaf satin
Fig. 982 . . .	20 × 20	10-leaf satin
Fig. 983 . . .	20 × 20	5-leaf satin
Fig. 984 . . .	20 × 20	5-leaf satin
Fig. 985 . . .	20 × 20	5-leaf satin
Fig. 986 . . .	20 × 20	5-leaf satin
Fig. 987 . . .	20 × 20	5-leaf satin
Fig. 988 . •. .	20 × 20	5-leaf satin
Fig. 989	24 × 24	8-leaf satin
Fig. 990	12 × 24	modified satin
Fig. 991	26 × 26	26-leaf satin
Fig. 992	11 × 22	modified satin

FIG. 997.   FIG. 998.   FIG. 999.

Fig. 993	26 × 26	26-leaf satin
Fig. 994	18 × 36	modified satin
Fig. 995	40 × 40	modified satin
Fig. 996	16 × 64	modified satin

CRÊPE BY TRANSPOSITION OF WEAVES IN CHECKER-- BOARD ORDER

Crêpe weaves are obtained by arranging a base weave in different positions in the different squares of the draft in regular and reversed form.

If, for example, an 8-leaf crêpe is wanted, the threads of the pattern are divided in each direction on the drafting paper into two equal parts, which divides the entire area into four equal parts. A balanced weave is then drafted in the lower left-hand square, as shown at Fig. 997.

The same weave reversed, risers and sinkers being transposed, is then drafted in the lower right-hand square, beginning with the last thread in the left-hand square so that the two threads will break with each other, Fig. 998. The upper half of the weave is then drafted, making the upper left-hand square like the lower right, and the upper right-hand square like the lower left, Fig. 999.

An unlimited number of attractive and useful crêpe weaves can be drafted by this method. Examples are shown at Figs. 1000 to 1027.

Fig. 1000	6 × 6
Fig. 1001	6 × 6
Fig. 1002	6 × 6
Fig. 1003	6 × 8
Fig. 1004	8 × 8
Fig. 1005	8 × 8
Fig. 1006	8 × 8

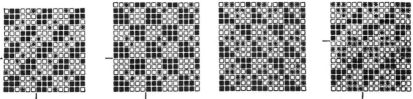

FIG. 1000.   FIG. 1001.   FIG. 1002.   FIG. 1003.

Fig. 1007 . . . . 8 × 8
Fig. 1008 . . . . 8 × 8
Fig. 1009 . . . . 8 × 8
Fig. 1010 . . . . 8 × 8
Fig. 1011 . . . . 10 × 10
Fig. 1012 . . . . 8 × 8
Fig. 1013 . . . . 8 × 8
Fig. 1014 . . . . 10 × 10
Fig. 1015 . . . . 10 × 10

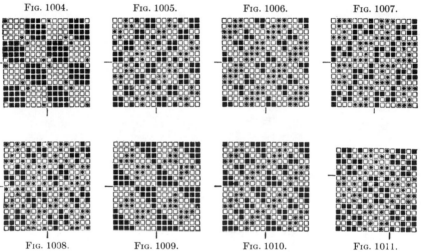

Fig. 1004.

Fig. 1005.

Fig. 1006.

Fig. 1007.

Fig. 1008.

Fig. 1009.

Fig. 1010.

Fig. 1011.

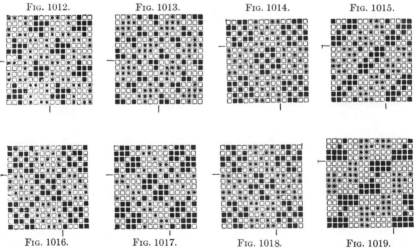

Fig. 1012.

Fig. 1013.

Fig. 1014.

Fig. 1015.

Fig. 1016.

Fig. 1017.

Fig. 1018.

Fig. 1019.

CRÊPE WEAVES BY REARRANGING OTHER WEAVES

Another method of drafting crêpe weaves consists in rearranging the threads of other weaves. A large number of crêpe weaves can be obtained by keeping the general character of the base weave unchanged, but changing the order in which the threads are arranged. The threads are either laid out in a predetermined order on a new draft, or the drawing-in draft is arranged to give the order desired.

Such rearrangements sometimes cause too long a

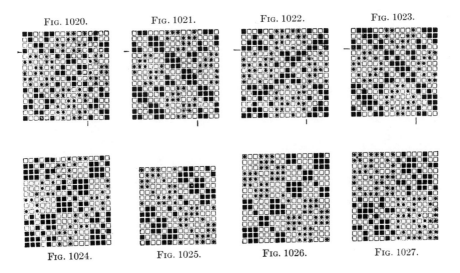

FIG. 1020.   FIG. 1021.   FIG. 1022.   FIG. 1023.

FIG. 1024.   FIG. 1025.   FIG. 1026.   FIG. 1027.

float of the filling threads, making it necessary to stitch the floats by inserting single points in order that the firmness of the fabric may not be impaired.

CRÊPE WEAVES BY REARRANGEMENT OF THE WARP THREADS

This method of crêpe weave construction is very useful because it enables the designer to combine twill and crêpe stripe effects in the same pattern without any increase in the number of shafts. The ground weave requires a straight drawing-in draft, while the crêpe is obtained by cross drafts. This method of drafting is illustrated at Fig. 1028, which shows four drawing-in drafts (a, b, c, d) with the same chain, giving the straight twill (a) and three crêpe effects (b, c, d).

In this way many weave effects can be produced in one pattern without an increase in the number of shafts. The method is very useful in weaving different patterns on one pattern warp. Other examples are shown at Figs. 1029 to 1067.

The foundation weave is either drafted at the upper left-hand corner, as at Fig. 1044, or indicated by a formula above the draft, as at Fig. 1029.

Fig. 1029 . . . . 11 × 11
Fig. 1030 . . . . 11 × 11
Fig. 1031 . . . . 11 × 11

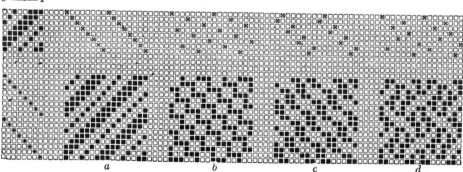

a   b   c   d

FIG. 1028.

Fig. 1032 . . . . 12 × 12
Fig. 1033 . . . . 12 × 12
Fig. 1034 . . . . 12 × 12
Fig. 1035 . . . . 14 × 14
Fig. 1036 . . . . 14 × 14
Fig. 1037 . . . . 14 × 14
Fig. 1038 . . . . 16 × 16
Fig. 1039 . . . . 16 × 16
Fig. 1040 . . . . 16 × 16
Fig. 1041 . . . . 16 × 16
Fig. 1042 . . . . 16 × 16
Fig. 1043 . . . . 16 × 16
Fig. 1044 . . . . 8 shafts

FIG. 1029.

$\frac{3\ 1\ 1}{2\ 2\ 2}$

FIG. 1030.

$\frac{3\ 1\ 1}{1\ 2\ 3}$

FIG. 1031.

$\frac{3\ 1\ 1}{2\ 3\ 1}$

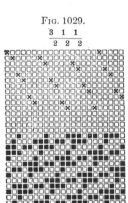

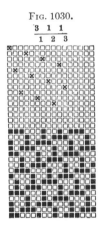

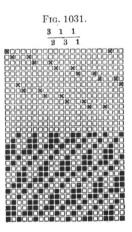

$\frac{3\ 1\ 1}{2\ 3\ 2}$

FIG. 1032.

$\frac{3\ 1\ 1\ 1}{1\ 2\ 2\ 1}$

FIG. 1033.

$\frac{3\ 2\ 1}{2\ 2\ 2}$

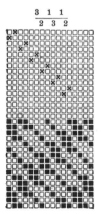

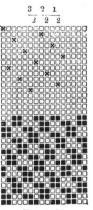

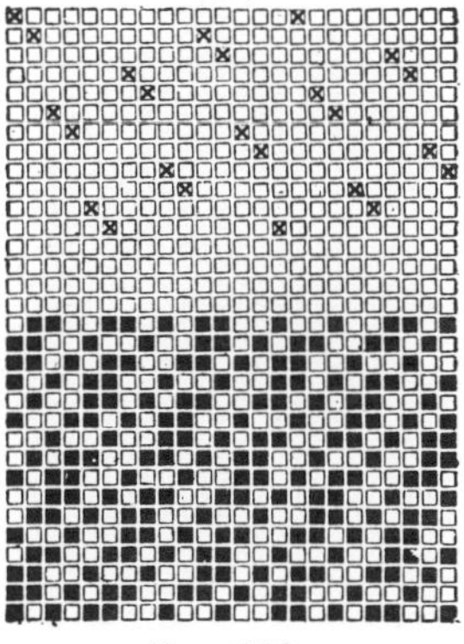

FIG. 1034.

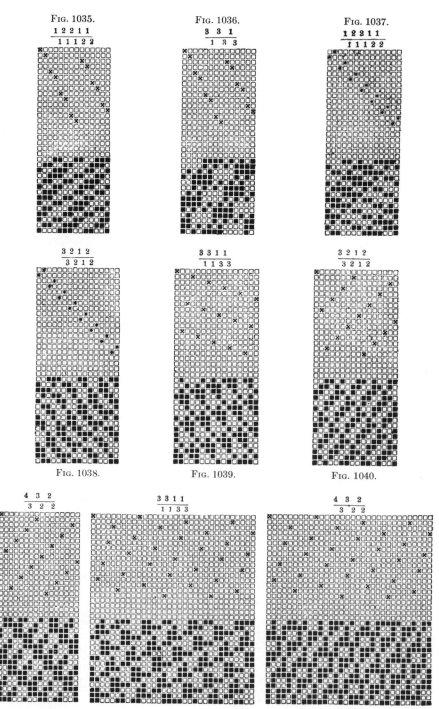

FIG. 1035.

$$\frac{1\ 2\ 2\ 1\ 1}{1\ 1\ 1\ 2\ 2}$$

FIG. 1036.

$$\frac{3\ 3\ 1}{1\ 3\ 3}$$

FIG. 1037.

$$\frac{1\ 2\ 2\ 1\ 1}{1\ 1\ 1\ 2\ 2}$$

$$\frac{3\ 2\ 1\ 2}{3\ 2\ 1\ 2}$$

$$\frac{3\ 3\ 1\ 1}{1\ 1\ 3\ 3}$$

$$\frac{3\ 2\ 1\ 2}{3\ 2\ 1\ 2}$$

FIG. 1038.

FIG. 1039.

FIG. 1040.

$$\frac{4\ 3\ 2}{3\ 2\ 2}$$

$$\frac{3\ 3\ 1\ 1}{1\ 1\ 3\ 3}$$

$$\frac{4\ 3\ 2}{3\ 2\ 2}$$

FIG. 1041.

FIG. 1042.

FIG. 1043.

FIG. 1044.

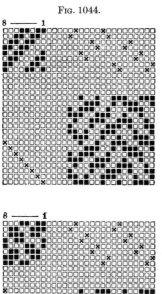

FIG. 1045.

FIG. 1046.

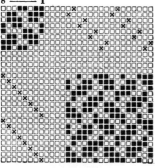

FIG. 1047.

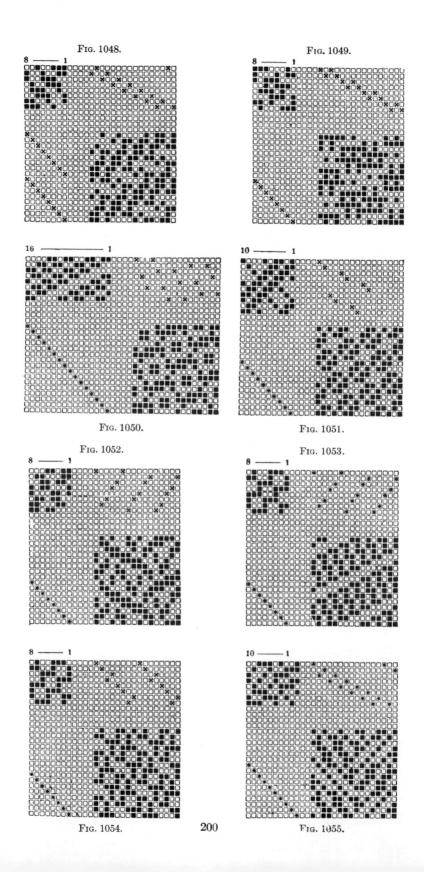

FIG. 1048.

FIG. 1049.

8 —— 1

8 —— 1

FIG. 1050.

FIG. 1051.

16 —————— 1

10 —— 1

FIG. 1052.

FIG. 1053.

8 —— 1

8 —— 1

8 —— 1

10 —— 1

FIG. 1054.

200

FIG. 1055.

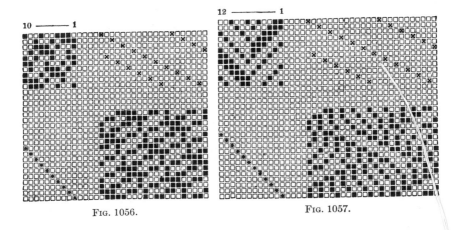

FIG. 1056. FIG. 1057.

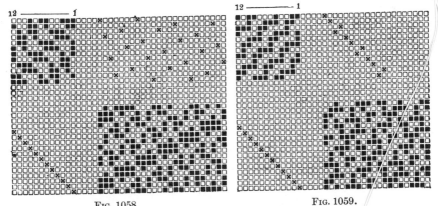

FIG. 1058. FIG. 1059.

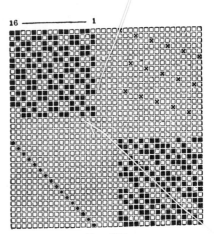

FIG. 1060. FIG. 1061.

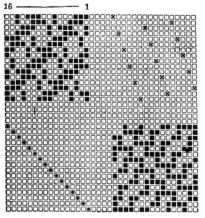

FIG. 1062.

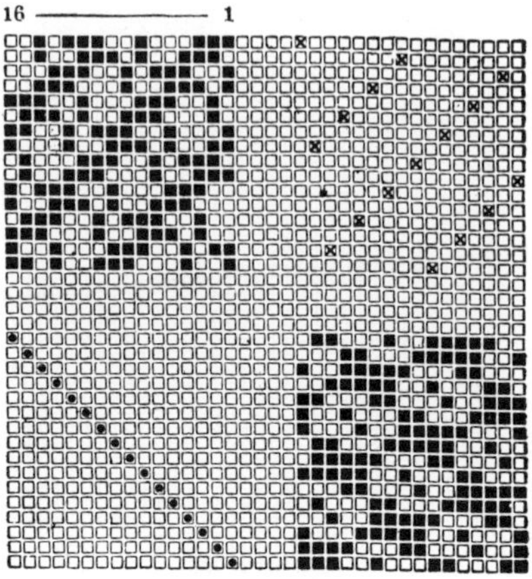

FIG. 1063.

FIG. 1064.

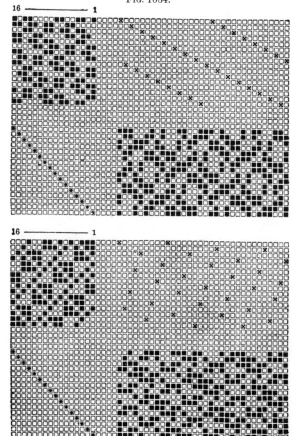

FIG. 1065.

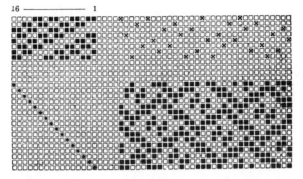

Fig. 1066.

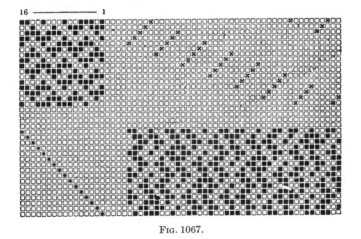

Fig. 1067.

CRÊPE WEAVES BY REARRANGING WARP AND FILLING

Much more interesting are the crêpe weaves produced by rearranging the threads in both warp and filling. This method enables different crêpe weaves

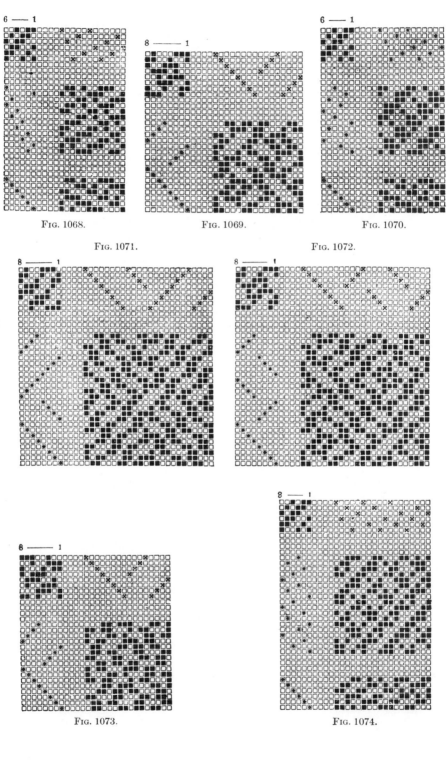

FIG. 1068.

FIG. 1069.

FIG. 1070.

FIG. 1071.

FIG. 1072.

FIG. 1073.

FIG. 1074.

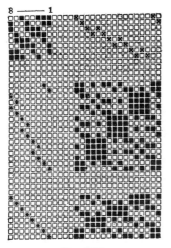

FIG. 1075.

FIG. 1076.

to be produced by changing the position of the filling threads on the same chain without change of the drawing-in draft.

The method of drafting is illustrated at Fig. 1068. The 6-leaf base weave is shown in the upper left-hand corner. The 6-shaft drawing-in draft appears at the top of the figure. The 12-thread weave resulting from this drawing-in draft is shown at the bottom.

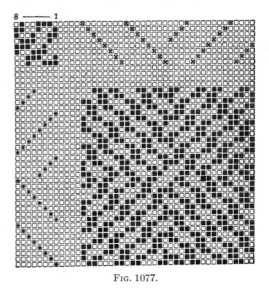

FIG. 1077.

At the left in the lower left-hand corner is the line of points indicating the 6 picks in the 12-thread weave at the bottom. Above this line and at the left side of the figure is given the order in which these 6 picks of the 12-thread weave are rearranged to produce the crêpe pattern at the right. The rearrangement of the picks is indicated by the method used for drawing-in drafts.

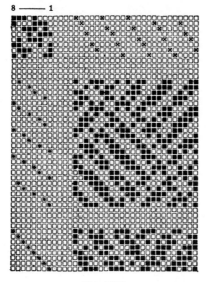

Fig. 1078.

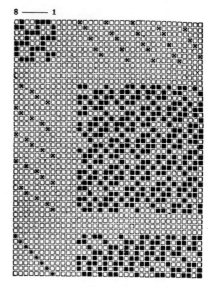

Fig. 1079.

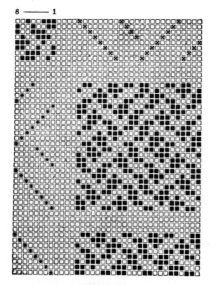

Fig. 1080.

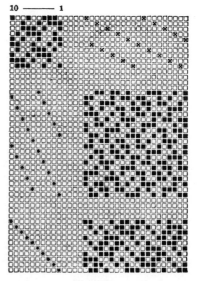

Fig. 108 .

This process of drafting is also illustrated in full in Figs. 1070, 1074, 1075, 1076 and 1078 to 1090. In the other drafts, Figs. 1069, 1071, 1072, 1073 and 1077,

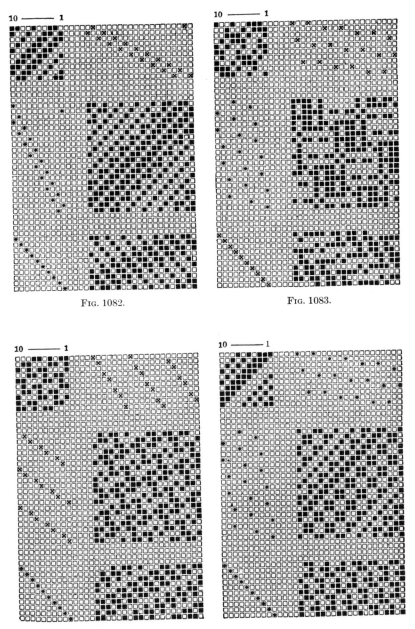

FIG. 1082.

FIG. 1083.

FIG. 1084.

FIG. 1085.

the weave obtained by rearranging the warp only is omitted.

Wide diagonals can be produced in this way with a small number of shafts, as shown at Figs. 1082, 1085, 1086 and 1088.

Fig. 1068 . . . . 6 shafts
Fig. 1069 . . . . 8 shafts
Fig. 1070 . . . . 6 shafts
Fig. 1071 . . . . 8 shafts
Fig. 1072 . . . . 8 shafts
Fig. 1073 . . . . 8 shafts
Fig. 1074 . . . . 6 shafts
Fig. 1075 . . . . 8 shafts
Fig. 1076 . . . . 8 shafts
Fig. 1077 . . . . 8 shafts
Fig. 1078 . . . . 8 shafts
Fig. 1079 . . . . 8 shafts
Fig. 1080 . . . . 8 shafts

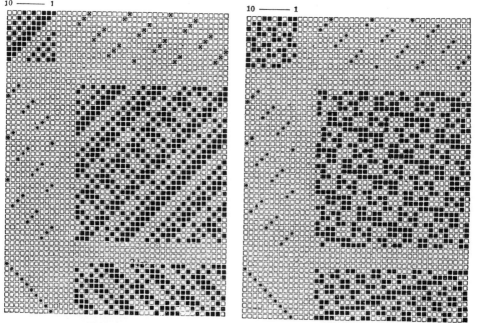

FIG. 1086.

FIG. 1087.

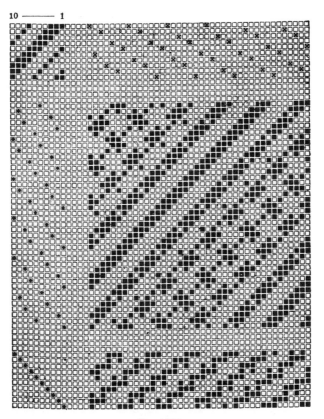

FIG. 1088.

CRÊPE WEAVES WITH GROUPS OF THREADS ON THE SAME SHAFT

Another method of constructing crêpe weaves consists in drawing a number of threads, each on a different shaft, as 1, 2, 3, 4, and then drawing two or mor'

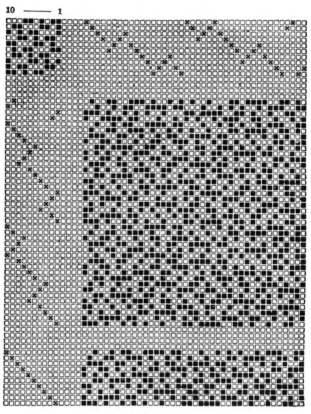

FIG. 1089.

threads on the same shaft. These groups are so arranged that the whole number of shafts is not divisible by the number of threads in the groups. For example, with 8 or 10 shafts the threads may be drawn in 2 single 1 double, total 3 shafts, or 1 single 2 double, total 3 shafts.

The object of this arrangement is to distribute the

double threads uniformly on all the different shafts. As neither 10 nor 8 is divisible by 3 it follows that the double threads will come on a different shaft at each passage of the drawing-in draft across the shafts, until

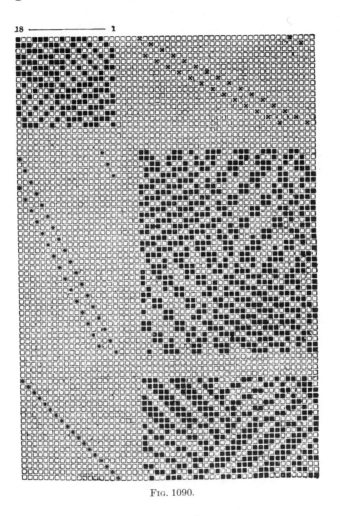

Fig. 1090.

every shaft carries a double thread, when the pattern is complete. The same rule is followed in the filling.

This method is illustrated at Figs. 1091 to 1094, in each of which the weave pattern resulting from the rearrangement of the warp threads only is shown at the bottom of the figure.

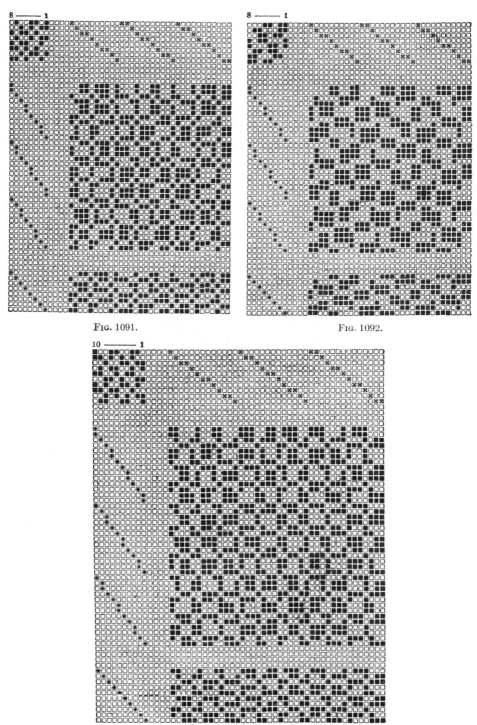

Fig. 1091.

Fig. 1092.

Fig. 1093.

From this draft the completed pattern, shown at the right of the figure is obtained by a similar rearrangement of the picks.

Fig. 1091 . . . . 8 shafts
Fig. 1092 . . . . 8 shafts
Fig. 1093 . . . . 10 shafts
Fig. 1094 . . . . 8 shafts

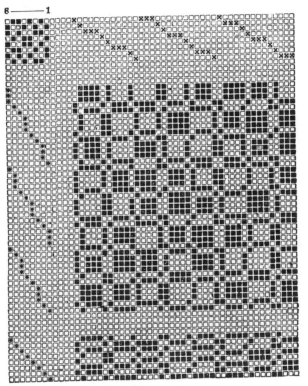

FIG. 1094.

CRÊPE BY INTERLOCKING A WEAVE WITH ITS REVERSE

This method consists in transferring the ground weave to a draft in which one or more warp threads are left blank at fixed intervals, the ground weave being sketched on the others. The blank threads are then filled in by inserting risers where sinkers are found at one side. If the blank threads are single, each one is drafted to break with the thread either to the right or left. In Figs. 1096 and 1098 the break is made with the thread at the left. The ground weaves for Figs. 1096 and 1098 are shown at Figs. 1095 and 1097.

If the blank threads occur in pairs, the left-hand thread of each pair breaks with the regular thread at the left and the right-hand thread breaks with the regular thread at the right, Figs. 1100 and 1102. The ground weaves for Figs. 1100 and 1102 are shown at Figs. 1099 and 1101.

CRÊPE BY INTERLOCKING TWO WEAVES

Crêpe effects can be obtained by interlocking two weaves. Fig. 1105 is the weave obtained by interlocking a twill, Fig. 1103, and a crêpe, Fig. 1104. Fig. 1108 is derived from two crêpe weaves, Figs. 1106

Fig. 1095.

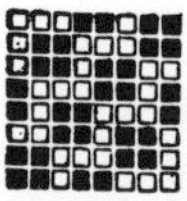

Fig. 1097.

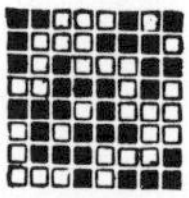

Fig. 1099.

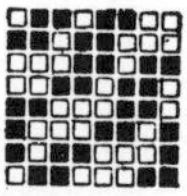

Fig. 1101

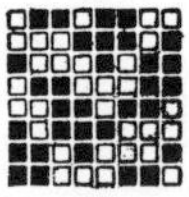

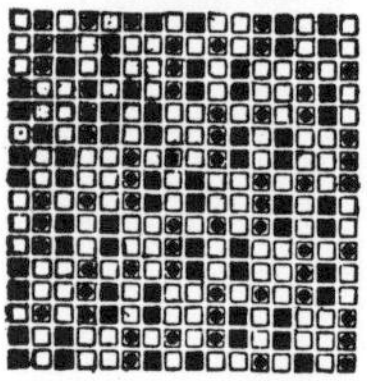

Fig. 1096.

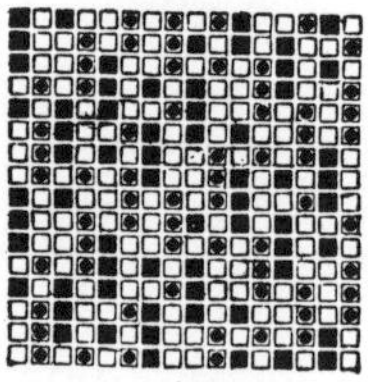

Fig. 1098.

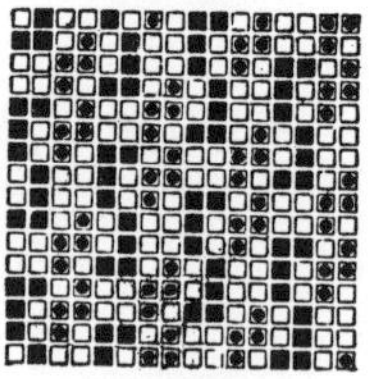

Fig. 1100.

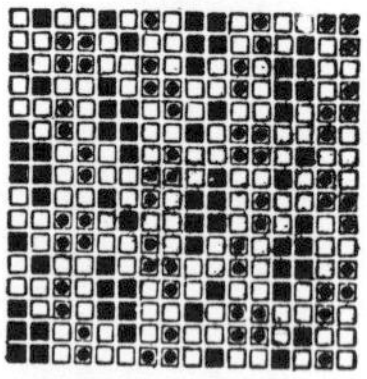

Fig. 1102.

Fig. 1103.   Fig. 1104.

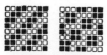

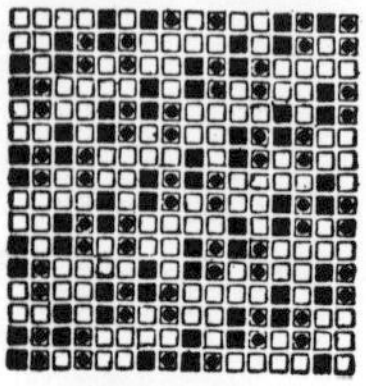

Fig. 1106.   Fig. 1107.

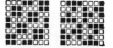

Fig. 1105.

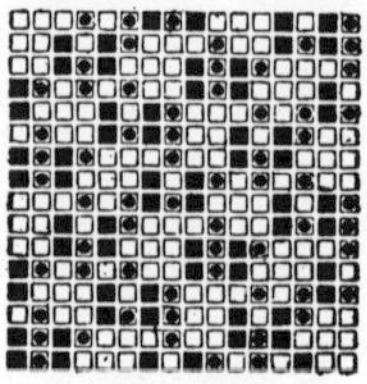

Fig. 1108.

and 1107. Other examples will be found under the head of Interlocking Weaves.

RIB CRÊPE

This form of crêpe weave results from the removal of single points at regular intervals from a ^{2}—$_2$ or ^{3}—$_3$ rib weave. When the riser is removed the filling floats over three warp threads, Figs. 1109 to 1115.

Fig. 1109	8 × 8
Fig. 1110	12 × 12
Fig. 1111 . . . . , . . .	12 × 12
Fig. 1112	14 × 12
Fig. 1113	6 × 12
Fig. 1114	12 × 12
Fig. 1115	16 × 16

CRÊPE WEAVES BY DRAFTING ONE WEAVE OVER ANOTHER

Crêpe effects can be obtained by superimposing one weave on another in the same draft. A weave is first sketched and then another is drafted over it without removing any of the risers of the first. For example, one twill is set over another, the two twills running in opposite directions. Or a satin may be

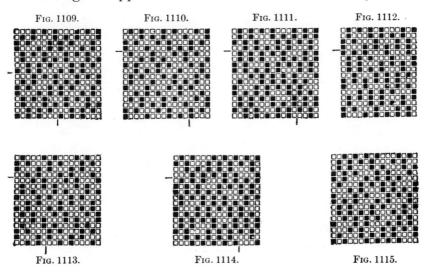

FIG. 1109.   FIG. 1110.   FIG. 1111.   FIG. 1112.

FIG. 1113.   FIG. 1114.   FIG. 1115.

sketched on a satin, the two weaves having a different number of threads. This method is used but little owing to the small number of good effects obtainable.

Fig. 1116	8 × 8
Fig. 1117	8 × 8
Fig. 1118	8 × 8
Fig. 1119	8 × 8
Fig. 1120	12 × 12
Fig. 1121	12 × 12
Fig. 1122	12 × 12
Fig. 1123	12 × 12
Fig. 1124	12 × 12
Fig. 1125	16 × 16

FIG. 1116.

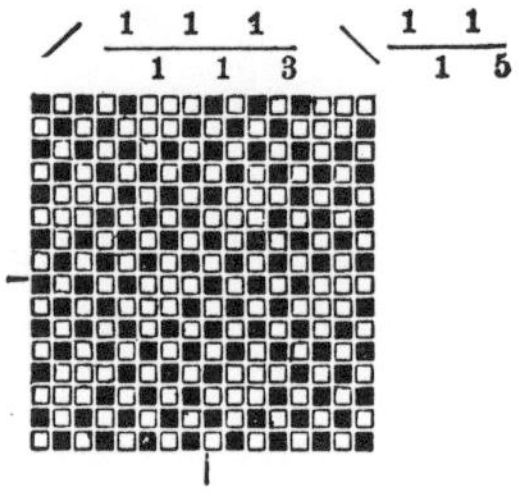

FIG. 1117.

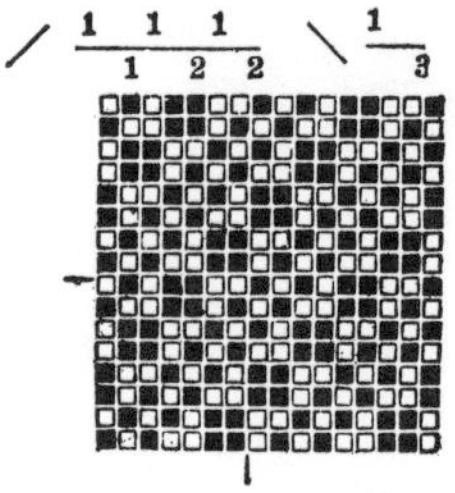

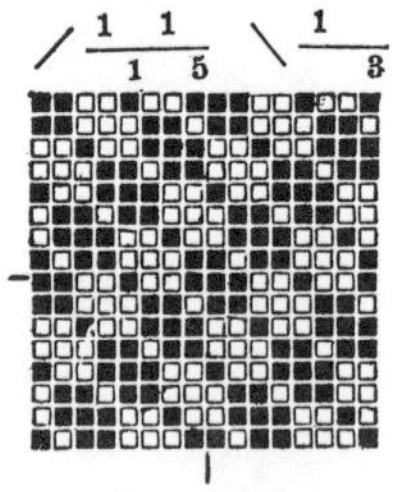

FIG. 1118.

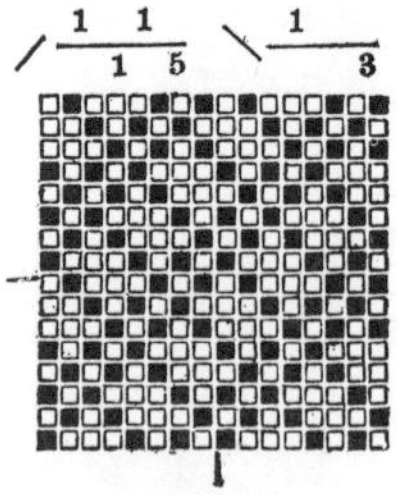

FIG. 1119.

The formulas for the two twills, with slanting lines to indicate the direction of the twill line, are shown above each combination weave, Figs. 1116 to 1125.

CRÊPE WEAVES BY DRAFTING A WEAVE IN FOUR SQUARES

This method consists in drafting a weave on alternate warp and filling threads, then turning the foundation weave draft quarter way around and transferring it in this position to alternate warp and filling threads of a new draft, repeating the process for each of the other two positions.

Each of the two sets of alternate warp and filling threads receives two of the transferred weaves. This method is illustrated at Figs. 1126 to 1130. Fig. 1130 is the completed crêpe weave derived from a ^{2}—$_2$ twill.

The twill is transferred to the first set of alternate warp and filling threads of the draft, Fig. 1126.

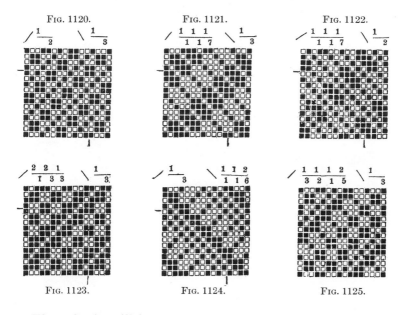

FIG. 1120.   FIG. 1121.   FIG. 1122.

FIG. 1123.   FIG. 1124.   FIG. 1125.

The 4-leaf twill is next turned one-quarter way round and transferred in this position, to the second set of alternate warp and filling threads of Fig. 1127.

Another quarter turn and a transfer gives the twill shown at Fig. 1128.

The twill is again turned one-quarter way around and transferred to Fig. 1129.

These four transfers are shown on four separate drafts, Figs. 1126, 1127, 1128 and 1129, for the sake of clearness. They are in fact transferred to the same draft, making the crêpe weave shown at Fig. 1130.

The operation is made easier by using ink of a different color for each transfer.

Other examples of this method are shown at Figs. 1132, 1134 and 1136, which are derived from Figs. 1131, 1133 and 1135 respectively.

A variation of the method consists in reversing the ground weave for two of the transfers, making the sinkers risers.

This completes the study of crêpe weaves. Methods for the production of an unlimited number of effects have been described and illustrated by several hundred weave patterns: Designing these effects requires not only imagination for the conception of new ideas, but also skill in drafting and the ability to determine in advance what effect the weave will have in the goods.

Fig. 1126.

Fig. 1127.

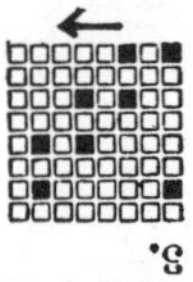

Fig. 1128.

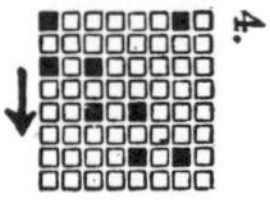

Fig. 1129.

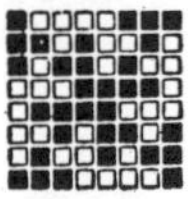

Fig. 1130.

Fig. 1131.

Fig. 1133.

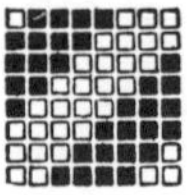

Fig. 1135.

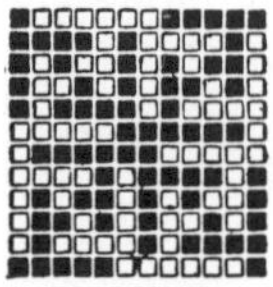

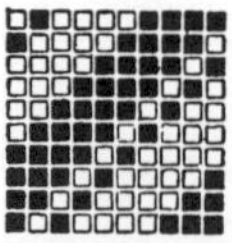

Fig. 1132.

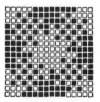

Fig. 1134.

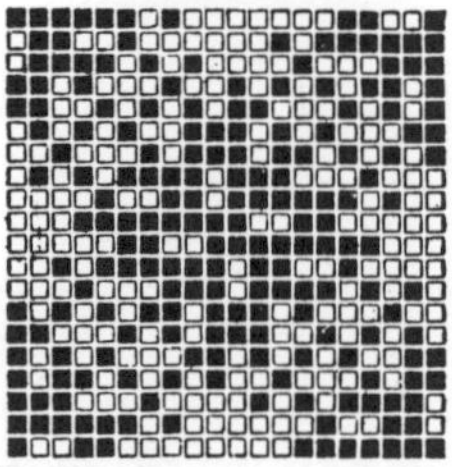

Fig. 1136.

REFORM WEAVES WITH WARP THREADS AL-
TERNATING ON FACE AND BACK

A firmer texture is obtained when each warp thread is transferred at regular intervals alternately to the face and back. The threads when on the face may

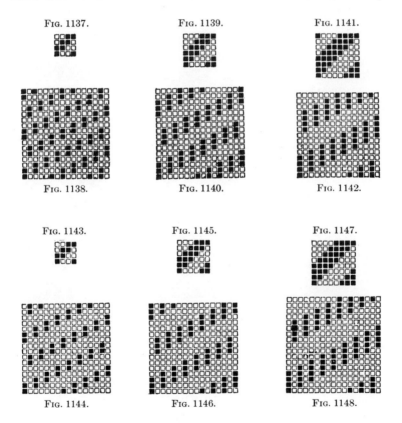

FIG. 1137. FIG. 1139. FIG. 1141.

FIG. 1138. FIG. 1140. FIG. 1142.

FIG. 1143. FIG. 1145. FIG. 1147.

FIG. 1144. FIG. 1146. FIG. 1148.

be woven with a twill, satin or other weave, while they float under the filling when on the back. These are sometimes called reform weaves.

The advantage of such a method as compared with

the use of separate sets of threads for the face and back warp are:

1. Greater durability.
2. Uniform take-up.
3. Imperfections in the yarn are less apparent.

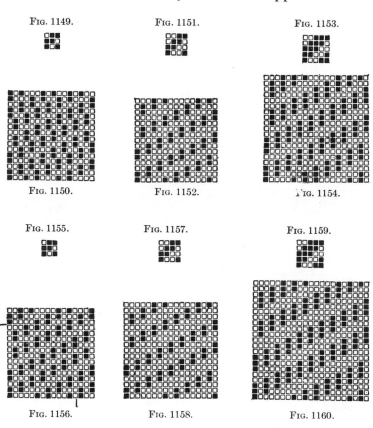

FIG. 1149.   FIG. 1151.   FIG. 1153.

FIG. 1150.   FIG. 1152.   FIG. 1154.

FIG. 1155.   FIG. 1157.   FIG. 1159.

FIG. 1156.   FIG. 1158.   FIG. 1160.

Reform weaves were used at first for ladies' dress goods, vestings and similar fabrics, but frequently in the reverse order, that is, with the warp floating on the face and stitched on the back. In recent years they have also been used for men's wear worsteds.

Each thread passes to the face and back at regular intervals. When warp threads 1, 3, 5, 7, etc., form a face twill, threads 2, 4, 6, 8, etc., float on the back; when threads 2, 4, 6, 8, etc., form the face twill, threads

1, 3, 5, 7, etc., float on the back. As a result of this arrangement, two adjacent warp threads are required for each thread line of the weave on the face.

Following are the rules for constructing the weaves of this class :

REFORM WEAVES IN WHICH THE WARP IS 1 FACE 1 BACK

1. If the weave is an ordinary twill in which the twill line rises one pick at each thread, the number of threads in the pattern is either one more or one less than double the number in the ground weave. Thus, for an 8-shaft twill, 15 or 17 threads are required.

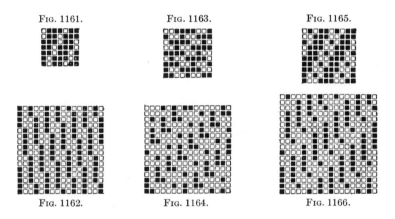

FIG. 1161.   FIG. 1163.   FIG. 1165.

FIG. 1162.   FIG. 1164.   FIG. 1166.

A twill is first marked on threads 1, 3, 5, 7, etc.

If the weave pattern covers one less than double the number of threads in the ground weave, the second twill is placed on threads 2, 4, 6, 8, etc., as far above the twill of the adjacent thread as there are threads in the ground weave. Examples are shown at Figs. 1138, 1140 and 1142, the ground weaves being given at Figs. 1137, 1139 and 1141 respectively.

Fig. 1138 is a reform weave made by drafting a 4-leaf twill, Fig. 1137, on 7 threads, the twill line rising 4 picks at every warp thread. Fig. 1140 is a 6-leaf twill, Fig. 1139, drafted on 11 threads, the twill line rising 6 picks at a time. Fig. 1142 is an 8-leaf twill,

Fig. 1141, drafted on 15 threads, the twill line rising 8 picks at each warp thread.

If the weave pattern contains one more than double the number of threads in the ground weave, the second twill is placed one more than the number of threads in the ground weave above the twill on the adjacent thread :

For a 4-leaf twill on 9 threads, 5 picks higher, Figs. 1143 and 1144 ;

For a 6-leaf twill on 13 threads, 7 picks higher, Figs. 1145 and 1146 ;

For an 8-leaf twill on 17 threads, 9 picks higher, Figs. 1147 and 1148.

2. If each warp thread is brought to the face to form two twill lines while the adjacent thread is float-

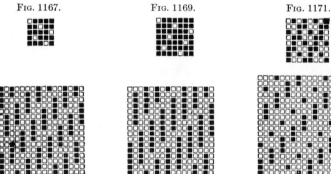

FIG. 1167. FIG. 1169. FIG. 1171.

FIG. 1168. FIG. 1170. FIG. 1172.

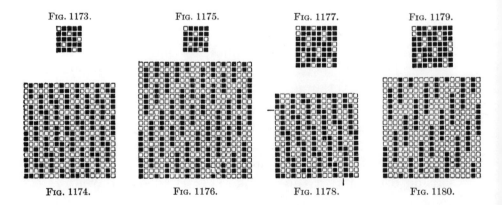

FIG. 1173. FIG. 1175. FIG. 1177. FIG. 1179.

FIG. 1174. FIG. 1176. FIG. 1178. FIG. 1180.

ing on the back, the threads in the pattern must number one less or one more than four times the number in the ground weave; for a 4-leaf twill, 15 or 17 threads; for a 6-leaf twill, 23 or 25 threads.

If there is one thread less than four times the ground weave, the twill on the adjacent thread is placed twice as many picks above the corresponding twill on the preceding thread as there are threads in the ground weave:

For a 3-leaf twill on 11 threads, 6 picks higher, Figs. 1149 and 1150;

For a 4-leaf twill on 15 threads, 8 picks higher, Figs. 1151 and 1152;

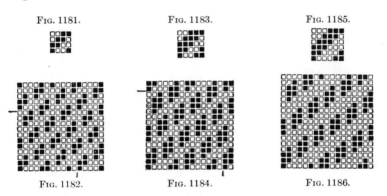

FIG. 1181.   FIG. 1183.   FIG. 1185.

FIG. 1182.   FIG. 1184.   FIG. 1186.

For a 5-leaf twill on 19 threads, 10 picks higher, Figs. 1153 and 1154.

If the reform weave covers one thread more than four times the number of threads in the ground weave, the twill on each thread is placed one more than double the number of threads in the ground weave above the corresponding twill on the preceding thread.

For a 3-leaf twill on 13 threads, 7 picks higher, Figs. 1155 and 1156;

For a 4-leaf twill on 17 threads, 9 picks higher, Figs. 1157 and 1158;

For a 5-leaf twill on 21 threads, 11 picks higher, Figs. 1159 and 1160.

3. For satin weaves in which the rising number is 2

(for example, 5 or 7 shaft satins), likewise for steep twills in which the twill on each warp thread rises two filling threads above the twill on the preceding warp thread, the number of threads in the reform weave is either 2 more or 2 less than double the number of threads in the ground weave; thus, for a 7-shaft ground weave, 12 or 16 threads, instead of 14 threads.

If the reform weave has two threads less than double the number of threads in the ground weave, the twill is raised on each warp thread as far above the twill of

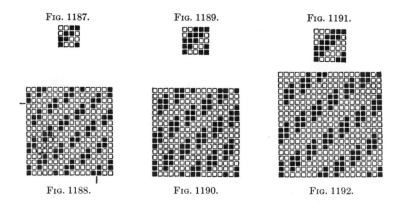

FIG. 1187.   FIG. 1189.   FIG. 1191.

FIG. 1188.   FIG. 1190.   FIG. 1192.

the preceding warp thread as there are threads in the ground weave:

For a 7-shaft weave on 12 threads, 7 picks higher, Figs. 1161 and 1162;

For a 9-shaft weave on 16 threads, 9 picks higher, Figs. 1163 and 1164;

For a steep twill with 5 threads and 10 picks on a reform weave with 9 threads and 18 picks, 10 picks higher, Figs. 1165 and 1166.

If the reform weave has two threads more than double the number of threads in the ground weave, the twill is set two picks more than the number of threads in the ground weave above the twill on the preceding thread:

For a 5-leaf satin on 12 threads, 7 picks higher, Figs. 1167 and 1168;

For a 7-leaf satin on 16 threads, 9 picks higher, Figs. 1169 and 1170;

For a steep twill with 4 threads and 8 picks, on a reform weave with 9 threads and 18 picks, 10 picks higher, Figs. 1171 and 1172.

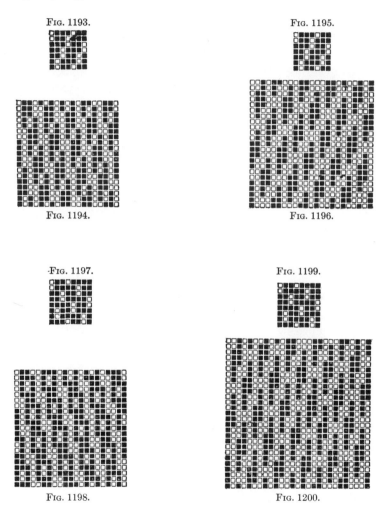

FIG. 1193.

FIG. 1195.

FIG. 1194.

FIG. 1196.

-FIG. 1197.

FIG. 1199.

FIG. 1198.

FIG. 1200.

4. If each warp thread of a satin weave is brought to the face twice in succession before the adjacent thread is raised, the reform weave will cover either two threads less or two more than four times the number of threads in the ground weave:

A 5-shaft ground weave will cover 18 or 22 threads in the reform weave.

If the reform weave has two less than four times the number of threads in the ground weave, the twill is raised at each warp thread twice as many picks as there are threads in the ground weave:

For a 5-leaf satin on 18 threads, 10 picks higher, Figs. 1173 and 1174.

If the reform weave has two more than four times the number of threads in the ground weave, the twill

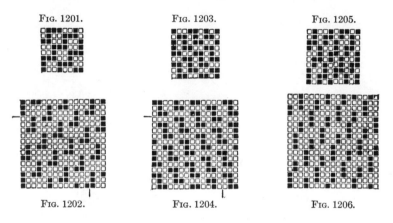

Fig. 1201.   Fig. 1203.   Fig. 1205.

Fig. 1202.   Fig. 1204.   Fig. 1206.

is raised at each warp thread two more than double the number of threads in the ground weave:

For a 5-leaf satin on 22 threads, 12 picks higher, Figs. 1175 and 1176.

5. For ground weaves in which the rising number is 3, such as an 8- or a 10-shaft satin, the threads in the reform weave number three more or three less than double the number of threads in the ground weave. Thus an 8-shaft ground weave would have either 13 or 19 threads in the reform weave.

For an 8-shaft steep twill of this kind on 13 threads, the rising number in the reform weave is 8, equal to the number of threads in the ground weave, Figs. 1177 and 1178.

For the same 8-shaft steep twill on 19 threads, the rising number in the reform weave is 11, which is 3 more than the number of threads in the ground weave, Figs. 1179 and 1180.

Where the warp threads float for a considerable distance on the back, they are frequently stitched by raising a warp thread over 1 pick, at a point where there is a raised thread at each side of the stitched thread.

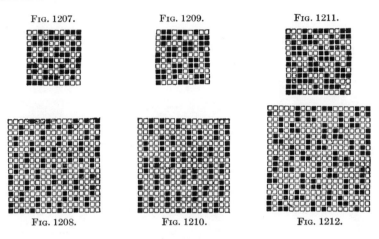

FIG. 1207. FIG. 1209. FIG. 1211.

FIG. 1208. FIG. 1210. FIG. 1212.

REFORM WEAVES WITH TWO THREADS ON THE FACE FOR ONE ON THE BACK

To make the face closer, reform weaves are sometimes arranged to bring two threads to the face for each one on the back. They are constructed according to the following rules:

1. The pattern covers either one more or one less than three times the number of threads in the ground weave. Three twills are thus formed in one pattern.

If the weave covers one thread less than three times the ground weave, the rising number is double the number of threads in the ground weave:

For a 4-shaft twill on 11 threads, 8 picks higher, Figs. 1181 and 1182;

For a 5-shaft twill on 14 threads, 10 picks higher, Figs. 1183 and 1184;

For a 6-shaft twill on 17 threads, 12 picks higher, Figs. 1185 and 1186.

If the threads in the pattern number one more than three times those in the ground weave, the rising number is one more than the number of threads in the ground weave.

For a 4-shaft twill on 13 threads, 5 picks higher, Figs. 1187 and 1188.

For a 5-shaft twill on 16 threads, 6 picks higher, Figs. 1189 and 1190.

For a 6-shaft twill on 19 threads, 7 picks higher, Figs. 1191 and 1192.

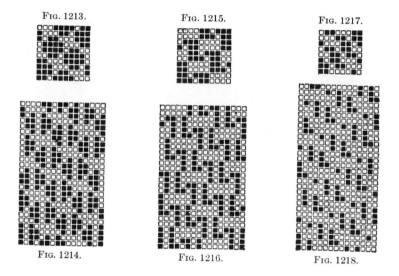

FIG. 1213.

FIG. 1215.

FIG. 1217.

FIG. 1214.

FIG. 1216.

FIG. 1218.

2. With 2 for the rising number in a steep twill or satin weave forming the ground weave, the reform pattern covers either two less or two more than three times the number of threads in that weave; thus, for a 7-shaft weave, either 19 or 23 threads.

If the reform weave has two less than three times the number of threads in the ground weave, the rising number in the reform weave is double the number of threads in the ground weave:

For a 7-shaft steep twill on 19 threads, 14 picks higher, Figs. 1193 and 1194.

If the reform weave has two more than three times

the number of threads in the ground weave, the twill on each warp thread is set two picks more than the number of threads in the ground weave above the corresponding twill on the preceding thread :

For the same 7-shaft steep twill, Fig. 1193, on 23 threads, the twill rises 9 picks at each thread, Figs. 1195 and 1196.

3. If the ground weave is a satin with 3 for its riser, the weave will cover three less or three more than three times the number of threads in the ground weave.

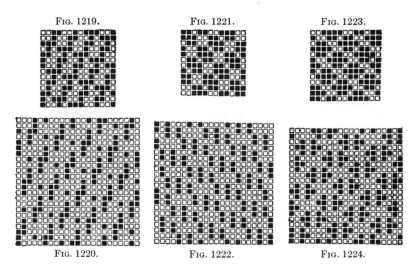

FIG. 1219.   FIG. 1221.   FIG. 1223.

FIG. 1220.   FIG. 1222.   FIG. 1224.

If 3 threads less, the riser of a reform weave is double the number of threads in the ground weave. Fig. 1198, rising 16 picks, is a 21-thread reform weave. The 8-shaft steep twill, Fig. 1197, is the ground weave.

If 3 threads more, the riser of the reform weave is 3 more than the number of threads in the base weave. Fig. 1200, rising 11 picks, is a 27-thread reform weave with the same 8-shaft steep twill, Fig. 1197, as a base, Fig. 1199.

Reform weaves can be so constructed that each thread forms three or four twills before passing to the back.

Figs. 1201 to 1230 illustrate additional forms of these weaves.

Fig. 1201, 8-thread weave on 13 threads, Fig. 1202.
Fig. 1203, 9-thread weave on 13 threads, Fig. 1204.
Fig. 1205, 10-thread weave on 17 threads, Fig. 1206.
Fig. 1207, 10-thread weave on 17 threads, Fig. 1208.
Fig. 1209, 10-thread weave on 17 threads, Fig. 1210.
Fig. 1211, 12-thread weave on 19 threads, Fig. 1212.

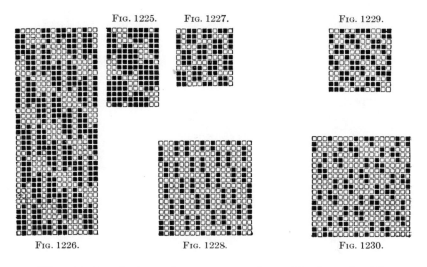

FIG. 1225.   FIG. 1227.   FIG. 1229.

FIG. 1226.   FIG. 1228.   FIG. 1230.

Fig. 1213, 10-thread weave on 13 × 26 threads, Fig. 1214.

Fig. 1215, 10-thread weave on 13 × 26 threads, Fig. 1216.

Fig. 1217, 8-thread weave on 15 × 30 threads, Fig. 1218.

Fig. 1219, 14-thread weave on 23 threads, Fig. 1220.
Fig. 1221, 12-thread weave on 22 threads, Fig. 1222.
Fig. 1223, 13-thread weave on 21 threads, Fig. 1224.
Fig. 1225, 10 × 15-thread weave on 13 × 39 threads, Fig. 1226.
Fig. 1227, 11-thread weave on 18 threads, Fig. 1228.
Fig. 1229, 12-thread weave on 19 threads, Fig. 1230.

REFORM WEAVES WITH STUFFING PICKS

It is frequently necessary to increase the weight of cloths made with reform weaves by introducing extra filling threads, called stuffing picks, which do not show on either side of the fabric. When the stuffing pick is inserted those threads are raised which float on the face before and after that pick, while those threads are lowered which at that point are floating on the back. This construction is illustrated at Fig. 1232, which shows a stuffing pick inserted after every third pick of Fig. 1231. As there are 13 threads in the pattern at Fig. 1231, two of these patterns are required for the weave at Fig. 1232, making with the stuffing picks a total of 39 picks.

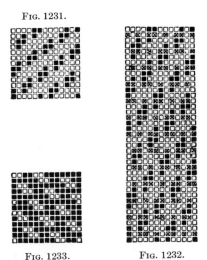

FIG. 1231.

FIG. 1233.

FIG. 1232.

WEAVES IN WHICH THE FILLING THREADS ALTERNATE ON FACE AND BACK

These weaves are obtained by turning the reform weaves already described so as to bring the side at the top of the draft, making the risers sinkers and the sinkers risers. Fig. 1233 shows such a reform weave obtained by turning Fig. 1231, the ground weave being a 4-leaf twill, Fig. 1187. The object of this construction is to obtain a closer set than is possible with the ordinary single cloth.

BACK WARP FABRICS

Weaves with an extra set of warp threads on the back are used for increasing the weight of fabrics. If a face thread alternates with a back in the warp, the set is called 1 and 1. If there are 2 threads on the face to 1 on the back, the set is 2 and 1. If a warp satin is used for the face and a filling satin weave for the back, the warp being dressed 1 gray, 1 white, the face of the cloth will be gray and the back white.

These weaves are not suitable for heavy woolen cloths, as the necessarily close set of the warp makes it difficult to form a good shed with coarse woolen yarn. They can be used for medium-weight woolen fabrics, 18 to 20 ounces per yard, 55 inches wide, but for heavier cloths a back filling answers much better for increasing the weight, as the number of picks can be increased more easily than can the threads in the warp, and a much closer face can thus be obtained.

The back warp weaves answer very well, however, for fine worsted fabrics for men's wear, in which as many as 10,000 or 12,000 ends are sometimes used for 6/4 cloths.

In drafting back warp weaves the first rule to be observed is that the riser of a back thread should have the face warp raised on each side of it. It is sometimes necessary to vary the regular order of stitching the back to prevent single risers from coming next to single sinkers and causing an irregularity in the fabric.

Figs. 1234 to 1260 illustrate various forms of these weaves.

Fig. 1243 shows a 3 up 1 down broken twill on the face with a back warp. The warp is dressed 1 back 1 face. The back warp is woven with a 1 up 3 down broken twill. This makes the cloth the same on both back and face.

The back and face weaves, Fig. 1234, must be adjusted so that no single stitcher of the face warp comes next to a single stitcher of the back warp. This can be accomplished with only one of the four possible combinations. This weave is used for hair-line effects, which are obtained by a suitable arrangement of colors in warp and filling to make a continuous warp line.

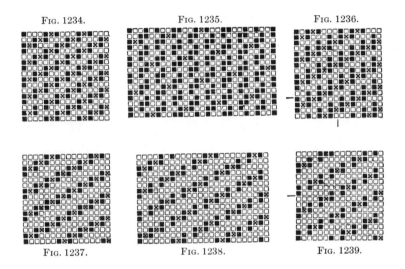

Fig. 1234. Fig. 1235. Fig. 1236.

Fig. 1237. Fig. 1238. Fig. 1239.

Fig. 1234, 1 and 1, face 2 up 1 down twill; back 1 up 2 down twill.

Fig. 1235, 2 and 1, face 2 up 1 down twill; back 9-leaf satin.

Fig. 1236, 1 and 1, face 3 up 1 down twill; back 1 up 3 down twill.

Fig. 1237, 1 and 1, face 2 up 2 down twill; back 1 up 3 down twill.

Fig. 1238, 1 and 1, face 2 up 2 down twill; back 12-leaf.

Fig. 1239, 1 and 1, face 2 up 2 down twill; back 8-leaf satin.

Fig. 1240, 1 and 1, face 3 up 2 down twill; back 1 up 4 down twill.

Fig. 1241, 2 and 1, face 3 up 2 down twill; back 10-leaf satin.

Fig. 1242, 1 and 1, face 3 up 3 down twill; back 1 up 5 down twill.

Fig. 1243, 1 and 1, face 3 up 1 down broken twill; back 1 up 3 down broken twill.

Fig. 1244, 1 and 1, face 5-leaf satin; back 5-leaf satin.

Fig. 1245, 1 and 1, face 7-leaf satin; back 7-leaf satin.

Fig. 1246, 1 and 1, face 8-leaf satin; back 8-leaf satin.

Fig. 1247, 2 and 1, face 8-leaf double satin; back 16-leaf.

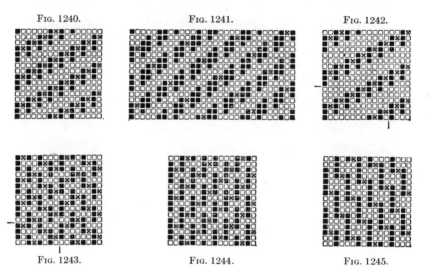

FIG. 1240. FIG. 1241. FIG. 1242.

FIG. 1243. FIG. 1244. FIG. 1245.

Fig. 1248, 1 and 1, face 8-leaf double satin; back 8-leaf satin.

Fig. 1249, 1 and 1, face 10-leaf double satin; back 10-leaf satin.

Fig. 1250, 2 and 1, face 10-leaf double satin; back 10-leaf.

Fig. 1251, 2 and 1, face 4-leaf basket; back 1 up 3 down broken twill.

Fig. 1253, 1 and 1, face crêpe, Fig. 1252; back 8-leaf satin.

Fig. 1254, 1 and 1, face 13-leaf twill rib; back 26-leaf.

Fig. 1256, 2 and 1, face crêpe, Fig. 1255; back 10-leaf.

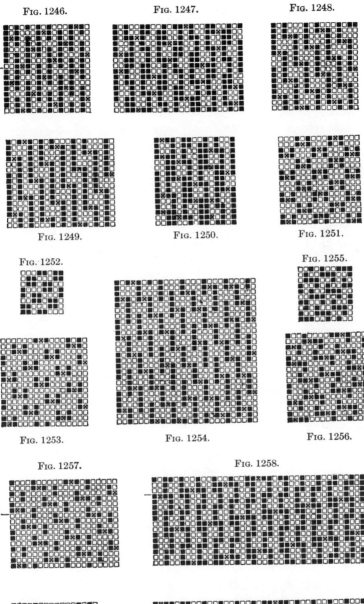

Fig. 1246.

Fig. 1247.

Fig. 1248.

Fig. 1249.

Fig. 1250.

Fig. 1251.

Fig. 1252.

Fig. 1255.

Fig. 1253.

Fig. 1254.

Fig. 1256.

Fig. 1257.

Fig. 1258.

Fig. 1259.

Fig. 1260.

Fig. 1257, 1 and 1, face crêpe, Fig. 1255; back 10-leaf.

Fig. 1258, 2 and 1, face twill rib, Fig. 472; back 13-leaf.

Fig. 1259, 1 and 1, face crêpe, Fig. 1028 c; back 8-leaf.

Fig. 1260, 2 and 1, face twill rib, Fig. 472; back 13-leaf.

Fig. 1243 is well suited for kersey fabrics. The warp for kerseys is set closer than the filling in order that the nap may be raised mainly from the parallel fibers of the warp and thus produce a smooth effect lengthways of the piece.

Hair lines on the contrary are generally sheared close, as a sandy feel is desired. For this reason the warp and filling are more nearly balanced. The following layouts for a kersey and a hair line, both woven with the weave at Fig. 1243, illustrate the difference between the proportions of warp and filling:

KERSEY

Warp, 88 ends per inch finished.

Filling, 67 ends per inch finished.

21 threads (33 per cent) more per inch in warp than in filling.

HAIR LINE

Warp, 70 ends per inch finished.

Filling, 65 ends per inch finished.

5 threads (8 per cent) more per inch in warp than in filling.

By turning Fig. 1243 one-quarter way around the back filling weave shown at Fig. 1283 is obtained.

A divided drawing-in draft, No. 8, Figs. 25 and 26, is used for a back warp weave and arranged to bring the back threads on the back shafts and the face threads on the front shafts nearest to the reed.

When weaving cloth with a worsted face warp and woolen back warp, it is a better plan to reverse this order, bringing the back warp on the front shafts nearest to the reed.

Every filling thread in these weaves should be stitched by the back warp. This is necessary in order that the picks may be held in the same relative position and the face remain smooth and uniform.

WEAVES WITH BACK WARP AND STUFFING PICKS

It is sometimes necessary to introduce stuffing picks in worsted fabrics to obtain sufficient weight. A stuffing pick is woven so as to lie between the face and back warp in the center of the fabric. The usual

FIG. 1261.

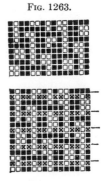

FIG. 1263.

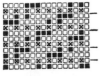

FIG. 1262.

FIG. 1264.

order is 2 regular picks, 1 stuffing pick. When the stuffing pick is woven, all the face warp threads are raised, and all back warp lowered.

Fig. 1262 shows Fig. 1261 woven with a stuffing pick, the warp being dressed 1 face, 1 back; filling, 2 regular picks, 1 stuffing pick.

Fig. 1264 shows Fig. 1263 woven with a stuffing pick, the warp being dressed 2 face, 1 back; filling, 2 regular picks, 1 stuffing pick.

The stuffing picks are indicated by the lines at the side of the drafts and are drafted with crosses (×), Figs. 1262 and 1264.

BACK FILLING FABRICS

Back filling is used to make cloths thicker and heavier. It also enables the cost to be reduced by the use of cheaper material for the back. For this purpose the back filling is usually spun heavier than the face filling or the warp. If, however, the difference between the size of the face and back filling, woven 1 and 1, is too great, the appearance of the face will be injured, as the coarse backing will prevent the filling threads from lying close together to form a smooth face. This difficulty can be remedied only by weaving two or three face picks to one back pick. Even then there is a limit to the size of the back filling that can be advantageously used.

The back filling may be interlaced either with the regular warp, making one set of warp threads and two sets (face and back) of filling threads; or it may be interlaced with a separate set of back warp threads, making the regular double cloth.

For fabrics made with one set of warp and two sets (face and back) of filling, the two principal rules of construction are:

1. The back filling must be interlaced so as not to disturb the position of the warp and filling on the face.

2. The interlacing of the warp and back filling should not hinder the approach of any two adjacent picks to each other. The back shed should be formed so as to allow the face pick to slide over and cover the preceding back pick. This is made plain by Fig. 1265, in which the face pick cannot pass readily to its position above the back pick because warp threads 4, 8, 12, etc., which are under the back pick, are raised above the

adjacent face pick, forming a barrier to the free passage of the latter.

Likewise a back pick cannot pass under a preceding face pick when a warp thread that is raised above the adjacent face pick is lowered below the back pick. In Fig. 1266, threads 4, 8, 12, etc., which are raised above the face pick are lowered below the back pick and thus hinder the passage of the back pick to its proper position below the face pick.

This rule applies to regular smooth faced fabrics. The arrangement of the filling threads in a back filling weave as shown at Figs. 1265 and 1266 is sometimes used to produce tricot effects, which will be described later.

3. When a back pick is stitched by lowering a warp thread below it, this warp thread should be under

FIG. 1265.    FIG. 1266.    FIG. 1267.

both the preceding and succeeding picks as shown in Fig. 1267. This rule cannot be followed in the case of double cloths having a plain weave on the face.

4. The face and back picks should alternate with each other in regular order. Where both are of the same size it is advisable, especially for close fabrics, to arrange them 1 face 1 back. For loose fabrics, such as those woven with 6- and 8-leaf satins, the order may be 2 face 2 back. If the back filling is much coarser than the face, the filling is woven 2 face 1 back, or 3 face 1 back.

5. If the face filling is woven with long floats, the stitchers for the back filling should come as nearly as possible opposite the center of the face filling float. The stitchers for the back filling should come where the back filling yarn will be covered by the adjacent face filling threads.

The back filling should rise above but one warp

thread at a time. If, however, the face filling floats over as many as five or six consecutive warp threads, the back filling can be stitched over two adjacent warp threads at a time, providing the face and back colors do not contrast too sharply.

6. To secure a uniform tension on the warp threads, it is desirable that the stitching of the back filling be distributed uniformly over all the warp threads. If some of the warp threads are not stitched to the face, they may become slack and cause an imperfect shed in weaving.

To draft a back filling weave, the order of face and back picks is first marked on the cross-section paper. The face weave is then drafted, leaving the back

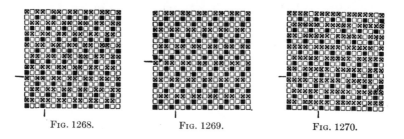

FIG. 1268.   FIG. 1269.   FIG. 1270.

filling spaces unmarked. The back weave is then drafted in accordance with the preceding rules.

Following are examples of the more important back filling weaves:

Fig. 1268, twill face 1 up 2 down; twill back 2 up 1 down; woven 1 × 1.

Fig. 1269, twill face 1 up 2 down; twill back 2 up 1 down; woven 2 × 1.

Fig. 1270, twill face 1 up 2 down; twill back 5 up 1 down; woven 1 × 1.

Fig. 1271, plain face; twill back 3 up 1 down; woven 1 × 1.

Fig. 1272, plain face; 8-leaf satin back; woven 1 × 1.

Fig. 1273, twill face 1 up 3 down; twill back 3 up 1 down; woven 1 × 1.

Fig. 1274, twill face 2 up 2 down; twill back 3 up 1 down; woven 1 × 1.

Fig. 1275, twill face 2 up 2 down; twill back 7 up 1 down, woven 1 × 1.

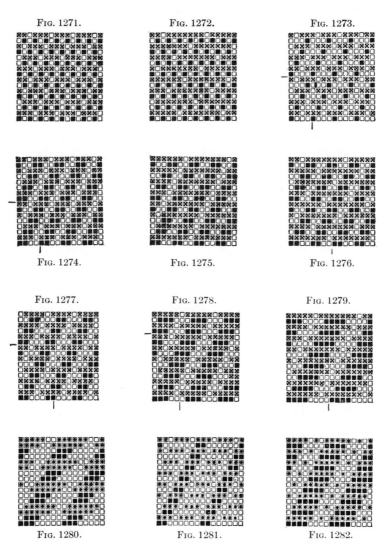

FIG. 1271. FIG. 1272. FIG. 1273.

FIG. 1274. FIG. 1275. FIG. 1276.

FIG. 1277. FIG. 1278. FIG. 1279.

FIG. 1280. FIG. 1281. FIG. 1282.

Fig. 1276, twill face 2 up 2 down; 8-leaf satin back; woven 1 × 1.

Fig. 1277, twill face 2 up 3 down; twill back 4 up 1 down; woven 1 × 1.

Fig. 1278, twill face 3 up 3 down; twill back 5 up 1 down; woven 1 × 1.

Fig. 1279, twill face 4 up 4 down; twill back 7 up 1 down; woven 1 × 1.

Fig. 1280, twill face 3 up 5 down; twill back 6 up 2 down; woven 2 × 2.

Fig. 1281, twill face 2 up 6 down; twill back 3 up 1 down; woven 1 × 1.

Fig. 1282, twill face 4 up 4 down; twill back 5 up 1 down 1 up 1 down; woven 1 × 1.

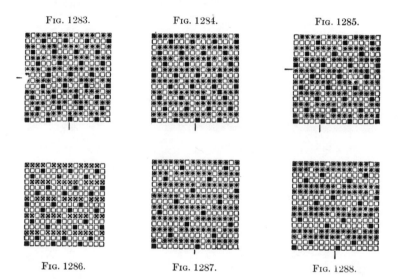

FIG. 1283.   FIG. 1284.   FIG. 1285.

FIG. 1286.   FIG. 1287.   FIG. 1288.

Fig. 1283, broken twill face 1 up 3 down; broken twill back 3 up 1 down; woven 1 × 1.

Fig. 1284, broken twill face 1 up 3 down; 8-leaf satin back; woven 1 × 1.

Fig. 1285, 5-leaf satin face; 5-leaf satin back; woven 1 × 1.

Fig. 1286, 5-leaf satin face; 5-leaf twill back; woven 2 × 1.

Fig. 1287, 8-leaf satin face; 8-leaf satin back; woven 1 × 1.

Fig. 1288, 8-leaf satin face; 8-leaf satin back; woven 2 × 2.

Fig. 1289, twill face 2 up 2 down; 12-leaf back; woven 1 × 1.

Fig. 1290, twill face 2 up 2 down; 8-leaf back; woven 1 × 2.

Fig. 1291, modified broken twill face; 8-leaf satin back; woven 2 × 1.

Fig. 1292, 8-leaf modified satin face; 8-leaf satin back; woven 2 × 1.

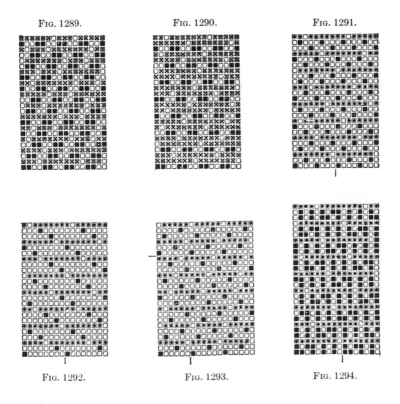

FIG. 1289.   FIG. 1290.   FIG. 1291.

FIG. 1292.   FIG. 1293.   FIG. 1294.

Fig. 1293, modified 6-leaf satin face; 6-leaf back; woven 2 × 1.

Fig. 1294, corkscrew twill face; 5 up 4 down, Fig. 457; 9-leaf back; woven 2 × 1.

Fig. 1295, 8-leaf double satin face; 8-leaf satin back; woven 1 × 1.

Fig. 1296, 3-leaf pointed twill face; 6-leaf back; woven 1 × 1.

Fig. 1297, 4-leaf broken twill face; 4-leaf broken twill back; woven 1 × 1.

Fig. 1298, interlocking twill (Fig. 510) face; 9-leaf back; woven 1 × 1.

Fig. 1301, 7-leaf double satin face; 7-leaf satin back; woven 2 × 1.

Fig. 1303, 6-leaf satin face; 6-leaf satin back; woven 1 × 1.

Fig. 1304, twill face 2 up 2 down; woven 1 face pick 1 back pick 3 up 1 down, 1 back pick 7 up 1 down.

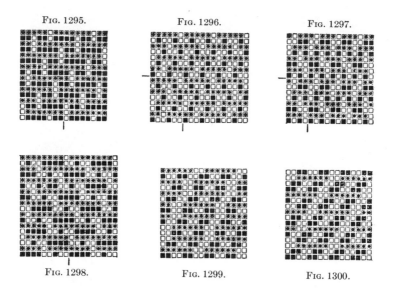

FIG. 1295.   FIG. 1296.   FIG. 1297.

FIG. 1298.   FIG. 1299.   FIG. 1300.

Fig. 1305, 7-leaf satin face; 7-leaf satin back; woven 2 × 1.

Fig. 1307, 5-leaf warp satin face; 10-leaf warp satin back; woven 1 × 1.

Fig. 1308, twill face 2 up 3 down, 10-leaf satin back; woven 2 × 1.

Fig. 1309, twill face 2 up 2 down; woven 1 face 2 up 2 down, 1 stuffing pick 1 down 4 up 1 down 1 up 1 down 4 up, 1 back pick 1 down 11 up; this may also be considered as woven 2 face 1 back, making a 12-leaf diagonal.

Fig. 1310, basket face 3 up 3 down; woven 1 face, 1 back, 1 face.

Fig. 1314, crêpe face, Fig. 1311; back 9 up 1 down 5 up 1 down; woven 2 × 1.

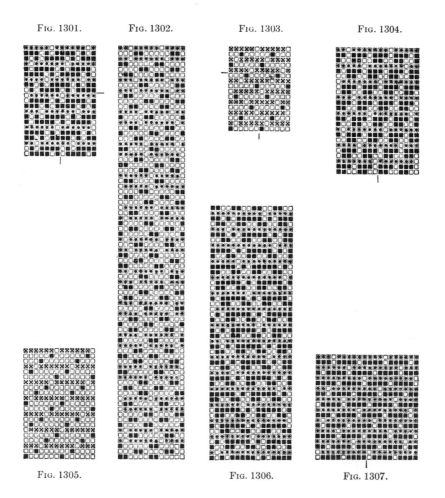

FIG. 1301.   FIG. 1302.   FIG. 1303.   FIG. 1304.

FIG. 1305.   FIG. 1306.   FIG. 1307.

A heavier fabric can be made with Fig. 1270 than with either Fig. 1268 or Fig. 1269, as the back filling in Fig. 1270 is stitched but once in six threads instead of every third thread.

As both Figs. 1271 and 1272 are woven with a plain weave on the face, rule 3, already given, cannot be followed. These weaves are in common use.

When a warp thread passes below and stitches a back pick, it should also lie below the preceding face pick. For example, in Fig. 1271 thread 4, which stitches pick 2 (back) is below pick 1 (face).

A fabric can be made much heavier with either Fig. 1275 or Fig. 1276, in which the back filling is stitched every eighth thread, than if woven with Fig. 1274, in which the back filling is stitched every fourth thread.

These three back filling weaves, Figs. 1274, 1275 and 1276, have the same weave, a 4-leaf twill, on the face. When, however, the back filling weave covers twice as many warp threads as the face weave, the back stitchers must be brought on alternate face twills in order to prevent them from affecting the appearance of the face. If the back stitchers are all brought on the same face twill, this twill will appear flatter and narrower than the other twill under which the back picks float without stitchers.

Fig. 1275 shows all the back stitchers on the same twill line, producing an uneven face, while in Fig. 1276 the face twills will be uniform because the back stitchers come on alternate twills.

Fig. 1289 is also arranged, like 1276, to give a smooth face.

The arrangement of 1 face 2 back, shown at Fig. 1290, is for the purpose of reducing the cost of the fabric, cheaper material being used for the back than for the face.

Back filling cloths are sometimes made firmer by stitching the back filling two or more times in each weave pattern, as shown at Figs. 1281 and 1282.

Fig. 1280 shows the back pick stitched by being raised above two adjacent warp threads. This method is admissible for weaves with long floats, but the contrast in color or quality between the face and back should not be too sharp.

Fig. 1283 gives a very firm fabric. As the filling is woven 1 face 1 back the yarn on the back and face should be about the same size. This weave is well adapted for a close finish on woolen fabrics. In checks and plaids two adjacent threads of one color in the warp are required to balance one face thread of the same color in the filling.

Plain wool and silk mixtures are made with this weave. The warp and back filling are usually black, the face filling being all 2-ply made of 1 single black, 1 organzine silk.

Fig. 1283 is Fig. 1243 turned one-quarter way round to transpose the warp and filling.

Fig. 1283 may be used for a cotton warp frieze, the warp being hid by both face and back. The use of cotton warp for friezes is of doubtful economy owing to the necessity of increasing the number of picks to obtain the required weight. A cotton warp frieze woven with Fig. 1283 can be striped in the warp by weaving fancy woolen warp threads on an extra harness in 5 up 3 down broken twill order.

Fig. 1293 is suited for cotton warp piece dyed chinchillas.

Figs. 1283, 1284, 1285, 1286, 1287, 1288, 1291, 1292, 1293, 1303 and 1305 are weaves in which the filling predominates on the surface of both face and back, the warp being covered. Such weaves are often used for cheap fabrics in which the warp is cotton yarn and the filling medium wool or shoddy. If the filling is made of shoddy and spun to a coarse count, the 1 and 1 or 2 and 2 order is usually changed to 2 face 1 back in order to improve the appearance of the face. The face weave is arranged to give a regular stitching of the back filling. This arrangement is shown at Figs. 1291, 1292 and 1293.

When cloth in which the warp predominates on the face is woven with a back filling, the latter must float at least twice as far as the face filling and be so interlaced that stitchers shall come on every twill line. In such weaves it is not always possible to have the

stitching warp thread below the face thread both before and after the back pick.

This difficulty is illustrated at Fig. 1307, in which
the warp thread that stitches a back pick is below the
preceding face pick, but above the succeeding face
pick. If, however, the face weave is a double warp
satin, instead of single, the stitchers can be inserted
so that the warp thread lies below the face pick on each
side of the stitched back pick, Figs. 1295 and 1301.

For fine stripes a 3-leaf twill, pointed in the filling,
is used, with the face picks stitched successively on
warp threads, 1, 2, 3, 2, Fig. 639. Fig. 1296 shows
such a weave with the back filling stitched only on
warp threads, 1, 3, 4, 6. The absence of back stitchers
on warp threads 2 and 5 does not cause irregularity
of tension because these two threads are woven plain
and thus interlace the face filling more closely than the
other warp threads, which are woven 1 up 2 down.

It is evident from Fig. 1296 that the face of back filling weaves need not be regular twills or satins. Most
weaves are suited for the face of back filling fabrics,
especially those in which the warp passes below two
successive filling threads.

Fig. 1297 is a broken 2 up 2 down twill, Fig. 382,
on the face, with a broken 3 up 1 down twill on the
back.

Fig. 1294 is a corkscrew, Fig. 457, on the face, with
a 9-leaf back weave.

Fig. 1298 is an interlocking twill, Fig. 510, on the
face with a 9-leaf back weave. All three are suitable
for heavy goods.

Two back picks can be inserted between each face
pick. In such a case one back pick passes below the
other and floats twice as far. Fig. 1304 shows such a
weave in which one back pick, stitched with an 8-leaf
satin, passes under the other back pick, which is stitched
with a 3 up 1 down twill, the face weave being a 2 up
2 down twill.

Fig. 1309 shows the diagonal, Fig. 326, woven with back filling. This weave can be designated as 2 face, 1 back or 1 face, 1 stuffing pick, 1 back.

In Fig. 1310 each warp thread stitches the back filling twice in each filling pattern. The face is a 6-leaf basket. The filling is woven 1 face, 1 back, 1 face, 1 back, 1 face.

Fig. 1314 shows the crêpe weave, Fig. 1311, with each back pick woven 9 up 1 down 5 up 1 down. The filling is woven 2 face, 1 back.

Figs. 1302 and 1315 are often used for fine worsteds.

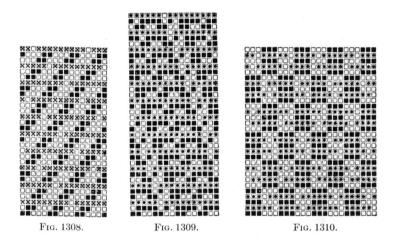

FIG. 1308.   FIG. 1309.   FIG. 1310.

The twill form in which the back picks are stitched causes a diagonal break or recess on the face.

Figs. 1306, 1313 and 1316 are used for military diagonals and cloth for riding breeches.

Fig. 1306 is woven 1 face, 1 stuffing pick, 1 back.

Fig. 1313, 1 face, 1 back.

Fig. 1316, 2 face, 1 back.

A diagonal recess is obtained by stitching the back picks as shown at Figs. 1299 and 1300.

A familiarity with the construction of back filling weaves is important, especially when dissecting cloths of this kind which may have been fulled hard.

When drafting back filling weaves in which it is

difficult to stitch the back picks regularly, the stitchers are arranged to conform to the face weave. For this purpose a space is left between each two face picks, and on each of these lines risers are marked where the back pick should be stitched. The face weave is then drafted so that as many of the back stitchers as possible may come where the warp is below both the preceding and succeeding picks. The remaining stitches are then rearranged to effect the same result while disturbing the regular order as little as possible.

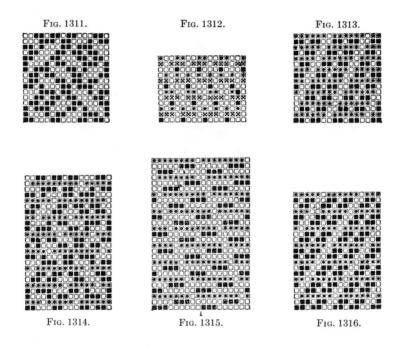

Fig. 1311.   Fig. 1312.   Fig. 1313.

Fig. 1314.   Fig. 1315.   Fig. 1316.

Fig. 1302 is a back filling weave, 3 face, 1 back, 1 face, 1 back.

Fig. 1312, used for woven felt, is a broken 1 up 3 down twill on the face and a broken 3 up 1 down twill on the back, woven 1 face, 1 back, 1 stuffing pick. After each two picks (1 face, 1 back) there is inserted a stuffing pick which lies between the face and back. Above this pick is raised every warp thread that is raised above the preceding or succeeding face pick.

Fig. 1306, 16-shaft, woven 1 face, 1 stuffing pick, 1 back.

Fig. 1312, woven 1 face, 1 back, 1 stuffing pick.

Fig. 1315, woven 2 face, 1 back.

Fig. 1316, 7-shaft, woven 2 face, 1 back.

TRICOT WEAVES

Cloths having the face broken with narrow and uniform furrows or ridges to resemble knitted fabrics are called tricots, the name being derived from the French *tricoter*, to knit. When the furrows run lengthways or in the direction of the warp, the weave is called "tricot long." If the furrows run crossways or with the filling, it is called "tricot cross."

The simplest way of obtaining a tricot effect is by alternating a thread of right twist with one of left twist in both warp and filling on a plain weave. The reversal of the twist causes a ridge or tricot, which is very effective in light fabrics. Combinations of tricot long and tricot cross effects can be made by a suitable arrangement of threads of different twist in both warp and filling.

TRICOT LONG

In the weaves at Figs. 1317 and 1318 tricot effects are produced by alternating two threads of a warp weave with two threads of a filling weave.

Fig. 1317, 2 threads woven 3 up 1 down, 2 threads woven 1 up 3 down.

Fig. 1318, 2 threads woven 4 up 1 down, 2 threads woven 1 up 4 down.

Combinations of 2 up 1 down with 1 up 2 down can also be used for this purpose.

At Fig. 1319 a group of 4 warp threads is woven plain on alternate picks, the other picks floating on the back. The plain weave and float are transposed for the next 4 threads, the back pick interlacing the warp in plain weave order, while the plain pick floats on the back. This exchange of position after each

4 warp threads causes a rib or tricot line and produces an elastic fabric. It is suited for a tricot effect in worsted dress goods with 150 to 170 picks of 1/70s to 1/80s worsted per inch.

For heavy tricot cloths, transposed double weaves, as shown at Fig. 1320, are used. In Fig. 1320 the first 4 warp threads form two plain cloths, one above the other, and not stitched in any way. After the fourth thread every back pick comes to the face, while the face picks pass to the back. In this new position two

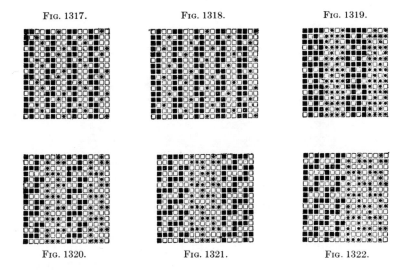

FIG. 1317.   FIG. 1318.   FIG. 1319.

FIG. 1320.   FIG. 1321.   FIG. 1322.

plain cloths are again made for 4 threads when the back and face picks again are transposed, resuming their original position for another four threads. The transfer of the filling from face to back and from back to face makes one compact fabric.

At the point where the face and back picks are transposed a back warp thread, woven 1 up 3 down, breaks with the adjacent face warp thread, woven 3 up 1 down, as shown by threads 4 and 5, Fig. 1320. This sharp break tends to separate the two adjacent face warp threads, 3 and 5, Fig. 1320, causing the face warp to form groups of two threads each. Threads

1 and 3 lie close together, as do threads 5 and 7, developing the tricot effect.

Fig. 1320 may also be considered as a back warp weave with a broken 3 up 1 down twill on the face and a broken 1 up 3 down twill on the back, the two weaves being so adjusted as to cause the break already described. By an increase in the width between the breaks the double plain weave is clearly developed as shown at Figs. 1321 and 1322. The face and back picks are transposed every 6 threads in Fig. 1321, and every 8 threads in Fig. 1322.

Fig. 1323 shows a pattern with tricot stripes of different widths.

Very heavy tricot cloths are made with extra back

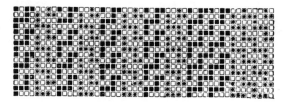

FIG. 1323.

warp or filling. Fig. 1324 shows the tricot long, Fig. 1320, with a back filling stitched in 7 up 1 down order.

Tricot long effects are frequently used for fine woolen goods in which the face warp consists of woolen yarn twisted with organzine silk.

TRICOT CROSS

Tricot cross effects are obtained by turning the tricot long weaves one-quarter way around, thus transposing the warp and filling. Fig. 1325 shows 2 picks of a broken 3 up 1 down twill alternating with 2 picks of a broken 1 up 3 down twill. The filling threads are arranged to avoid a sharp break like that in the warp of the tricot long, Fig. 1317. The tricot effect can be made more pronounced by using heavier filling for the picks that float on the back.

Fig. 1326 is a cross tricot weave obtained by turning Fig. 1320 one-quarter way around to bring the back threads in the filling. It is shown at Fig. 1327 with a stuffing pick in each stripe to increase the weight of the cloth.

Fig. 1326 may be considered a double plain weave with face and back warp threads transposed every 4 picks. As the tricot effect covers the same number of threads as in Fig. 1320, it may be considered a back filling weave with the face a broken 1 up 3 down twill, and the back a broken 3 up 1 down twill, the two weaves being adjusted to cause a break by bringing a

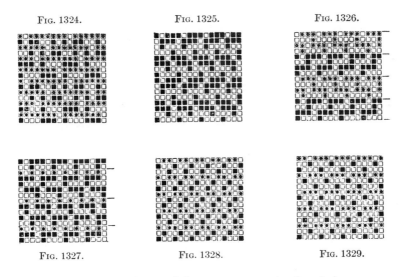

FIG. 1324.   FIG. 1325.   FIG. 1326.

FIG. 1327.   FIG. 1328.   FIG. 1329.

single riser on a face pick next to a single sinker on a back pick.

Fig. 1328 shows a back filling tricot weave, 2 face, 1 back. The face weave is a 1 up 2 down twill to the right; the back weave a 2 up 1 down twill to the left. Each sinker on the back pick comes next to a riser on the preceding face pick, producing the break or tricot effect.

Fig. 1329 shows a similar arrangement with a broken 1 up 3 down twill on the face and a 3 up 1 down twill to the right on the back; woven 2 face, 1 back.

Figs. 1328 and 1329 are suited for very fine tricot effects.

In tricot fabrics the effect depends in large measure upon the correct adjustment of the set of warp and filling, and upon the relative size of the warp and filling yarn.   Thus in Fig. 1326 the tricot effect is made more pronounced by increasing the relative size of the filling yarn as compared with the warp.

CLOTHS WITH AN EXTRA INNER FABRIC

If the threads of a fabric float for long distances, it is frequently necessary, in order to prevent slipping of the warp and filling and to make the cloth more durable, to introduce an extra inner fabric, which is usually woven with a plain weave.

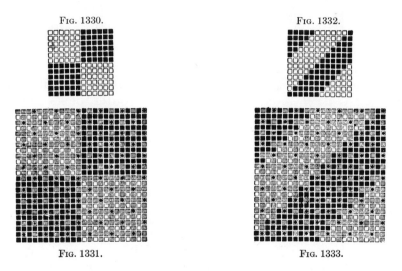

FIG. 1330.

FIG. 1332.

FIG. 1331.

FIG. 1333.

Fig. 1331 is a 6 up 6 down basket, Fig. 1330, woven 1 and 1 with an inner plain weave. It is drafted as follows:

1. The warp and filling threads for the inner fabric are shaded to distinguish the inner from the outer threads.

2. The inner plain weave is drafted with dotted circles on the shaded threads.

3. The weave for the outer threads is drafted with black squares.

4. The inner and outer weaves having been drafted

as above, it is now necessary to raise the outer warp threads above the inner picks when the outer threads float on the face. Where the outer warp is above an outer pick, the outer warp thread is also raised above the succeeding inner pick, thus bringing the inner pick below the outer warp.

It is also necessary to raise the inner warp threads above the outer picks where the latter float on the back. Where an outer warp thread is raised above an outer

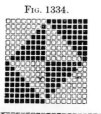

FIG. 1334.

pick, the inner warp thread at the right is also raised above the same outer pick, thus bringing the inner warp thread above the outer filling.

No additional risers are necessary in the squares where the outer picks float on the face, because the outer picks come above the adjacent inner picks, while the outer warp threads float on the back.

This fourth and last operation of drafting may be stated thus:

FIG. 1335.

Place a riser to the right and also above each riser of the outer weave.

The completed draft is shown at Fig. 1331.

Figs. 1331, 1333 and 1355 are weaves for cloths with extra inner fabrics, the outer weaves being shown at Figs. 1330, 1332 and 1334 respectively.

When the fabric is laid 2 inner, 1 outer, the fourth operation is changed to the following:

Place a riser at the right and left as well as above and below each riser of the outer weave, as shown at Fig. 1337, for which Fig. 1336 is the ground weave.

On the other hand, when the cloth is laid 2 outer,

1 inner, the fourth operation is changed to the following:

Place a riser above every riser on each outer pick that is followed by an inner pick; and place a riser at the right of every riser of each outer warp thread that is followed by an inner warp thread, as shown at Fig. 1340, for which Fig. 1339 is the ground weave.

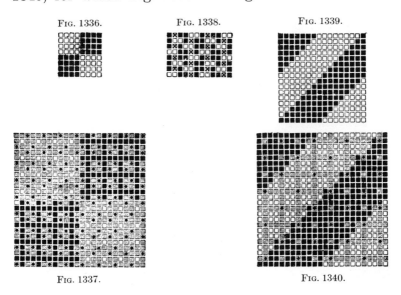

FIG. 1336.   FIG. 1338.   FIG. 1339.

FIG. 1337.   FIG. 1340.

Fabrics are also woven with plain stitch threads running in only one direction, warp or filling, and which are completely covered by the other threads.

Fig. 1338 shows a broken 3 up 1 down twill to which an extra warp thread is stitched plain, 1 up 1 down with the filling. The warp is 2 regular, 1 extra. The two weaves are so adjusted that the extra warp threads are covered by the regular threads.

DOUBLE CLOTHS

A double cloth consists of two distinct fabrics, face and back, which are generally stitched together by interlacing the face threads with the back threads. The various applications of double cloth construction are as follows:

1. Tubular fabrics, such as lamp wicking, fire hose, seamless bags, woven felt for covering pipes, etc. The face and back are joined at both sides, forming a tubular fabric.

2. To produce a fabric of uniform density. Frequently the face does not permit the addition of a back filling only, in which case a separate set of warp threads for the back must be added to carry the back filling.

3. To make the fabric thicker and heavier than is possible with back filling alone. It is evident that in double cloth, the warp threads being divided into two parts, a much smaller number of threads are inserted in one texture than is the case with back filling cloths, in which all the warp threads are woven together. The more open the set of the warp, the more easily will it receive the filling, and thus the thicker and heavier can the cloth be made.

4. For the better production of plaids and checks in both light and heavy goods. If such patterns are made in filling back fabrics, the set of the filling is likely to be too coarse, as it is impossible to insert as many face picks per inch in a filling back cloth as in a cloth without back filling. The result of the more open filling set is that each square of the weave represents

a space which in the cloth itself is longer than it is wide. The chief defect of such a texture is that the warp colors are more prominent than the filling. This is due to the more open set of the filling, which leaves the warp threads more exposed. This difficulty may be relieved by laying the warp with a more open set, using finer yarn for the back filling and inserting more picks.

5. Cloths are also made double in order that the cost may not increase in proportion to the increase in the weight and thickness. Double textures not only permit the insertion of more filling, but offer the advantage that in both warp and filling the backing yarn can be made of much cheaper material than that used for the face. This is especially true of the back filling yarn which in double cloths is often very heavy and made of exceedingly low stock. Such yarn, if used for the backing of regular back filling cloths, would be likely to show through on the face. Moreover, the heavy backing would make it impossible to drive the required number of picks into back filling fabric.

6. Cloths with face and back of contrasting colors, such as plaid-back overcoating. The set and weave of the back of a double cloth are usually made to conform to those of the face. This, however, is not essential. Both the set and weave of the back may be entirely different from those on the face. This is not to be understood as permitting the use of any and every possible combination of diverse weaves and sets for back and face, as the shrinking or fulling properties of the different textures must be considered. Judgment must be used on this point as no fixed rules can be laid down.

The face and back threads in both warp and filling are arranged so that one back thread comes after one, two, three, or four face threads. Following are some practical combinations:

Face Weave	Back Weave	Set
Plain	Plain	1 face 1 back
Plain	Plain	2 face 1 back
Plain	Twill 2 up 2 down	1 face 1 back
Plain	Basket 2 up 2 down	1 face 1 back
Basket 2 up 2 down	Basket 2 up 2 down	1 face 1 back
Basket 2 up 2 down	Plain	2 face 1 back
Basket 3 up 3 down	Plain	2 face 1 back
Basket 3 up 3 down	Plain	3 face 1 back
Twill 2 up 1 down	Plain	2 face 1 back
Twill 2 up 2 down	Plain	2 face 1 back
Twill 2 up 2 down	Twill 2 up 2 down	1 face 1 back
Twill 2 up 2 down	Twill 3 up 1 down	1 face 1 back
Twill 2 up 2 down	Broken twill 3 up 1 down	1 face 1 back
Broken twill 3 up 1 down	Broken twill 3 up 1 down	2 face 1 back
Broken twill 3 up 1 down	Plain	2 face 1 back
Satin 5-leaf	Satin 5-leaf	2 face 1 back
Twill 3 up 3 down	Plain	3 face 1 back
Twill 3 up 3 down	Plain	2 face 1 back
Twill 3 up 3 down	Twill 2 up 1 down	2 face 1 back
Tricot long	Plain	4 face 1 back

Fig. 1341.   Fig. 1342. 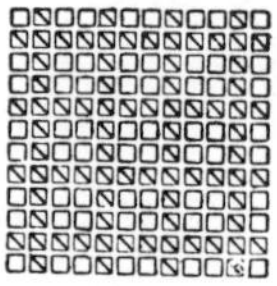   Fig. 1343. 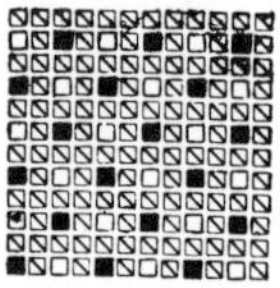   Fig. 1344.

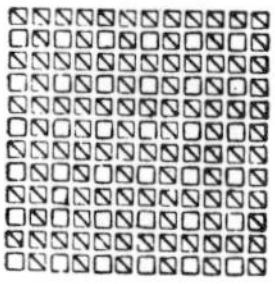

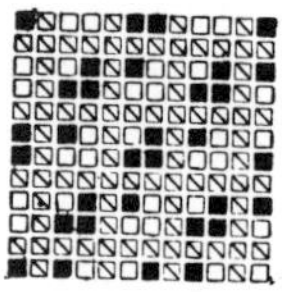

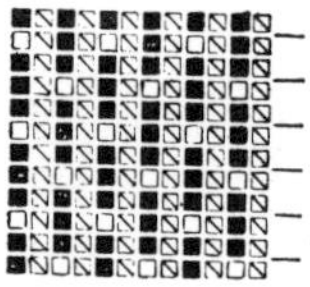

Fig. 1345. 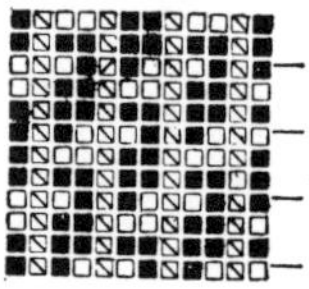   Fig. 1346. 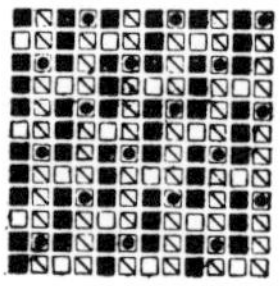   Fig. 1347. 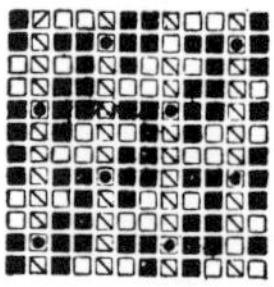   Fig. 1348.

The arrangement of face and back in the warp may be different from that in the filling. For example, the warp may be dressed 1 face, 1 back and the filling 2 face, 1 back, or the warp may be 3 or 4 face, 1 back, and the filling 2 face, 1 back. The object of such variations is to increase the proportion of filling in the goods, on account of the lower cost of the back filling, and to obtain a better cover on the back.

Weaves for double cloths are drafted as follows:

1. The spaces for the back threads are indicated by the diagonal lines, Figs. 1341 and 1342, in which

the set is 1 face, 1 back and 2 face, 1 back respectively. This is to distinguish the back threads from the face, and serves no other purpose. The back threads can be distinguished by any other means desired, such as painting the space instead of marking it.

2. The face weave is next drafted with black squares indicating warp risers, and blank squares for warp sinkers. For example, Fig. 1343 shows a plain woven face on Fig. 1341; Fig. 1344, a 2 up 2 down twill face on Fig. 1342.

3. All face warp threads are now raised above the back picks. This is shown by Fig. 1345 for Fig. 1343; by Fig. 1346 for Fig. 1344.

4. The weave intended for the back is drafted on the back warp and filling threads.. The dotted squares indicate warp risers. Figs. 1347 and 1348 show a plain weave on the back of Figs. 1345 and 1346 respectively.

For cloths set 2 face, 1 back, the draft is usually begun 1 face, 1 back, 2 face, 1 back, etc.

All double fabric weaves are drafted in the manner just described. It is evident that face and back each form separate textures, which may be of different colors.

TUBULAR FABRICS

Tubular fabrics, such as lamp wicking, fire hose and seamless bags, are usually woven with a plain weave. The warp is made with an odd number of threads. For example, a warp for lamp wicking may be made with 67 ends, of which 34 are for the upper and 33 for the lower fabric. This arrangement is necessary to prevent two adjacent threads at the edge from being woven alike.

The double plain weave is shown at Figs. 1347 and 1358, the picks being thrown alternately on face and back. Two threads are drawn in the outside dent of the reed; 3 threads in each of the next two dents; and 4 threads in each dent for the rest of the warp. The object of the more open set at the edges is to counteract the tendency of the filling to contract more at the sides than in the center of the cloth.

Fire hose is often made of hemp yarn: warp, 3-ply; filling, 5-ply twisted slack. Two threads are drawn in each heddle. The filling is set very close, causing a warp take-up of 20 to 25 per cent. The weave is shown at Fig. 1347.

Bags without seams at the bottom are woven with 2 back picks alternating with 2 face picks. The shuttle passes from right to left and return. In this way the right side is closed, forming the bottom, and the left side is open, forming the top or mouth of the bag. The weave is shown at Fig. 1349.

Each side of the bag is closed by weaving the entire warp (face and back) for a short distance into a single fabric with the weave shown at Fig. 1353. The projecting edges are turned inside the bag.

Seamless bags are frequently woven like fire hose with the weave shown at Fig. 1347. At the beginning the whole warp is woven single for a short distance, as just described, to close the bottom of the bag. The sides are woven seamless and the edges at the top are hemmed after the bag comes from the loom.

Tubular fabrics are sometimes made to cover cylindrical objects. In Europe the cylinders of rotary cloth presses are sometimes covered with a tubular woven felt, which must be accurately made in order that the covered surface of the cylinder may be smooth.

The first and last three dents in the reed should each

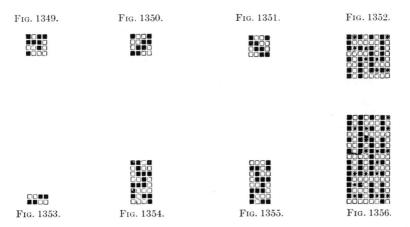

Fig. 1349.   Fig. 1350.   Fig. 1351.   Fig. 1352.

Fig. 1353.   Fig. 1354.   Fig. 1355.   Fig. 1356.

have one third less threads than are drawn in the other dents. Thus if the body of the warp is reeded 6 threads in a dent, the edges should be reeded 4 in a dent. This is for the purpose of avoiding tight edges.

Usually these fabrics are woven with a 4-leaf twill, 2 up 2 down. In order that the twill may run in the same direction throughout the circumference of the tubular fabric, the twill of the upper weave is run in a direction opposite to that of the lower weave as both are viewed in the loom.

If this requirement is not observed, the twill in one half of the completed fabric will be to the left, that of the other half to the right. Fig. 1352 shows the draft

to be used for this purpose; the upper twill is shown at
Fig. 1350; the lower twill at Fig. 1351.

For very thick double felt the face and back are
each woven with back filling, frequently with a broken
1 up 3 down twill, Fig. 1283. In drafting the weave
the order for the filling threads should first be determined. Two methods are available. The two picks
for the outer texture (the upper pick of the upper
fabric and the lower pick of the lower fabric) can be
inserted in succession, and followed by the two picks
from the inner texture (the lower pick of the upper
fabric and the upper pick of the lower fabric); or the
two inner picks of the cloth (the lower pick of the face
and upper pick of the back) can be woven first and
then followed by the exterior picks of the cloth (upper
pick of the face and lower pick of the back).

Figs. 1354, 1355 and 1356 show a broken 3 up 1 down
back filling twill in the first-named order, Fig. 1354
being the face, Fig. 1355 the back, and Fig. 1356 the
complete double weave. The upper picks of the face
and the lower picks of the back weave form the filling
on the outside of the tubular fabric.

REGULAR DOUBLE FABRICS

Double weaves are chiefly used, not for tubular goods, but to increase the weight and thickness of a fabric. For this purpose it is necessary that the two textures should be carefully and regularly stitched together, by interlacing the threads of one fabric with those of the other. This is accomplished either by raising the back warp above the face filling or by lowering the face warp below the back filling.

Raising the back warp above the face filling is called stitching from back to face. Lowering the face warp below the back filling is called stitching from face to back.

The method of stitching has great influence on the appearance and handle of the cloth.

Following are the principal points to be observed:

1. Uniform distribution of the stitchers.

2. The right number of stitchers. General rules on this point are as follows: For 1 face, 1 back weaves, 2 stitchers are inserted in an area of 8 threads square; for cloths set 2 face, 1 back, 2 stitchers are inserted in an area of 6 threads square; or, 2, 4 or 8 stitchers in an area 12 threads square.

3. So far as possible stitch with each back warp thread, when stitching from back to face.

4. Insert so far as possible each stitcher where the stitching warp thread is above both the preceding and following picks; also where both warp threads next to the stitching thread are likewise raised so as to cover the back stitcher. This rule refers to stitching from back to face.

5. Arrange the stitchers so as to disarrange the color pattern and weave as little as possible.

Most double cloths are stitched from back to face, because the back warp is usually finer than the back filling and is, consequently, covered better by the face threads when raised to stitch the fabric. Stitching from face to back brings the back filling to the face.

The simplest double weave is the double plain, shown at Fig. 1347 without stitchers. It is difficult to lay down a general rule as to whether a double

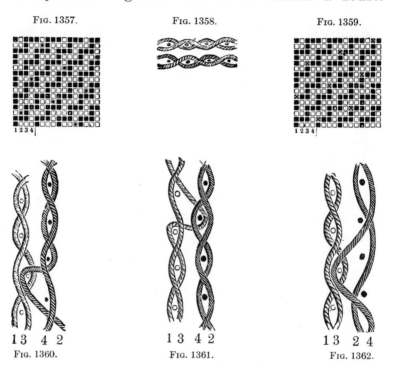

FIG. 1357.

FIG. 1358.

FIG. 1359.

1 3   4 2
FIG. 1360.

1 3   4 2
FIG. 1361.

1 3   2 4
FIG. 1362.

plain cloth should be stitched from back to face or from face to back. The quality, color and size of both face and back yarn must be considered, as well as the arrangement of the colors in checks and stripes. If a double cloth is made with a dark back warp and a light-colored plaid on a dark ground on the face, stitching from back to face has a tendency to subdue the light colors of the face filling. Stitching the same cloth from face to back would, on the other hand, subdue the light colors of the face warp.

Fig. 1357 is a 1 and 1 double plain weave stitched from back to face; the stitchers are risers indicated by the dotted circles.

Fig. 1359 shows the same weave stitched from face to back, the crosses representing stitchers, which are sinkers.

The stitchers in both weaves are arranged regularly in 8-leaf satin order, but both have the defect, which is inherent in double plain weaves, that the stitching thread passes directly from one side of the cloth to the other. This is shown in Fig. 1360, which is a longitudinal section of Fig. 1357. The first four warp threads and the ends of 8 picks are shown.

In the sectional drawings, Figs. 1360, 1361 and 1362, the light threads are face warp; the dark threads, back warp.

Fig. 1361 is a longitudinal section of the 1 and 1 plain weave shown at Fig. 1359, stitched from face to back. This face-to-back method is objectionable in double plain cloths made with a coarse back filling because of the increased curvature of the stitching thread, which must pass under the back filling.

The curvature of the stitching thread is less where the weave of either face or back allows the stitching thread to pass on the same side of (above or below) two consecutive picks of the same texture (face or back).

Figs. 1362 and 1363 show this construction. The back weave is a 2 up 2 down twill; the face weave is plain. The stitching thread passes from back to face so as to bring it above both the preceding and succeeding back picks, bringing three risers together on the stitching thread. In this way the curvature of the stitching thread is gradual, as shown by the longitudinal section, Fig. 1362, instead of abrupt, as in Figs. 1360 and 1361.

The first four warp threads in each of the weaves, Figs. 1357, 1359 and 1363 are indicated by corresponding numbers, 1, 2, 3 and 4 in the respective sections, Figs. 1360, 1361 and 1362.

Fig. 1364 shows a 1 and 1 fabric having a plain weave on the face and a 2 up 2 down basket on the back. Only a part of the stitchers are favorably placed to reduce the curvature of the stitching thread.

In Fig. 1365 the face is a 2 up 2 down basket, the back a plain weave. The set in both warp and filling is 2 face 1 back (beginning 1 face 1 back). The face-to-back stitchers, which are sinkers indicated by

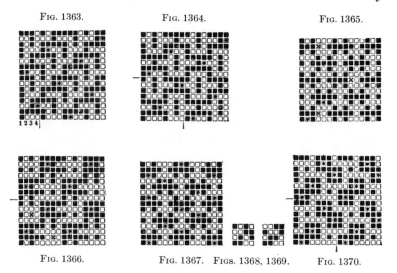

FIG. 1363.　　　FIG. 1364.　　　FIG. 1365.

FIG. 1366.　　　FIG. 1367.　FIGS. 1368, 1369.　　FIG. 1370.

crosses, are favorably placed so that the stitching thread passes below a face, a back and a face pick in succession.

As the face threads work in pairs, being down for two picks in succession, the stitching from face to back is to be preferred. If, however, the low grade of the back filling makes stitching from back to face necessary, the stitchers can be inserted on the dotted squares, threads 2 and 5.

In Fig. 1366 each texture is woven with a 2 up 2 down basket and stitched in both ways. Stitchers from back to face are risers indicated by dotted squares; from face to back, sinkers indicated by crosses.

Fig. 1367 shows a 2 up 2 down basket face and a plain back stitched in modified broken twill order, as in Fig. 1451.

Fig. 1370 shows the two broken twill weaves, Figs. 1368 and 1369 (for back and face respectively) stitched, in broken 4-leaf twill order, 1, 2, 4 and 3. Here each stitcher has risers at the right and left as well as before and after.

Fig. 1371 shows two 3-leaf twills stitched in twill order; the warp set is 1 and 1; the back set, 2 and 1.

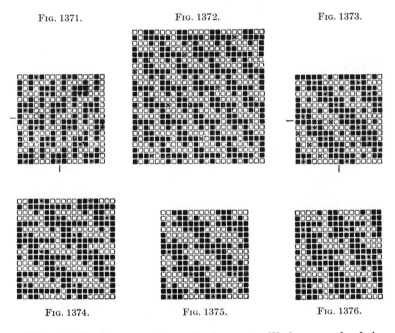

FIG. 1371.   FIG. 1372.   FIG. 1373.

FIG. 1374.   FIG. 1375.   FIG. 1376.

Fig. 1372 shows a 2 up 2 down twill face and plain back, set 2 and 1. The stitching, indicated by crosses, is from face to back in 8-leaf satin order. Such weaves are frequently stitched twice in a 6-thread square, Fig. 1380; or four times in a 12-thread square, Fig. 1381.

Fig. 1373 shows a double 2 up 2 down twill set 1 and 1 in warp and filling. The dotted squares, risers, indicate stitchers from back to face; the crosses, sinkers, are the stitchers from face to back.

In Fig. 1374 the face is a 3 up 3 down twill; the back, a 1 down 2 up twill, the set 2 face 1 back, stitched from back to face.

Fig. 1375 has a 3 up 3 down twill face and plain back; the set is 3 face 1 back; stitched from back to face. A better cover is given to the back of this fabric by setting the filling 2 face 1 back 1 face 1 back with every 2 back picks interlacing the filling alike, as shown at Fig. 1376.

The arrangement of the face and back threads in Figs. 1363 to 1376 is well suited for stitching the two

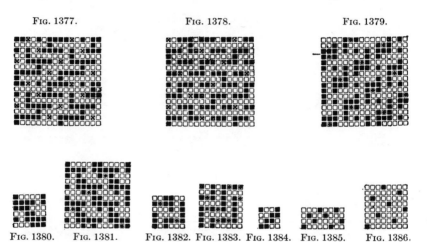

FIG. 1377. FIG. 1378. FIG. 1379.

FIG. 1380. FIG. 1381. FIG. 1382. FIG. 1383. FIG. 1384. FIG. 1385. FIG. 1386.

weaves. This would not have been the case if the back weave had been begun at a different place. For example, if in Fig. 1372 the plain back weave, instead of beginning 1 up 1 down, had started with 1 down 1 up, the draft would have been as shown at Fig. 1382, which cannot be stitched to good advantage.

Again, if the twill of the back weave in Fig. 1373 instead of beginning 1 up 2 down 1 up had begun 1 down 2 up 1 down, the draft would have been as shown at Fig. 1383, which offers no good places for stitching.

These examples show the necessity of constructing double weaves so as to leave a favorable place for the insertion of the stitchers.

While desirable, it is nevertheless impossible to draft double weaves by fixed rules. The only general rule that can be given is to bring the risers of the back weave next to the risers of the face weave.

Fig. 1377 is a broken 1 up 3 down twill on the face and a 2 up 2 down twill on the back. The set is 1 and 1 in warp and filling. The face-to-back stitchers are indicated by crosses (×), sinkers, arranged in broken 4-leaf twill order.

Fig. 1378 is a 6-leaf satin face with a plain weave

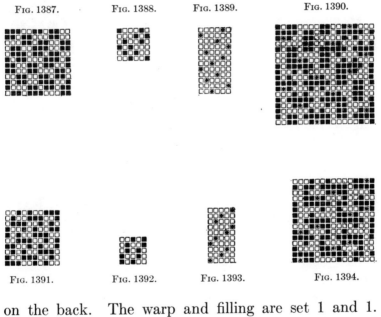

FIG. 1387.   FIG. 1388.   FIG. 1389.   FIG. 1390.

FIG. 1391.   FIG. 1392.   FIG. 1393.   FIG. 1394.

on the back. The warp and filling are set 1 and 1. The face-to-back stitchers (×), sinkers, are arranged in 6-leaf satin order.

Such weaves are used for plaid backcloths in which the back and face are made of contrasting colors, the face usually one color and the back plaided. The stitchers are from face to back to prevent the back threads from showing on the face.

The weave at Fig. 1379 is adapted for worsted goods having a 2 up 2 down twill face. The back weave is a broken twill, while the stitchers are in-

serted in 8-leaf satin order. The warp is set 1 and 1;
the filling, 2 and 1.

For this class of goods the face is often woven with
crêpe and similar weaves, while the back weave is so
arranged that the warp comes to the surface on the
back of the cloth, the back filling being concealed in
the center of the fabric.

This construction is shown at Figs. 1379, 1390,
1394, 1398, 1402 and 1406. The face weave, back

FIG. 1395.   FIG. 1396.   FIG. 1397.   FIG. 1398.

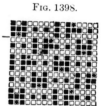

FIG. 1399.   FIG. 1400.   FIG. 1401.   FIG. 1402.

weave and order of stitching for the respective double
weaves are shown as follows:

Figs. 1384, 1385 and 1386 for Fig. 1379.
Figs. 1387, 1388 and 1389 for Fig. 1390.
Figs. 1391, 1392 and 1393 for Fig. 1394.
Figs. 1395, 1396 and 1397 for Fig. 1398.
Figs. 1399, 1400 and 1401 for Fig. 1402.
Figs. 1403, 1404 and 1405 for Fig. 1406.

These weaves are set as follows:

Fig. 1379, warp, 1 and 1; filling, 2 and 1.
Fig. 1390, warp and filling, 2 and 1.

Fig. 1394, warp and filling, 2 and 1.

Fig. 1398, warp, 1 and 1 ; filling, 2 and 1.

Fig. 1402, warp and filling, 2 and 1.

Fig. 1406, warp, 1 and 1 ; filling, 2 and 1.

The face and back in Fig. 1402 are stitched by bringing the back warp thread above two adjacent face picks, indicated by dotted squares. This method of joining double weaves should be used only when the back and face warp are of the same quality and color and the stitchers are well covered by warp risers on either side, as in Fig. 1402, which is suited for worsted cloths.

The back weave is often plain when the cloth is made with a worsted face and woolen back. This is

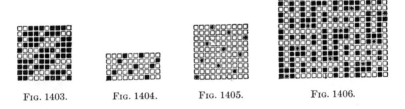

FIG. 1403.   FIG. 1404.   FIG. 1405.   FIG. 1406.

the usual course when both face and back are woolen, the object being to make the fabric firmer. At Figs. 1410 and 1414 are shown two weaves in which the face is crêpe and the back plain. The face and back weaves and order of stitching for Fig. 1410 are shown at Figs. 1407, 1408 and 1409; for Fig. 1414, at Figs. 1411, 1412 and 1413.

Attention is called to two other weaves for heavy woolen fabrics, the army tricot, Fig. 1415, and the army diagonal, Fig. 1416.

The first, Fig. 1415, is the tricot long, Fig. 1320, with a plain back. The warp is set 4 face 1 back; the filling, 2 face 1 back; stitched from face to back.

The face of the army diagonal, Fig. 1416, is the diagonal shown at Fig. 313, the back being woven with the cross-rib weave, Fig. 208. The warp is set 4 face

1 back; the filling, 2 face 1 back; the stitching is from back to face.

Warp weaves, preferably the broken 3 up 1 down twill, are used for the face of face-finished goods. The back is often woven plain and the stitching so arranged that 2 stitchers come in each square of 6 threads, 4 stitchers in a 12-thread square or 8 stitchers in a

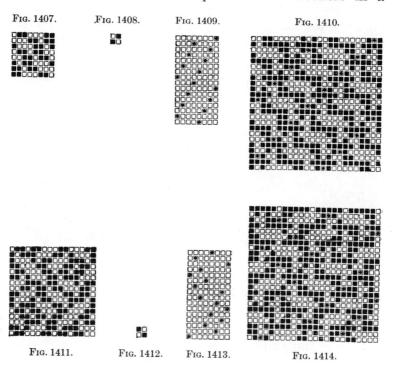

FIG. 1407.   FIG. 1408.   FIG. 1409.   FIG. 1410.

FIG. 1411.   FIG. 1412.   FIG. 1413.   FIG. 1414.

24-thread square, as shown in Figs. 1418, 1425 and 1429, respectively.

The face and back weaves and stitching order for Fig. 1418 are shown at Figs. 1419, 1420 and 1421; for Fig. 1425, at Figs. 1422, 1423 and 1424; for Fig. 1429, at Figs. 1426, 1427 and 1428; for Fig. 1439, at Figs. 1430, 1431 and 1432; for Fig. 1440, at Figs. 1433, 1434 and 1435; for Fig. 1441 at Figs. 1436, 1437 and 1438; for Fig. 1451, at Figs. 1442, 1443 and 1444; for Fig. 1452, at Figs. 1445, 1446 and 1447; for Fig. 1453, at Figs. 1448, 1449 and 1450.

Lighter fabrics are sometimes woven with a 3-leaf twill face and plain back, as shown at Fig. 1417. The order of stitching covers 6 back warp threads and 12 face picks.

The heavy overcoating cloth known as double satin, president and Eskimo cloth, is woven with a broken 3 up 1 down twill or a 5-leaf warp satin on both face and back. The two weaves are stitched tightly, but so carefully and regularly that the smoothness of the face is not affected. A stitcher with a riser at both right and left is inserted at each face pick. Figs. 1430 to 1453 show examples of these weaves. Figs. 1452 and 1453 are better adapted for goods of lighter

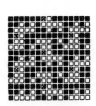

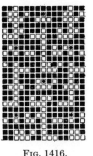

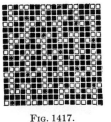

FIG. 1415.   FIG. 1416.   FIG. 1417.

weight, on account of the greater firmness resulting from the plain back with which they are woven.

The warp in each of these six weaves is 2 face 1 back. The filling in Fig. 1439 is set 1 face 1 back; in Fig. 1441, 3 face 1 back; in the others, 2 face 1 back.

The warp of these fabrics is sometimes set 3 or 4 face to 1 back, as shown at Figs. 1454 and 1455, in order to obtain a closer set on the face. The filling in these two weaves is set 2 face 1 back.

Two combinations of 5-leaf satin weaves for Eskimo overcoating cloths are shown at Figs. 1456 and 1457.

Fig. 1456 has a warp satin on back and face. Fig. 1457 has a warp satin on the face and a filling satin on the back, which is made double to avoid the long filling floats.

Two back weaves for beaver cloths are shown at Figs. 1460 and 1461, with blank spaces showing the position of the face picks. Fig. 1460 is a rib, Fig. 208; Fig. 1461 shows a double 5-leaf warp satin. The filling is set 2 face 2 back, the two face picks being inserted between two back picks woven alike. This arrangement is sometimes adopted when a thick nap is wanted on the back.

Overcoating cloths with curled or looped effects on the face resembling Persian lamb skins are made with

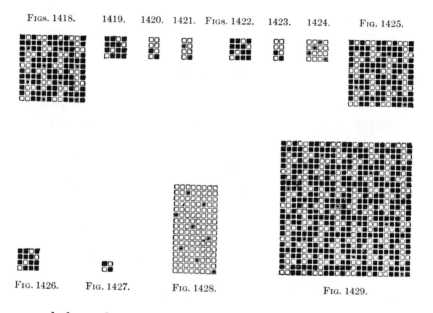

Figs. 1418.   1419.   1420. 1421. Figs. 1422.   1423.   1424.   Fig. 1425.

Fig. 1426.   Fig. 1427.   Fig. 1428.   Fig. 1429.

carded woolen warp and back filling, the face filling being made by doubling a fine thread with a coarse thread of luster wool. In twisting the ply yarn, the coarse thread is run slack on the fine thread as a base, thus forming loops or curls. About two inches of the coarse thread is twisted on every inch of the fine yarn. A very fine thread, called the binder, is twisted in the opposite direction around the other two and develops the loop.

The face is usually woven with a broken 4-leaf filling twill or a filling satin, the back with a 2 up 2 down

twill or a weave which throws the filling on the back.
Fig. 1458 is a weave of this kind with a broken 1 up 3
down twill on the face, and a 2 up 2 down twill on the
back. It is set 1 and 1 in the warp, and 1 face 2 back
in the filling.

Fig. 1462 is woven 1 face 2 back in the warp and
1 face 3 back in the filling. The weave is a 4-leaf
broken filling twill on the face, and a 2 up 2 down twill

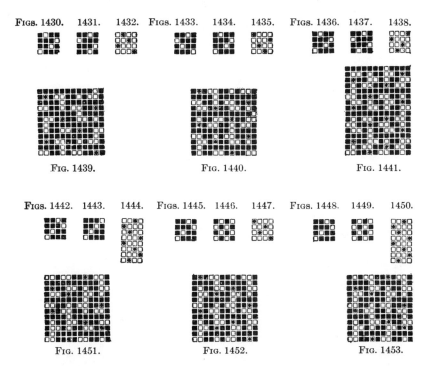

Figs. 1430. 1431. 1432. Figs. 1433. 1434. 1435. Figs. 1436. 1437. 1438.

Fig. 1439.   Fig. 1440.   Fig. 1441.

Figs. 1442. 1443. 1444. Figs. 1445. 1446. 1447. Figs. 1448. 1449. 1450.

Fig. 1451.   Fig. 1452.   Fig. 1453.

on the back. Both weaves should be stitched from
face to back, as shown in the draft, in which the stitchers,
sinkers, are indicated by crosses (×).

In Fig. 1463 the face filling is woven with an 8-leaf
satin; the back filling, with a modified broken twill;
filling, 1 face 2 back. This is a single fabric woven with
a back filling, and not a regular double fabric.

The illustrations that have been given show the
method of constructing double weaves, of which the
number is unlimited. The principal difficulty in draft-

ing double cloths is in stitching the face and back fabrics together. The rules already given should be strictly observed and care taken when drafting a new weave for a double texture to have the stitchers in the right place.

The divided drawing-in draft, No. 8, Figs. 25 and 26, is best for double cloths, the face and back warp com-

Fig. 1454.

Fig. 1455.

ing on separate sets of shafts. In some mills it is customary to draw in the warp straight, using as many shafts as there are threads in the weave pattern. It is usually better, however, to draw the back warp and face warp on separate groups of shafts. In many cases this enables the warp to be drawn on a less number of shafts than with a straight draft.

Fig. 1459 shows a double cloth weave, 2 face, 1 back in warp and filling, a broken 4-leaf warp twill on the face, and plain weave on the back, with the face and back warp drawn on separate groups of shafts.

Fig. 1456.   Fig. 1457.   Fig. 1458.   Fig. 1459.

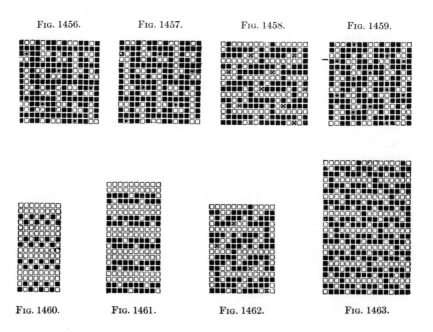

Fig. 1460.   Fig. 1461.   Fig. 1462.   Fig. 1463.

So far as possible the warp of double cloths should be reeded as follows:

1 face 1 back: 4, 6 or 8 threads per dent.
2 face 1 back: 3 threads (1 face 1 back 1 face) per dent; 4 and 5 alternate per dent; or, 6, 9 or 12 threads per dent.
3 face 1 back: 4 threads (1 face 1 back 2 face) per dent; or 8 threads per dent.

When there are 2 or more face threads for 1 back thread, the back thread should not come first or last in the dent.

DOUBLE CLOTHS WITH STUFFING THREADS

Stuffing threads are inserted in the cloth when the requisite weight and thickness cannot be obtained with the

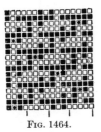

FIG. 1464.   FIG. 1465.

regular double weaves. These stuffing threads, which may be in warp or filling, lie between the face and back. They do not come to the surface on either side of the cloth and can, therefore, be of any color or quality desired, provided the contrast is not so sharp that the color of the inner threads shows to an objectionable extent on the face or back. These stuffing threads often serve to increase the prominence of stripes and figured effects as in piqué and matelassé.

Stuffing warp threads lie above every back pick and below every face pick. If the stuffing threads are in the filling, all face warp threads must be raised above and all back warp threads lowered below each

stuffing pick.   Fig. 1464 shows stuffing warp threads
in a double cloth with a 2 up 2 down twill face and
plain back.   Fig. 1465 shows the same face and back
weaves woven with a stuffing pick.   In both cases
the order is 1 face 1 back 1 face 1 stuffing thread.

THREE OR MORE PLY CLOTHS

Three or more fabrics are woven one above the other and stitched together when very thick and heavy goods are to be made.

In drafting a 3-ply weave the procedure is as follows:

The position of the threads for each fabric, face, center and back is first indicated on the draft.

The face weave is then drafted on the face threads, the center and back threads being left blank.

The face warp threads are now raised above all the center picks.

The center weave is drafted, the back threads being left blank.

The face and center warp threads are raised above all the back picks, and the draft is completed by drafting the back weave. The stitching can be effected in various ways:

1. From back to center and from center to face.
2. From face to center and from center to back.
3. From back to center and from face to center.
4. From center to face and from center to back.

Fig. 1466 shows a 3-ply weave, each fabric woven plain, and stitched in 8-leaf satin order, according to the first method given above. Warp and filling are set 1 face 1 center 1 back.

Fig. 1467 is a longitudinal section of the same weave and shows plainly the construction of the fabric.

Fig. 1470 shows a ply weave used for drying-felt for cotton cloth, also for belting. Five sets of warp and 6 sets of filling threads lie over each other. The sixth set of filling is in fact a back filling on the 5-ply fabric. The first or face fabric is stitched to the second; the second is stitched to the third; the third, to the fourth; and the fourth, to the fifth. The two outside fabrics (1 and 5) have the same set and weave, broken 4-leaf twill, except that the risers of one weave correspond to the sinkers of the other.

Of each 12 warp threads, 3 belong to the first or face weave, 3 to the back weave, and 2 to each of the three interior weaves. Fig. 1468 is the weave for the face; Fig. 1469, the weave for the second, third and fourth fabrics; and Fig. 1471 the weave for the back texture.

FIGS. 1468.   1469.

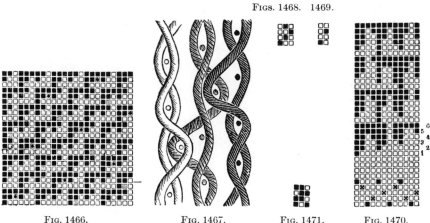

FIG. 1466.   FIG. 1467.   FIG. 1471.   FIG. 1470.

The complete draft is shown at Fig. 1470. The division and distribution of the warp threads are indicated at the bottom of the draft; of the filling threads, by the figures 1 to 6 at the side. The warp is reeded 12 threads in a dent. A fabric that is quite common is woven with this weave and reeded with $13\frac{1}{2}$ dents per inch.

THREE OR MORE PLY CLOTHS STITCHED WITH EXTRA WARP OR FILLING

The ordinary method of stitching 3 or more ply cloths tend to solidify the fabric by drawing the separate textures together. This method is satisfactory when a firm and durable cloth is desired.

For thick, bulky goods, it is sometimes necessary to weave separately each of the textures that form the cloth and without interlacing the threads of one fabric with those of another. The different textures are stitched together by extra warp or filling threads, which pass by degrees from one side of the cloth to the other. An extra warp beam is required for these extra threads if they are introduced in the warp.

This method of stitching is frequently used for cloaking fabrics, of which the face color is plain or fancy, and the back plaided. The binding thread is fine cotton yarn. One stitching thread is usually inserted

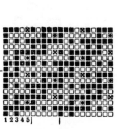

FIG. 1472.

FIG. 1473.

FIG. 1474.

after every four of the regular threads. The stitching threads are raised above a face pick and lowered below a back pick, thus binding the separate fabrics together. When not so raised or lowered, they lie between the upper and lower textures.

Weaves for these fabrics are drafted by first coloring the stitching warp threads on the draft to distinguish them.

The weaves for the different textures are then drafted in the remaining spaces.

The stitching warp threads are then raised above all the back picks.

These stitching threads are next raised above certain face picks (dotted squares), and lowered below certain back picks, so as to bind face and back together.

If the stitching threads are in the filling, all of the face warp threads are first raised above them. Then a back warp thread is raised and a face warp thread lowered below a stitching pick to bind the face and back fabrics together. These stitchers are brought to face or back only where the adjacent threads are in a position to conceal them.

Figs. 1472 to 1484 show different weaves of this class. The accompanying cross sections make the construction clearer. The dotted squares indicate risers; the crosses, sinkers.

Fig. 1472 is a double cloth, each weave being a 2 up 2 down twill. After every group of 2 face and

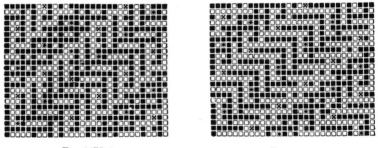

FIG. 1475.   FIG. 1476.

2 back warp threads, a binding thread is inserted. The numbers of the warp threads in the longitudinal section, Fig. 1473, correspond with the numbers in Fig. 1472. The dotted line, not numbered, is the second binding thread, which is the tenth thread in Fig. 1472.

Fig. 1474 shows two 3 up 3 down twill weaves stitched with 1 binding warp thread after every group of 2 face and 2 back threads.

Fig. 1475 shows a 3 up 1 down twill face and 3 up 3 down twill back stitched with 1 binding warp thread after every group of 2 face and 2 back threads.

Fig. 1476 shows a 3 up 3 down twill face and 2 up 2 down twill back stitched with 1 binding warp thread after every group of 2 face and 2 back threads.

Fig. 1478 and the corresponding cross section, Fig. 1477, show two 2 up 2 down twills stitched together with an extra pick following every group of 2 face and 2 back picks. The picks are numbered the same in both draft and section.

Fig. 1479 is a ply weave for a very thick cloth. Four picks lie one above the other. The face and back weaves are 6-leaf satin with back filling. The fifth pick serves as a binding thread, as shown by the cross section, Fig. 1482. The first 5 picks are numbered to correspond with the first 5 picks at Fig. 1479. The

FIG. 1477.

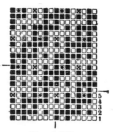

FIG. 1478.

FIG. 1479.   FIG. 1480.   FIG. 1481.

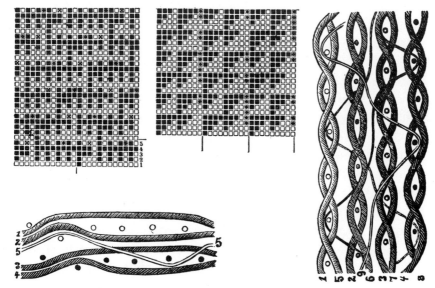

FIG. 1482.

face warp is indicated by the outline circles; the back warp, by the black circles. This cloth, which is from $\frac{1}{5}$ to $\frac{1}{4}$ inch thick and used for piano felt, is also made with six sets of filling; of which the sixth is a stuffing pick lying between the face and back, as at Fig. 1465.

Fig. 1480 is a weave for a 4-ply fabric with extra binding threads in the warp. Each of the four separate textures is woven with a plain weave. The position of the stitching warp is shown in the longitudinal section, Fig. 1481, in which the threads are numbered to correspond with the first 9 warp threads of Fig. 1480.

An excellent weave for woven felt is shown at Fig. 1483. The face weave is a broken 3-leaf filling twill;

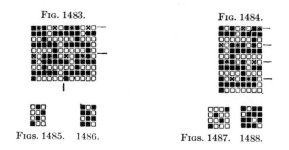

FIG. 1483.

FIG. 1484.

FIGS. 1485.   1486.

FIGS. 1487.   1488.

the back weave, a broken 3-leaf warp twill. This causes the face filling to predominate on the face, and the back filling to predominate on the back, making both sides of the cloth alike.

Every four regular picks are followed by one extra or stitching pick indicated by a straight line at the right. The stitching is effected by lowering a face warp thread below (crossed squares) and raising a back warp thread above (dotted squares) the stitching pick, thus binding both textures to this extra pick.

Another equally good weave for heavy felt is shown at Fig. 1484. Face and back are each woven with a broken 4-leaf twill, the face is 1 up 3 down; the back 3 up 1 down. After 1 face and 1 back pick of the regular weaves, there is a binding pick to which both face and back textures are bound, as in Fig. 1483. The stitchers are indicated by crosses (×), sinkers, and dotted squares, risers, on the binding pick.

Figs. 1485 and 1486 are the face and back weaves for Fig. 1483; Figs. 1487 and 1488, the face and back weaves for Fig. 1484.

WEAVES FOR WOVEN BELTING

Woven belting consists of several separate textures, which are more closely stitched together than the ply fabrics that have been described. In the belting fabrics a separate set of warp threads alternate on face and back, making a through and through fabric. This

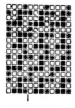

Fɪɢ. 1489.

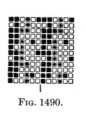

Fɪɢ. 1490.

results in a closer union of the different textures, and makes the whole fabric more solid and compact.

In the double plain weave, Fig. 1489, threads 1 and 4 alternate on face and back; thread 2 being on the back and thread 3 on the face continuously. The first warp thread passes under the first pick to the back, and above the fourth pick to the face, thus forming a part of both face and back textures. The fourth warp thread, on the other hand, passes below the fifth pick to the back, and above the eighth pick to the face, likewise forming a part of both the face and back. The threads are thus arranged as follows: warp, 1 binder 1 back 1 face 1 binder, bringing two binder threads together; filling, 1 back 1 face.

A similar weave is shown at Fig. 1490 and is used for cotton banding. It consists of two 3-leaf twills; 2 up 1 down for the face, 1 up 2 down for the back, making the back and face of the cloth alike. Warp threads 1 and 2 are face; 5 and 6, back threads. Threads 3 and 4 alternate on face and back, taking

290

the place of the third thread of the face twill and also of the back twill. Thread 3, for example, passes below picks 2 and 12 to the back, and above picks 5 and 7 to the face. Thread 4, on the other hand, passes above picks 1 and 11 to the face, and below picks 6 and 8 to the back.

Following are several weaves and lay-outs for belting fabrics:

(a) Double Banding, $4\frac{3}{4}$ inches wide. Weave, Fig. 1491. Warp, 6-ply No. 10 cotton. Filling, 8-ply No. 6 cotton, 410 ends in warp, 2 ends in each heddle, making 210 double ends. Four shafts, straight draft, beginning with shaft 2. Reeded, first dent (at left)

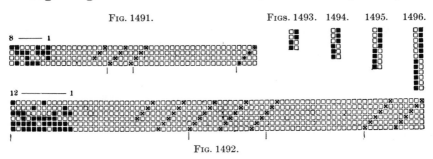

FIG. 1491.   FIGS. 1493. 1494. 1495. 1496.

FIG. 1492.

3 double ends, then 5 and 6 alternate for 36 dents, ending with 4 ends in last dent.

(b) Cotton Banding, $3\frac{9}{10}$ inches wide. Weave, Fig. 1492. Warp, 9-ply No. 16 cotton. Filling, 6-ply No. 10 cotton. 442 ends in warp. Six shafts, straight draft, beginning with shaft 3. Reeded, first dent (at left) 10 ends, then 15 ends in each of the next 28 dents, and 12 ends in last dent.

Certain kinds of double cloth, used for banding, belting, etc., are stitched by a separate set of threads introduced in the warp at intervals, each one passing alternately to the back and face so that when one passes to the face the other passes to the back, thus binding the two textures together.

Figs. 1493, 1494, 1495 and 1496 show four methods of interlacing these threads with the filling. These extra threads must be woven from a separate beam, and dressed considerably longer than the ground warp on account of the greater take-up. Following are several examples of this construction.

(c) 4-Ply Cotton Belting, $5\frac{3}{10}$ inches wide. Weave, Fig. 1497. Ground warp, 10-ply No. 16 cotton. Filling, 10-ply No. 6 cotton. 684 ends in ground warp; 54 ends of binding warp; making a total of 738 ends. 8 ground and 2 stitching shafts. Reeded, first dent (at left) 8 ends, second dent 24 ends, then 26 ends in each of the following 27 dents; last dent, 4 ends.

Fig. 1497.

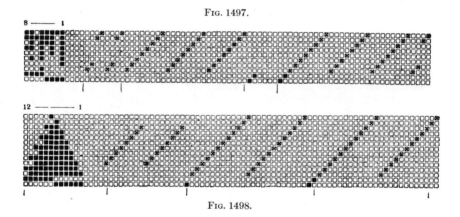

Fig. 1498.

Reed, 28 dents in 5 inches. The take-up of the ground warp is 22 per cent. Twenty-three yards of the binding warp is required for 10 yards of the ground warp.

(d) 6-Ply Hemp Belting, $5\frac{9}{10}$ inches wide. Weave, Fig. 1498. 664 ends 3-ply No. 8 hemp yarn in the ground warp; 53 ends double 3-ply No. 8 hemp yarn in binding warp; making a total of 717 ends. Twelve ground and 2 stitching shafts. Reeded, first dent 16 ground threads and 1 stitching thread, then 24 ground and 2 stitching threads in each of the next 26 dents, last dent 24 ground threads. Reed, 19 dents in 4 inches, $6\frac{3}{10}$ inches high. Take-up of ground warp, 22 per cent. From 25 to 26 yards of the binding warp is required for each 10 yards of the ground warp.

CORDED WEAVES

These are corrugated effects, or raised stripes running in the direction of either warp or filling.

CORDED STRIPES

The warp cords are usually produced by letting one pick float on the back under 4 to 16 ends, then raising it above one or two (seldom more than two) ends,

Fig. 1499.

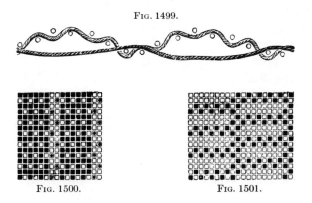

Fig. 1500.   Fig. 1501.

while the next pick interlaces the warp with a plain, twill or other weave.

In ladies' corded dress goods it is customary to let two floating picks alternate with two binding picks, Fig. 1501.

The warp threads under which the floating picks pass are pressed upward and form an arch, as shown in the cross section, Fig. 1499. If a woolen cloth woven in this way is well fulled, the raised stripe is made more prominent, because the floating picks shrink rapidly, while the other picks, being woven closely into the warp, full more slowly.

The weave at Fig. 1500 corresponds to the cross section at Fig. 1499. The raised stripe contains 6 ends; under which the floating picks lie, the latter being stitched plain on 2 warp threads.

Fig. 1501 shows the same weave as used for ladies' dress goods, the risers being indicated by the white squares; the sinkers, by the black squares.

In Fig. 1502 the raised cord is formed with 8 threads woven with a 2 up 2 down basket, while 2 threads form the recess or depression between the cords.

Fig. 1503 shows 10 threads woven with a 2 up 2 down twill, alternating with 2 recess threads. The twill runs alternately to the right and left, as shown.

In Fig. 1504 the warp is arranged as follows: 8

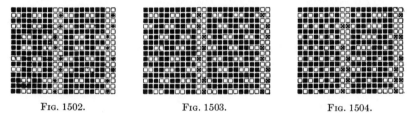

FIG. 1502.   FIG. 1503.   FIG. 1504.

threads woven plain, 2 recess threads, 8 threads woven with an 8-leaf diagonal, 2 recess threads; total, 20 threads.

If the face weave does not allow the weave for the recess threads to be drafted regularly, care must be taken to place the risers in the recess where they will break with the cord weave. A recess riser is inserted next to each cord sinker adjoining the recess, as shown at Fig. 1504.

Corded stripes can be woven without recess threads by making each pick float alternately on the back and interlace with the warp of the raised cord. In one stripe it floats on the back and in the next stripe it is woven on the face. The order is reversed on the next pick. Very pronounced corded patterns can be obtained in this way, as shown by the cross section, Fig. 1505, for which the weave is shown at Fig. 1506.

Each stripe is made with 8 threads woven plain on alternate picks.

Fig. 1507 shows a similar pattern with a 2 up 2 down twill substituted for the plain weave. The twill is reversed at each stripe.

Fig. 1508 shows a corded pattern, each stripe composed of 4 threads, a 2 up 2 down twill alternating with a plain weave.

Stuffing threads are introduced when a very full, round cord is wanted. In Fig. 1509 the cord is made with 6 ends woven plain and 4 stuffing ends. The latter are indicated by dotted squares and marked

FIG. 1505.

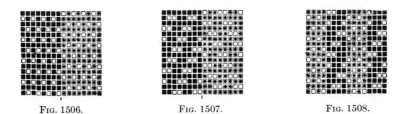

FIG. 1506. FIG. 1507. FIG. 1508.

with a line at the top of the draft. The recess is formed by 2 threads.

The durability of a corded cloth is increased by interlacing the stuffing threads with the picks floating on the back. In Fig. 1510 the stuffing threads and floating picks are woven plain. In other respects the pattern is the same as Fig. 1509.

A similar pattern is shown at Fig. 1511, in which a wide, 4-leaf basket cord alternates with a narrow twill cord, the two being separated by 2 recess threads. The back of the cord is woven plain.

Stitching the stuffing thread to the back or floating picks makes the cord less pronounced and results in two textures, one above the other.

Corded patterns without recess threads, Figs. 1506, 1507 and 1508, can be made with stuffing threads, if desired.

CROSS CORDS

These are usually made by letting every second or third warp thread float on the back for 4, 6, 8 or 10 picks while the other warp threads are woven with a plain weave, twill or similar weave. All the warp threads floating on the back are raised above the next one or two picks, thus producing a pronounced cross

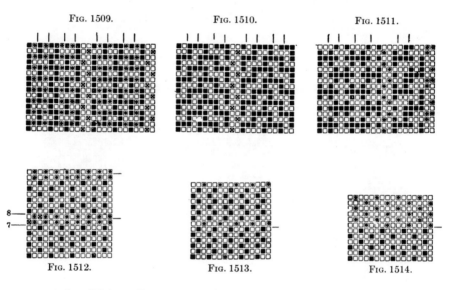

FIG. 1509.   FIG. 1510.   FIG. 1511.

FIG. 1512.   FIG. 1513.   FIG. 1514.

cord. This effect is made still more marked if the back warp threads are woven from a separate beam under greater tension than that on the face threads. In the cross-cord weave, Fig. 1512, threads 2, 4, 6, 8, etc., float on the back for 6 picks, and then rise above 2 recess picks. The other threads, 1, 3, 5, 7, etc., are woven plain for the first 6 picks, then passing under two recess picks, 7 and 8. The face warp can be interlaced with the recess picks, as shown by the crosses on threads 1 and 3, if desired.

In Fig. 1513, two warp threads are woven plain for six picks, then passing under 1 recess pick. Every third warp thread floats back of the six picks forming the cord, and then rises above the recess pick.

The recess is made finer by dispensing with recess threads and letting each warp thread float alternately back of the cord and interlace the filling, as shown at Fig. 1514.

The raised parts of filling cords are made more pronounced by introducing stuffing picks between

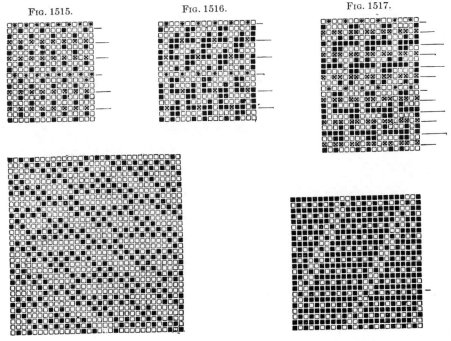

Fig. 1515.　　Fig. 1516.　　Fig. 1517.

Fig. 1518.　　Fig. 1519.

back and face, as shown at Fig. 1515. The risers over the stuffing picks are indicated by crosses; those over the recess picks, by the dotted squares.

The durability of the cloth is increased by interlacing the back warp with the stuffing picks. An example is shown at Fig. 1516, in which the back warp and stuffing picks are woven plain. The face warp is woven with a 2 up 2 down twill for 6 picks, followed by one recess pick.

A very pronounced filling cord can be obtained on thick fabrics by using both stitched and unstitched stuffing picks, as shown at Fig. 1517. The shortest lines at the left of the draft indicate the recess picks; the next longer lines, the unstitched stuffing picks; the longest lines, the stitched stuffing picks. In other respects this weave is the same as Fig. 1516.

DIAGONAL CORDS

In these effects the back or floating picks do not all float under the same face threads and intersect the

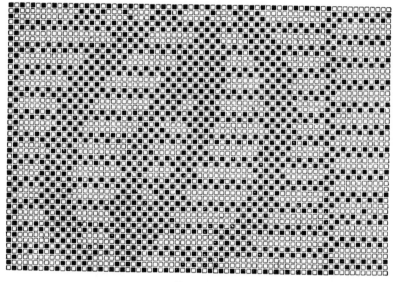

Fig. 1520.

same recess threads, but are arranged in twill order, as shown at Fig. 1519.

The raised effects obtained with corded weaves can be arranged to produce figured patterns, two examples being given at Figs. 1518 and 1520. The white squares are risers; the black squares, sinkers. The oval figure in Fig. 1520 is offset one half and inclined in the opposite direction in every other stripe.

DOUBLE WEAVES STITCHED TO FORM THE PATTERNS (MATELASSÉ)

Closely related to corded weaves, already described, are double weaves known as *matelassé* in which the

Fig. 1521.

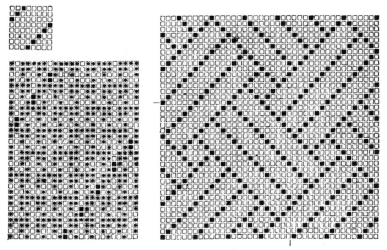

Fig. 1522.   Fig. 1523.

stitching forms the pattern. To this class belong the so-called piqué weaves. As a rule both warp and filling are set 2 face 1 back and stitched by raising the back warp above two adjacent face picks.

The double plain weave constructed in this way and shown at Fig. 1522 is set 2 face 1 back in the warp, 2 face 1 stuffing pick 1 back pick in the filling. The motif for the pattern is shown at Fig. 1521.

It is evident that a depression will be caused where the two textures are stitched, while the surface where the cloth is unstitched will be raised. The effect is heightened when the back or stitching warp is woven

299

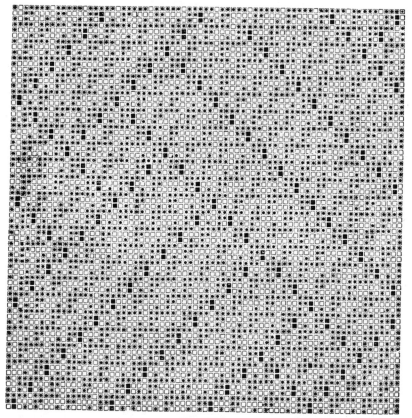

FIG. 1524.

FIG. 1525.

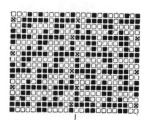

FIG. 1526.

FIG. 1527

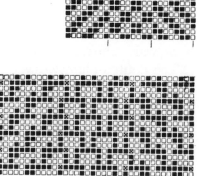

FIG. 1528.

from a separate beam under greater tension than is placed on the face warp. This raised effect is made more pronounced by introducing a stuffing pick of

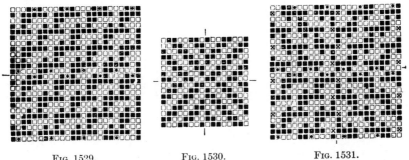

FIG. 1529.   FIG. 1530.   FIG. 1531.

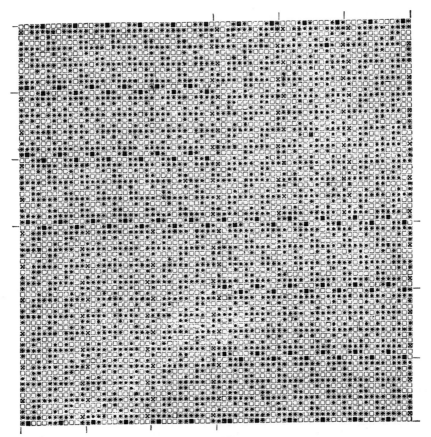

FIG. 1532.

coarser yarn, which, as shown by Fig. 1522, lies between the face and back.

The face is often woven with a twill, basket or similar weave; the back weave is usually plain. Fig. 1524 shows a 2 up 2 down twill on the face with a

FIG. 1533.   FIG. 1534.

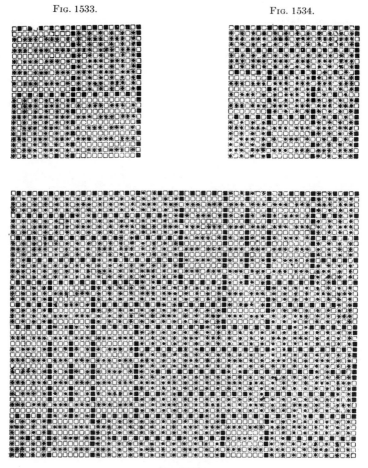

FIG. 1535.

plain back. The motif for the pattern is shown at Fig. 1523. The stitchers in Figs. 1522 and 1524 are indicated by the black squares, risers, on the back warp threads.

Many woolen and worsted cloths of this kind are stitched to produce a striped effect. The last face thread of one stripe and the first face thread of the next stripe are stitched in plain order by passing under every alternate back pick.

This construction is shown at Figs. 1526 and 1528, the back in both cases being plain. The crosses represent the stitchers, which are sinkers. Fig. 1525 is the face weave of Fig. 1526; Fig. 1527 is the face weave of Fig. 1528.

To run this matelassé effect across or filling ways of the cloth, the back warp is interlaced in plain weave order with two adjacent picks, as shown at Fig. 1529, in which the dotted squares represent the stitching risers.

Patterns are frequently made by stitching along both warp and filling lines to produce squares, cubes, braided and other effects. The weave of this kind, shown at Fig. 1531, consists of a twill face and a plain back. The stitching risers are shown by the dotted squares; the stitching sinkers, by the crosses. Fig. 1530 is the face weave.

In Fig. 1532 the warp and filling lines of stitchers form a checkerboard pattern. The face weave pattern is obtained by a combination of a 2 up 2 down twill with a 2 up 2 down basket. The back is a plain weave. The construction of these patterns is sometimes simplified by weaving the stitching threads in the warp or filling in 3 up 3 down order.

Figs. 1533, 1534 and 1535 show weaves frequently used for the so-called relief patterns in silk and worsted fabrics.

MONTAGNAC

The face of the montagnac fabric, used for over-coatings, is covered with loops of soft stock, part of which are intact while the others have been broken in finishing to form tufts of fibers. The fabric is loose and bulky, these qualities being obtained by the sacrifice of durability.

The warp has an open set to allow a large quantity

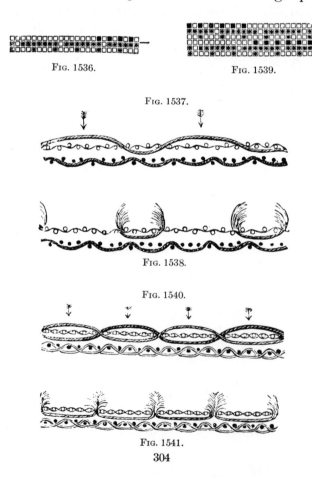

Fig. 1536.

Fig. 1539.

Fig. 1537.

Fig. 1538.

Fig. 1540.

Fig. 1541.

of filling to be driven into the cloth, which is woven narrow, as little, if any, fulling is required. The warp plays a subordinate part in the make-up, being almost completely hidden on both face and back. The ordinary grades of these goods are made with ground and effect filling; the better grades with ground, back and effect filling.

The effect filling, which is to form the tufts or loops on the face, is from 2- to 5-ply yarn and has only enough twist to stand the process of weaving. The effect pick floats over a number of face warp threads

Fig. 1542.   Fig. 1543.

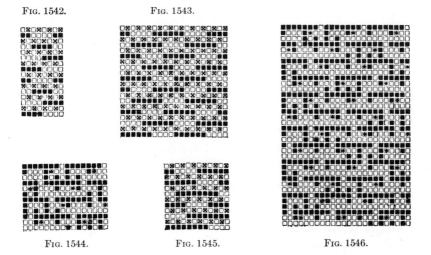

Fig. 1544.   Fig. 1545.   Fig. 1546.

and is then either stitched in plain weave order for a few warp threads or passed under them; the latter method is shown by the cross section at Fig. 1537.

The ground filling serves to bind the fabric together and give it durability, while the back filling increases the thickness of the cloth and enables a fluffy finish to be obtained on the back.

The slack twisted effect filling floating on the face is torn apart in the gigging or napping process at the points indicated by the arrows, Fig. 1537. The subsequent operations of beating and brushing raise the loose tufts and form them into clusters, which produce the well-known montagnac finish.

Fig. 1538 is a cross section of the cloth at Fig. 1537 after the effect filling has been torn apart and the tufts made to rise from the surface of the goods. A portion of the weave for this fabric is shown without stitchers at Fig. 1536, in which the filling is 1 ground 1 back 1 effect pick.

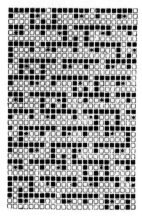

FIG. 1547.

FIG. 1548.

To increase the flaky effect and cover the face better, the effect picks are sometimes woven as shown at Fig. 1540, where each effect pick passes under the warp threads over which the preceding effect pick floated. This brings the tufts closer together, the face of the cloth being entirely covered with the effect filling. This construction is illustrated by Figs. 1540 and 1541, the first showing the woven cloth; the second, the gigged cloth. The weave is shown without stitchers at Fig. 1539. The effect picks are indicated by the short lines at the right of the draft.

The ground filling is usually woven plain. A plain weave, a 2 up 2 down twill, a 3 up 1 down twill or a 4-leaf broken twill is used for the back.

When it is desired to scatter the flakes or tufts irregularly over the face, the effect picks are woven with a 4-leaf broken twill or a 6-leaf satin weave. Striped montagnacs are made by arranging the effect floats in the form illustrated by Figs. 203, 204, 231 and 233. The effect floats are also arranged in straight, broken and herringbone twill order.

Figs. 1542 to 1548 are frequently used for monta-gnacs and correspond to the class of weaves shown at Fig. 1537 and 1538. None of them is constructed like Fig. 1540. The ground weave of each is plain; a broken 4-leaf twill or other suitable weave can, however, be used. In most cases a separate back texture is employed, the back filling interlacing with the back warp. Fig. 1542 is the face weave for Fig. 1543, the effect filling being woven in broken 4-leaf twill order.

In Figs. 1542, 1543, 1545 and 1547, the white

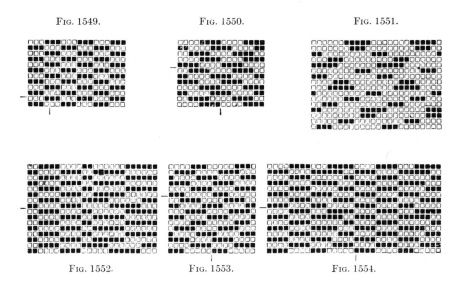

FIG. 1549. FIG. 1550. FIG. 1551.

FIG. 1552. FIG. 1553. FIG. 1554.

squares are warp risers; the marked squares (black and crosses) are warp sinkers.

In Fig. 1544 the back weave is a broken 3 up 1 down twill; the stitching is in the same order. The face weave is shown at Fig. 1542, the effect floats being distributed in broken 4-leaf twill order.

Fig. 1543 is a montagnac face weave, the effect floats being scattered in satin order.

In Fig. 1546 the back weave is a broken 3 up 1 down twill; the stitching is in the same order.

Fig. 1545 is the face weave for Fig. 1546. The effect floats are scattered in satin order.

Fig. 1547 is the face weave for Fig. 1548. The effect floats are scattered irregularly over 12 threads.

At Fig. 1548 the back weave is a broken 3 up 1 down twill. The weave is stitched from back to face in broken 1 up 3 down twill order.

Contrary to the usual custom, the marked squares in Figs. 1542, 1543, 1545 and 1547 indicate sinkers. The white or unmarked squares indicate risers. These four drafts are for the face only.

Figs. 1549 to 1558 show various arrangements of the effect picks only, with the construction illustrated

Fig. 1555.

Fig. 1556.

Fig. 1557.

Fig. 1558.

at Fig. 1540, which, as already explained, is used to cover the face more completely with the tufts or flakes.

This construction is better adapted for stripes, but can be used without difficulty for the production of checkerboard, twill, herringbone and other effects.

Usually an effect pick is followed by 1 ground and 1 back pick. Frequently two effect picks are woven before the ground pick.

In a third variety of montagnacs the ground filling is omitted. Instead, the effect pick is alternately floated on the face and woven plain, as shown at Fig. 1559, which shows the effect picks only. Every two adjacent effect picks form a plain pick and a continuous floating pick.

In drafting a weave of this kind it is advisable first to draft the motif for the design in the form of an ordinary weave, as shown at Fig. 1561. This motif is then transferred to the full-sized draft by leaving 2 unmarked warp threads next to each vertical line of the motif, and by alternating 2 vacant picks with 2 others corresponding to each horizontal line of the motif. Fig. 1560 shows the 8-thread motif at Fig. 1561 thus enlarged.

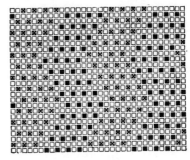

FIG. 1559.

This enlarged sketch, Fig. 1560, is a plan for the drafting of the effect picks. Each of the picks of every pair is made to float over the warp threads on which the other pick is woven plain; thus each pair forms a continuous floating pick and a continuous plain pick. The risers on the plan, Fig. 1560, are not transferred to the draft, Fig. 1562, but serve merely to indicate where the float and plain interlacing are transposed. The draft is completed by stitching the back picks, one form being shown at Fig. 1562.

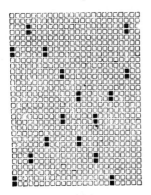

FIG. 1560.

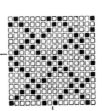

FIG. 1561.

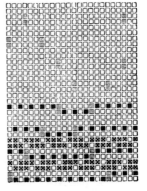

FIG. 1562.

Weaves with a broken 1 up 3 down twill, filling satin or similar weave on the face are also used for montagnacs. These are made either with a separate back texture, as shown at Fig. 1563, which is a broken 4-leaf twill on face and back, set 1 and 1 and stitched

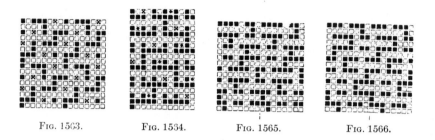

FIG. 1563.   FIG. 1564.   FIG. 1565.   FIG. 1566.

from face to back; or are made with a stuffing pick, Fig. 1564, in which the face is a 6-leaf satin, the back, a 3-leaf pointed twill. The warp is set 1 and 1; filling, 1 face 1 stuffing 1 back pick. Some fabrics are made with a single warp and a face and back filling, as shown at Figs. 1565 and 1566, in which the face is

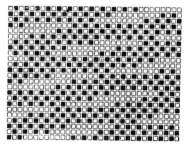

FIG. 1567.

a modified satin; the filling is set 1 face 1 back, two successive back picks interlacing the warp in the same order.

Fig. 1564 is stitched by extra inner picks, as shown at Figs. 1477, 1478, 1479, 1482 and 1483. The stuffing pick passes above a face warp and under a back warp thread, thus fastening both face and back to the stuffing pick.

The crosses in Figs. 1563 and 1564 are sinkers.

A modification of the montagnac fabric is the fulled bouclé cloth in which the filling is alternately floated and stitched plain for a considerable number of threads. The warp is usually cotton; the filling, mohair or similar stock. During the fulling the floating picks are formed into ringlets on the face of the cloth. Two weaves for this construction are shown at Figs. 1567 and 1568.

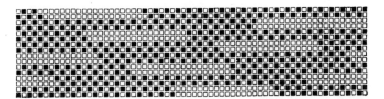

FIG. 1568.

COMBINATION WEAVES

Under this head are included all weave patterns in which two or more weaves are combined. In view of the vast number of weaves it is evident that only the general principles applicable to their combination can be illustrated.

Combination weaves may be divided into six classes: 1. Longitudinal stripes; 2, Cross stripes; 3, Plaids; 4, Checkerboard effects; 5, Broché patterns; 6, Transposed double cloths.

These classifications relate only to weave patterns and do not include color effects on a smooth face with a single weave.

LONGITUDINAL STRIPES

When two or more weaves are combined, care must be taken to have them break with each other at the line of junction. The risers of the first and last threads of each weave stripe should come opposite sinkers of the adjoining thread of the adjacent weave stripe. In this way the distinctive character and limits of each weave are preserved in the finished cloth as in the woven fabric.

If the two adjacent threads belonging to different weaves do not break with each other, the stripes are made irregular in width, owing to the floating of the threads across the dividing line, and the desired stripe effect is lost. In fulled goods an imperfect junction of two weaves may cause a thick or raised place in the cloth.

A break of a twill with a twill, or of a satin with a satin is effected by setting the twill line or ridge of each so that the risers of one come opposite the sinkers of the other, Figs. 1581 and 1582. This is a general rule which it is not always possible to follow exactly.

Fig. 1569 shows a plain weave for the ground with a rib stripe. It is not possible to obtain a perfect break between the two weave stripes, but the close

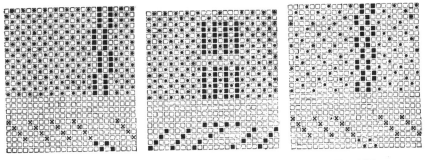

FIG. 1569.   FIG. 1570.   FIG. 1571.

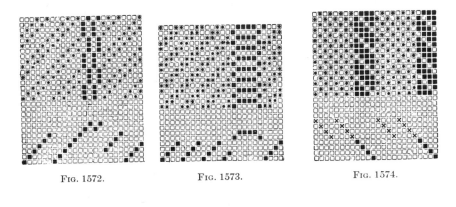

FIG. 1572.   FIG. 1573.   FIG. 1574.

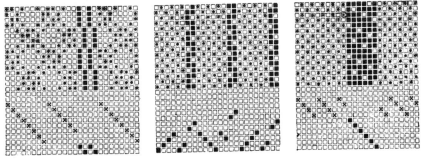

FIG. 1575.   FIG. 1576.   FIG. 1577.

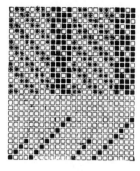

Fig. 1578.

interlacing of the plain weave prevents any serious irregularity.

Fig. 1570 is a plain ground with another form of rib stripe. In these patterns there are twice as many threads per dent in the stripe as in the ground. Thus if the ground is reeded 2 in a dent, the stripe will have 4 in a dent.

Figs. 1569 to 1584 show examples of weaves combined as follows:

Fig. 1569, plain and rib.
Fig. 1570, plain and rib.
Fig. 1571, broken 4-leaf twill and rib.
Fig. 1572, twill and rib.

Fig. 1579.

Fig. 1580.

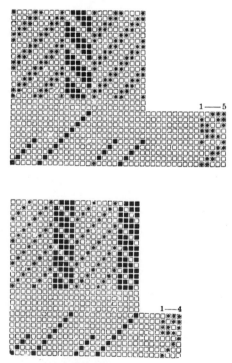

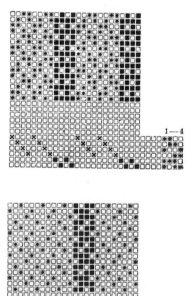

Fig. 1581.

Fig. 1582.

Fig. 1573, twill and filling rib.

Fig. 1574, plain and twill.

Fig. 1575, figured and rib.

Fig. 1576, plain and broken twill.

Fig. 1577, plain and 6-leaf satin.

Fig. 1578, twill and broken twill.

Fig. 1579, twill and twill.

Fig. 1580, broken twill and plain with floating picks.

Fig. 1581, filling twill and warp twill.

Fig. 1582, broken filling twill and broken warp twill.

Fig. 1583, 5-leaf filling satin and 5-leaf warp satin.

Fig. 1584, 6-leaf filling satin and 6-leaf warp satin.

The figures in Figs. 1579 to 1591, Fig. 1593 and Fig. 1594 indicate in each case the first and last picks in the chain draft.

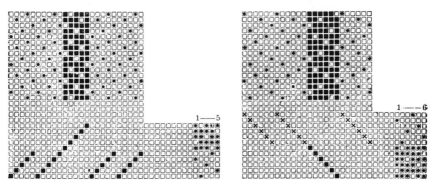

FIG. 1583. FIG. 1584.

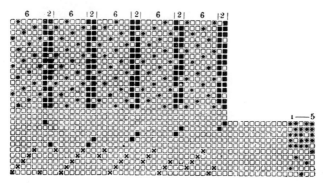

FIG. 1585.

It is more difficult to make satin weaves break with each other when the stripe does not include an even number of weave patterns.

When a warp satin is combined with a filling satin to form stripes of equal width, or of which one is a multiple of the other, the face float (sinkers) at the end of each weave should come opposite to the adjacent back float (risers) of the succeeding weave, as shown at Fig. 1583. If a certain number of warp threads, say 2, for example, are omitted at the end of the filling stripe, the break of the two weaves will be preserved if the same number of threads (2) are omitted at the beginning of the adjacent warp stripe.

If the threads in each stripe comprise an even number of weaves, each stripe is drawn in straight. If,

Fig. 1586.

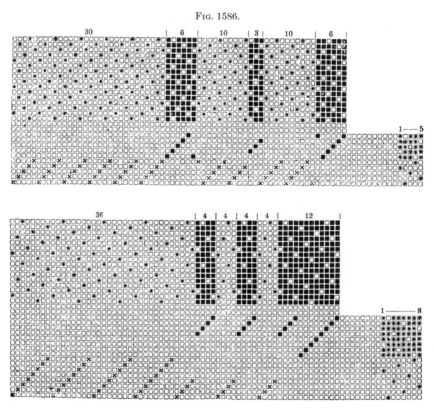

Fig. 1587.

Fig. 1588.

Fig. 1589.

Fig. 1590.

Fig. 1591.

Fig. 1592.

Fig. 1593.

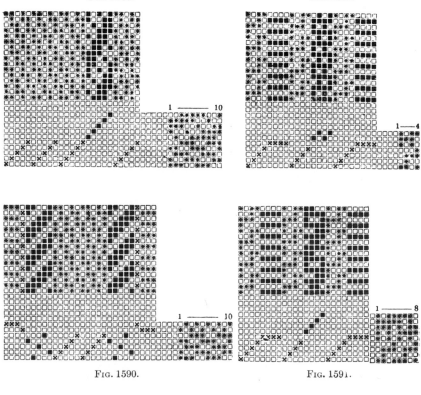

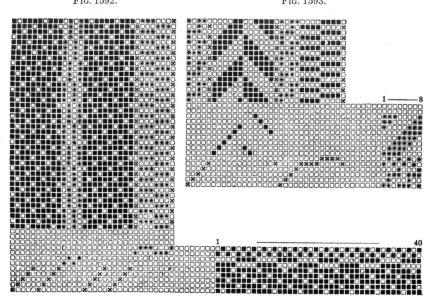

however, a number of threads are lacking to complete the last course of a stripe, an equal number of shafts belonging to the other weave are skipped before beginning the drawing-in of the next stripe. Figs. 1585, 1586, 1587 and 1594 are examples of this construction and show the method of drawing-in as well as the resulting break of the combined weaves.

FIG. 1594.

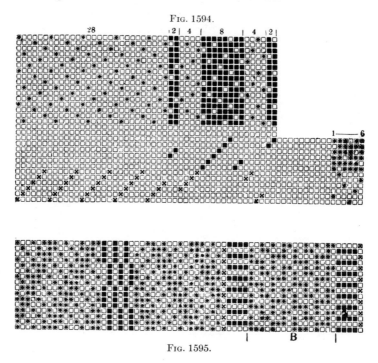

FIG. 1595.

Various stripes obtained by combining weaves are shown at Figs. 1585 to 1607:

Fig. 1585, 5-leaf filling satin and 5-leaf warp satin.
Fig. 1586, 5-leaf filling satin and 5-leaf warp satin.
Fig. 1587, 8-leaf filling satin and 8-leaf warp satin.
Fig. 1588, 5-leaf diagonal and 10-leaf diagonal.
Fig. 1589, double plain, filling rib and plain with stuffing pick.
Fig. 1590, 5-leaf diagonal, filling rib and twill.
Fig. 1591, double plain, filling rib and twill with floating picks.

Fig. 1592, 5-leaf warp satin, warp rib and filling rib.

Fig. 1593, double plain, filling rib and twill.

Fig. 1594, 6-leaf satin and 6-leaf satin.

Fig. 1595, diagonal warp rib and filling rib.

If a twill, satin, crêpe or other weave is to be combined with a filling rib, extra points are inserted to separate the rib from the weave with which it is combined, or an extra thread woven plain is inserted between the rib and adjacent stripe. The latter method is shown at Figs. 1573, 1590 and 1593.

Other combinations of weaves are shown at Figs.

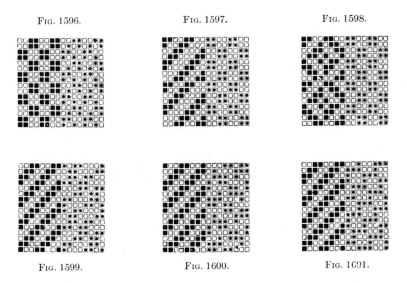

FIG. 1596.   FIG. 1597.   FIG. 1598.

FIG. 1599.   FIG. 1600.   FIG. 1601.

1596 to 1607, only eight threads of each weave being shown in each case.

It is evident that the threads of each weave in a combination weave must be drawn on a separate set of shafts when the weaves are of a distinctly different character. The shafts of the closer weaves, that is, those with more frequent intersections, should be placed in front next to the reed.

The number of picks or bars in the filling chain must embrace a whole number of each of the weave patterns. Thus, if a 3-pick and a 4-pick weave are combined, the filling chain must have at least 12 picks, as this is the least common multiple of 3 and 4. Again, if the separate weaves are 8-pick and 12-pick respectively, the filling chain must have at least 24 bars. In Fig. 1592 the filling pattern must cover at least 40 picks, since this is the smallest number that will include a whole number of each of the two separate weaves, which have 5 and 8 picks respectively.

In selecting weaves for combination, care should be taken to have them of such sizes that an excessively long filling chain may not be necessary. In Fig. 1595

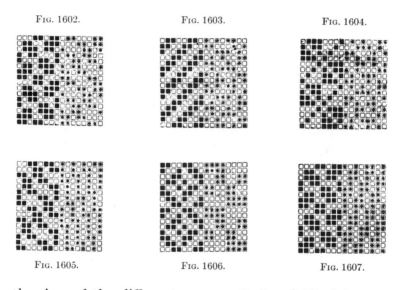

FIG. 1602. FIG. 1603. FIG. 1604.

FIG. 1605. FIG. 1606. FIG. 1607.

the sizes of the different weaves, 2, 8 and 15 picks respectively, necessitate at least 120 bars in the filling chain in order to include a whole number of repeats of each weave. If, however, a 16-pick weave is substituted for the one with 15 picks, the pattern can be woven with 16 bars on the chain and without affecting the appearance of the cloth.

CROSS STRIPES

The rules already given for forming longitudinal stripes with combination weaves apply also to cross stripes. The different weaves must, so far as possible, break against each other at the line of contact. In longitudinal stripes raised effects are produced by warp weaves and depressed effects by filling weaves. The conditions are reversed in cross stripes, the filling weaves giving raised effects and the warp weaves depressed stripes. Especially pronounced and arched

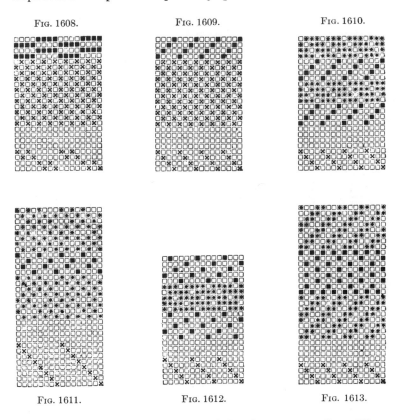

FIG. 1608.　　　　FIG. 1609.　　　　FIG. 1610.

FIG. 1611.　　　　FIG. 1612.　　　　FIG. 1613.

cross stripes are obtained with the cross ribs, Figs. 1512 to 1517. Several examples of cross stripes in combination weaves are shown at Figs. 1608 to 1615.

Fig. 1608 . . . . plain and rib
Fig. 1609 . . . . plain and twill
Fig. 1610 . . . . twill and twill
Fig. 1611 . . . . crêpe and twill
Fig. 1612 . . . . satin and satin

Fig. 1613 . . . twill and plain with floating warp
threads

Fig. 1614 . . . double warp satin and double filling satin

The cross stripe in Fig. 1615 is made by removing
points from the ground weave, which is a 13-shaft satin.

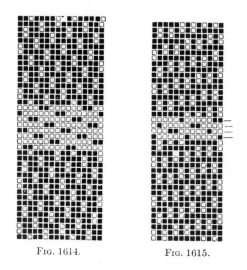

FIG. 1614.   FIG. 1615.

This method of con-
struction is especially
useful when the cross
stripe is made with
but a few picks. If
the weaves used for
cross stripes cover
an unequal number
of warp threads, the
combination weave
must be extended
until the different
weaves end with the
same thread. For
example, a 4-shaft
and a 5-shaft weave in a transverse stripe require
20 threads; a 5- and an 8-shaft weave, 40 threads.

PLAIDS

Plaided weave patterns are combinations of longitudinal and transverse stripes, and call for the appli-
cation of the rules already explained.

No general directions can be laid down for adjusting
the stripes to form plaids. The weave patterns must
be drafted so that as far as possible the weaves will break
with each other along all lines of contact. An unlimited
number of patterns can be made. A few typical examples are given at Figs. 1616 to 1633.

Fig. 1616 consists of a 2 up 2 down twill ground
with a 2 up 2 down basket stripe. To obtain a break
on each side of the stripe the ground must comprise

one thread more than an even number of twills. In this way the first and last threads of the ground are alike and break with the basket stripe.

If the twill ground is made the exact size desired, irrespective of the difficulty in effecting a break, it often becomes necessary to repeat the entire pattern several times before a break between the last and

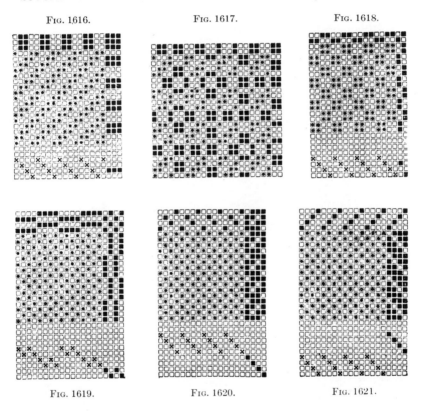

FIG. 1616.   FIG. 1617.   FIG. 1618.

FIG. 1619.   FIG. 1620.   FIG. 1621.

first threads is obtained. A case of this kind is shown at Fig. 1617, in which a 2 up 2 down twill ground is combined with a panama weave, and the pattern repeated four times before the desired break is reached.

Fig. 1618 is a panama ground with a rib plaiding. The plaiding is made with a material or color different from that of the ground.

Fig. 1624 shows a 2 up 2 down twill ground checked with 2 up 2 down basket stripes. The square formed at the intersection of the warp and filling stripes is woven in various ways. Thus in Fig. 1624 it is woven with the 2 up 2 down basket. When the weave of the warp stripe is different from that of the filling, the space at the intersection may be filled by a continuation of the warp stripe as in Fig. 1620; by the continuation of the filling stripe as in Fig. 1621; or with a weave different from either stripe as in Fig. 1619, in which the ground weave is used. The last-named method is usually adopted when the stripe weave tends to make the cloth thicker than the ground.

In combining a panama made of complete basket patterns with a 2 up 2 down twill weave the break is obtained more easily when the twill ground contains one thread less than an even number of twills; for

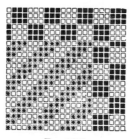

Fig. 1622.

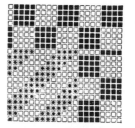

Fig. 1623.

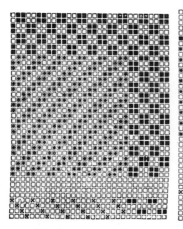

Fig. 1624.

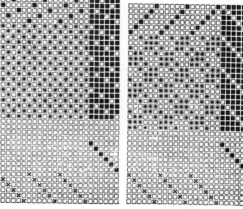

Fig. 1625.

Fig. 1626.

example, 7, 11, 15, 19 or 23 ground threads, the last-named number being shown at Fig. 1624.

With a 6-leaf 3 up 3 down twill combined with a

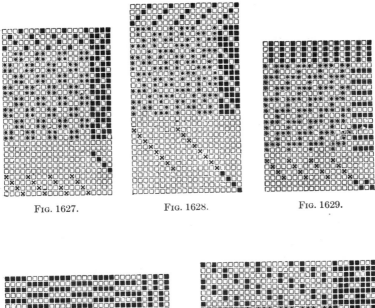

FIG. 1627.   FIG. 1628.   FIG. 1629.

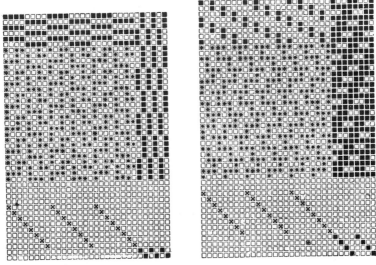

FIG. 1630.   FIG. 1631.

6-leaf panama stripe 2 threads should be omitted from the last twill, the threads in the twill portion numbering 10, 16, 22, 28, etc. With an 8-leaf 4 up 4 down twill, 3 threads should be dropped, the number of twill threads being 13, 21, 29, 37, etc. These rules are illustrated at Figs. 1622 and 1623.

In Fig. 1619 the ground is a plain weave, the checking a 4 up 4 down rib, while the intersection of the rib lines is woven plain.

Fig. 1625 shows a plain weave checked with 6-leaf satin stripe. To facilitate the breaking of the two weaves the 6-leaf satin is drafted 6, 4, 2, 5, 3, 1.

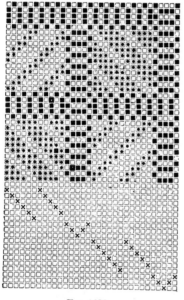

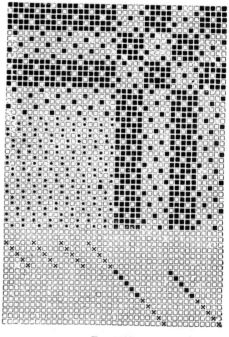

Fig. 1632.

Fig. 1633.

Fig. 1627 shows a panama ground and 4-leaf broken twill checking. Fig. 1628 is made with an 8-leaf crêpe ground and a 4-leaf twill plaiding, while Fig. 1626 is made with a 6-leaf crêpe ground checked with a 6-leaf twill checking.

Figs. 1629 to 1631 are weaves for heavier goods. Fig. 1629 has a double plain ground and rib overcheck. When, as in this weave, the longitudinal stripe is a filling rib, the cross stripe is made with a warp rib.

In Fig. 1630 the ground is a tricot long, the check,

a 4 up 4 down rib. At the intersection of the stripes the warp rib is continued, but changed to 3 up 3 down to match the width of the cross stripe.

In Fig. 1631 the ground is a broken 4-leaf twill with back filling. The overchecking is a 4-leaf twill with warp threads floating under the cross stripe and filling threads floating under the longitudinal stripe.

Fig. 1632 shows a pattern in which a 4 up 2 down twill alternates with a 2 up 4 down twill in the ground, the stripe being formed by a rib weave, which is separated from the ground by plain threads in both warp and filling.

At Fig. 1633 the overchecking is formed by alternate stripes of warp and filling satin weaves, the square at the intersection of these stripes being a checkerboard pattern.

CHECKERBOARD WEAVES

Combination weaves for checkerboard patterns are as interesting as the three groups that have been described. A sharp breaking of the weaves with each other is an essential feature. This is easily effected in twills and satins by running the twills of the warp and filling weaves in opposite directions.

In drafting satin weaves for checkerboard effects the warp stitcher on the first pick of each square should be as far from the first warp thread at the left as the warp stitcher on the last pick is from the last warp thread at the right. In the 5-leaf satin checkerboard effect at Fig. 1635, the first pick of the filling satin is stitched on the third warp thread counting from left to right, while the last pick is stitched on the third warp thread counting from right to left. By this arrangement each square of the same weave begins and ends in such a way that a perfect break is obtained between the warp and filling weaves.

Following is the order to be followed for 5-, 6-, and 8-leaf satin checkerboard effects:

5-leaf satin, 4, 1, 3, 5, 2.
6-leaf satin, 2, 6, 4, 1, 3, 5.
8-leaf satin, 6, 1, 4, 7, 2, 5, 8, 3.

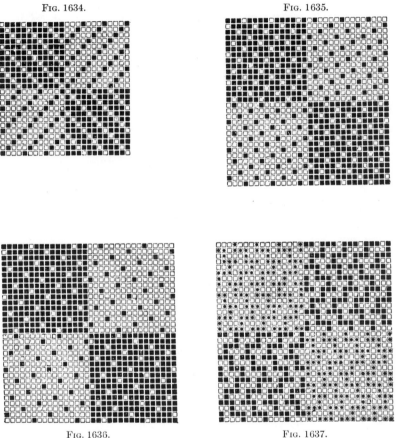

FIG. 1634.

FIG. 1635.

FIG. 1636.

FIG. 1637.

With the 5-leaf satin the warp stitcher (4) on the first pick is as far to the right of the first thread as the warp stitcher (2) on the last pick is to the left of the last thread.

With the 6-leaf satin the warp stitcher (2) on the first pick is as far to the right of the first thread as the warp stitcher (5) on the last pick is to the left of the last thread.

With the 8-leaf satin the warp stitcher (6) on the first pick is as far to the right of the first thread as the warp stitcher (3) on the last pick is to the left of the last thread.

Fig. 1634 shows 12 threads of a 4-leaf filling twill alternating with 12 threads of a 4-leaf warp twill.

Fig. 1635 shows 15 threads of a 5-leaf warp satin alternating with 15 threads of a 5-leaf warp twill.

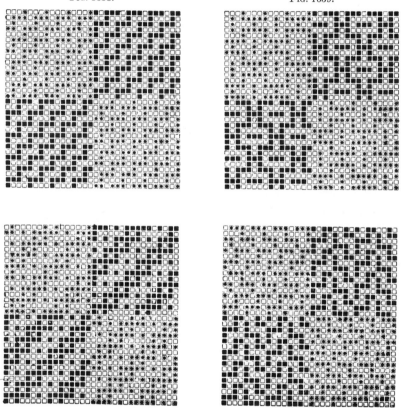

FIG. 1638.

FIG. 1639.

FIG. 1640.

FIG. 1641.

Fig. 1636 shows 16 threads of an 8-leaf warp satin alternating with 16 threads of an 8-leaf filling satin.

For bed blankets the squares are frequently made with a 4-leaf broken twill with back filling, woven 1 light 1 dark. The warp is often made of cotton, the filling of carded woolen, shoddy or silk waste. A weave for this class of goods is shown at Fig. 1637, in which the face and back picks are transposed at the beginning and end of every square of 16 threads.

Checkerboard patterns for heavy wearing apparel are usually made with a regular double weave, 1 back 1 face in both warp and filling, the two textures alternating on back and face to form the pattern. The color pattern is 1 light 1 dark, the two shades alternating on face and back.

Four examples are shown at Figs. 1638, 1639, 1640 and 1641.

Fig. 1638 shows two plain weaves transposed in a double cloth to produce a checkerboard effect.

At Fig. 1639 a plain weave is combined with a 2 up 2 down basket, the two being transposed to form the squares. The drawing-in draft for Fig. 1638 on 8 shafts is 1 to 4 four times and 5 to 8 four times, a total of 32 threads.

For Fig. 1639 on 8 shafts the following drawing-in draft is required: 1, 3, 1, 4, 2, 3, 2, 4 twice; 5, 7, 5, 8, 6, 7, 6, 8, twice.

Fig. 1640 consists of two 2 up 2 down twill weaves alternating on face and back.

A very attractive checkerboard pattern is shown at Fig. 1641 and is made by a combination of a cross tricot with a tricot long.

BROCHÉ FABRICS

Under this head are included cloths in which special threads are introduced in warp and filling to decorate the goods without forming a constituent part of the fabric. These threads are brought to the face only at isolated spots, being otherwise hidden from view. The ground weave and color predominate on the face where the broché effect does not appear.

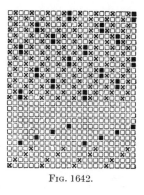

Fig. 1642.

If the ground and broché warp have the same set, they must be woven 1 ground, 1 broché, or 2 ground, 2 broché, the last-named order being usually employed with twill and satin weaves. If the broché warp is set more open, 1 broché thread alternates with 2 or more ground threads.

When the broché figure requires several adjacent threads of different colors, it is sometimes necessary to alternate 1 ground with 2 to 6 broché threads.

The set of the ground fabric remains uniform, and the broché threads are introduced as extra threads. For example, if the ground fabric is set 75 threads per inch and the broché and ground threads are woven 1 broché and 1 ground, the set for the warp where the broché effect is introduced would be 150 threads per inch. If the broché threads are in the warp, they are drawn in the reed as extra threads.

If a special broché attachment is used, the broché filling threads are passed over only the spots at which they are to appear in the cloth. The cloth is woven

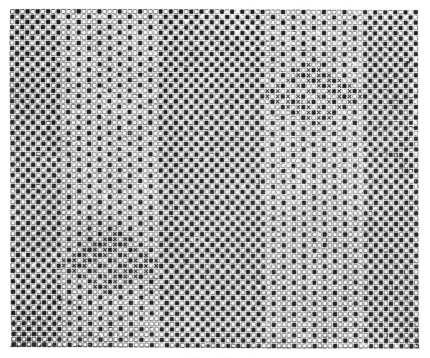

Fig. 1643.

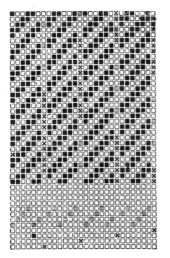

Fig. 1644.

Fig. 1645.

with the face down. The effect threads are usually stitched tighter at the edge of the spot in order to increase the durability of this part of the design.

In many cases the effect threads float loosely on the back side of the cloth when not shown on the face. These loose threads are often cut from the back of very thin fabrics, otherwise the color of the effect yarn would show on the face.

In medium and heavy cloths the broché threads are stitched occasionally during the float on the back from one spot where they show on the face to another.

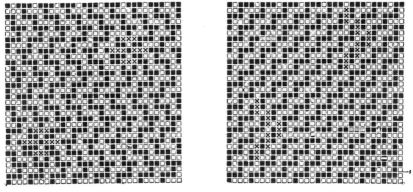

Fig. 1646.   Fig. 1647.

These stitchers are inserted in such a way that the broché thread will not be visible on the face.

In double fabrics the broché thread is preferably concealed by being passed like a stuffing thread, between back and face.

Fig. 1642 shows broché warp threads on a plain ground. The motif for the design is a broken 1 up 3 down twill. As the broché threads float but a short distance, no stitching is necessary.

At Fig. 1643 broché warp threads are woven on a plain ground. Owing to the long float, the effect threads are woven from a separate beam.

The ground weave in Fig. 1644 is a 2 up 2 down twill. The figure threads form short lines which are arranged in the form of a 2 up 2 down broken twill. These broché threads are stitched at intervals when floating on the back, as shown by the shaded squares.

The broché effect in Fig. 1648 is formed by extra threads in both warp and filling. The motif for the

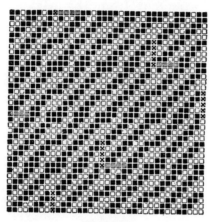

design is a broken 1 up 3 down twill. The ground weave is a 2 up 2 down twill. The shaded squares are sinkers.

When the float of the ground weave covers 2 or 3 threads, the broché float to be effective must cover 3, 4 or even 5 threads. When the broché float comes in a

Fig. 1648.

warp or filling twill, the stitching of an adjacent ground thread is changed so that the broché spot may not be obscured. An example is found at Fig. 1649, in which the ground weave is a 3 up 3 down twill.

A similar modification of the ground weave to make

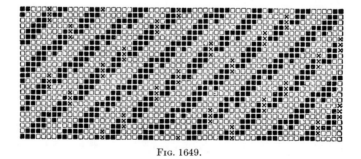

Fig. 1649.

the effect thread show plainly is shown at Fig. 1645, in which the broché threads are in the filling. The black squares indicate sinkers. Extra warp risers are inserted on the face pick adjacent to the broché float, causing the latter to stand out more prominently.

The ground is woven with a 3-leaf broken twill for the
face and a 6-leaf weave for the back filling. The
broché effect is stitched in 3-leaf order and is concealed
by the back filling.

In double cloths the back filling threads sometimes
serve as broché picks. The back picks that form the

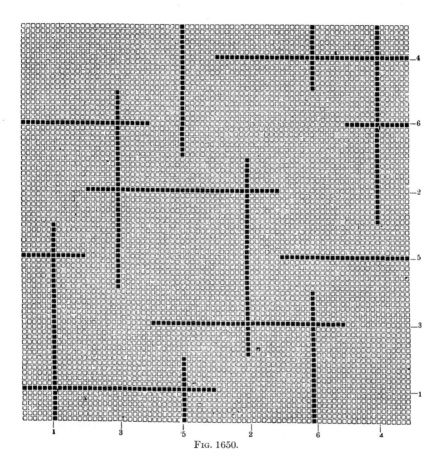

FIG. 1650.

pattern are usually of a different color from that of
the face in order to produce a more marked effect.
An example is shown at Fig. 1646. The crosses indicate sinkers. The ground weave is a broken 1 up 3
down twill with back filling. As the back pick floats
over but three threads, the same as the regular float

of the face pick, it is necessary to modify the adjacent face picks to make the spot distinct.

Fig. 1647 shows a double plain cloth in which both back warp and back filling are utilized to form the broché effect. The plain face threads cannot obscure the broché float of the back threads over two face

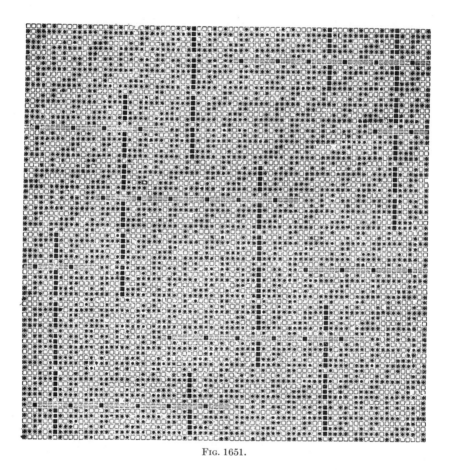

Fig. 1651.

threads and consequently no modification of the face weave is necessary. The shaded squares are sinkers.

If a mixed-up effect is desired, the broché lines are arranged in accordance with a motif having a scattered or promiscuous arrangement of the spots. A 6-leaf satin answers well for this purpose, each riser corresponding to a broché spot, as shown at Fig. 1650, in which both horizontal and upright lines are arranged in 1, 3, 5, 2, 6, 4 order. The ground and broché weaves are then drafted to conform to the motif, as shown in the completed draft, Fig. 1651. This is a double cloth with a 2 up 2 down twill on the face and a plain back. Warp and filling are each set 1 face 1 back 1 face. The broché threads when not on the face lie between the back and face.

DOUBLE TRANSPOSED TEXTURES

In many heavy cloths, such as cotton vestings, table covers and suitings, the pattern is often produced by bringing each of the two textures of the double fabric alternately to the face and back. The face fabric in the groundwork is on the back where the figured effect is formed, while the back fabric of the groundwork becomes the face of the figured effect.

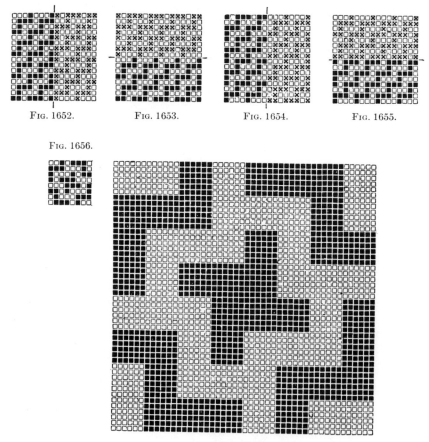

FIG. 1652.　　FIG. 1653.　　FIG. 1654.　　FIG. 1655.

FIG. 1656.

FIG. 1657.

Usually face and back are set alike, 1 face 1 back. The draft is very simple where each weave is plain. The exchange of face and back threads is then made by offsetting the stair effect for one thread, as shown in Figs. 1652 to 1655 and Fig. 1658.

Either 2 face or 2 back threads come together when the back and face textures exchange places. Thus in Fig. 1652, one transposition of face and back takes place at threads 1 and 16, both of which are on the back.

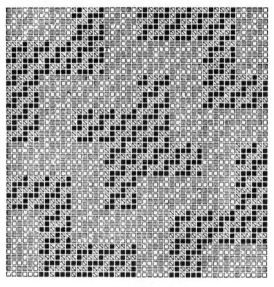

FIG. 1658.

The other transposition occurs at threads 8 and 9, both of which are on the face.

When large designs are to be made in a double plain weave, a motif, as shown at Fig. 1656, is transferred to the full-sized draft, Fig. 1657, from which the weave is then drafted, as shown at Fig. 1658.

If, for example, the complete draft is to consist of 48 threads, and to be developed from an 8-leaf motif, Fig. 1656, each thread of the motif will correspond to six threads of the full-sized pattern, Fig. 1657. The pattern is indicated on the draft by some bright color, usually yellow. The two weaves are then transposed,

as shown in Fig. 1658, in accordance with this enlarged motif.

Each thread in a motif corresponds to at least two
threads (1 face and 1 back) of the completed draft.

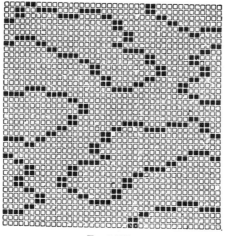

FIG. 1659.

Fig. 1660 shows the
lower half of the
motif at Fig. 1659
enlarged in the pro-
portion of 2 to 1.
This 2 to 1 enlarge-
ment gives the small-
est pattern that can
be obtained by de-
veloping a motif.

If the motif con-
tains many single
risers, it is difficult to
draft the weaves in
the right order for
transposing the textures. In such a case the ground is
filled in with the plain or stair pattern, and when a figure
space is reached, the same weave is counted off, but the
points are not inserted until the figure space is passed.
When the ground is again reached, the points are in-

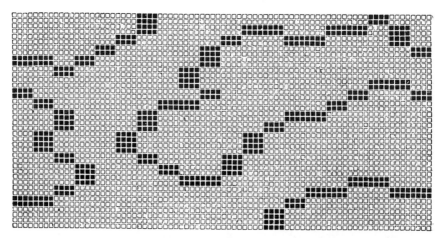

FIG. 1660.

serted in the position they would occupy if the figure
space formed a portion of the ground and points had
been inserted without interruption.   The figure is then
filled in by the same method, offsetting the figure weave
to make the required transposition of face and back.

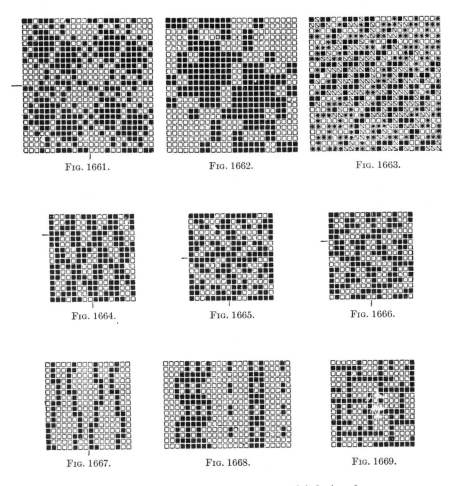

FIG. 1661.   FIG. 1662.   FIG. 1663.

FIG. 1664.   FIG. 1665.   FIG. 1666.

FIG. 1667.   FIG. 1668.   FIG. 1669.

An example is shown at Fig. 1663, which is the weave
draft for the motif at Fig. 1661, enlarged at Fig. 1662.

The motifs for transposed weave patterns may be
of any desired form.   Several motifs for this class of
weave patterns are shown at Figs. 1664 to 1673.

Usually the weave for the face is the same as for the
back, as in Figs. 1652 to 1663, in which the ground

and figure are each drafted with the respective weave as if that weave covered the whole draft. The operations of drafting are as follows:

1. The face warp threads are filled in throughout

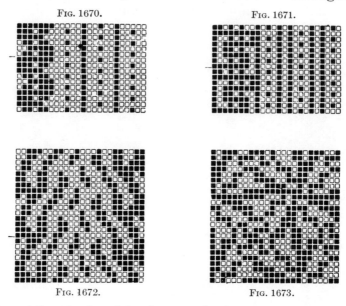

FIG. 1670.

FIG. 1671.

FIG. 1672.

FIG. 1673.

the entire draft with the required weave on the face picks. Risers are then inserted to bring the back warp threads to conform to the figure of the motif. Fig. 1674 is the motif. Fig. 1675 shows a plain weave (dotted squares) on the face warp and face filling, the back warp threads being raised (black squares) to correspond with the figure of the motif.

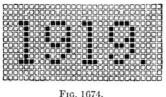

FIG. 1674.

2. The back warp threads are next filled in with the required weave on the back filling, and the face warp threads raised above the back picks to correspond with the blank space on the motif. Fig. 1676 shows a plain weave (crosses) on the back picks, and the face warp threads raised (black squares) above these picks to correspond with the blank squares of the motif, Fig. 1674.

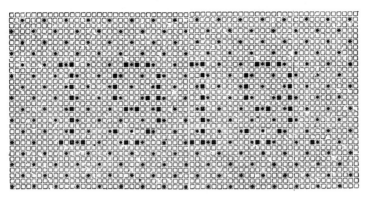

FIG. 1675.

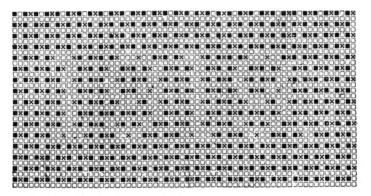

FIG. 1676.

FIG. 1677.

Figs. 1675 and 1676 belong to the same pattern and are shown separately in order to illustrate the method of construction. The completed weave, Fig. 1677, shows that the transposition of the two textures and

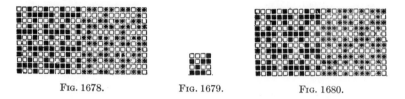

FIG. 1678.   FIG. 1679.   FIG. 1680.

the drafting of the weaves are the same as in Figs. 1652 to 1663.

When the warp and filling are set 2 face 1 back or 2 back 1 face and each texture is brought alternately to back and face without changing the weave, the method shown at Figs. 1678, 1680 and 1681 is adopted.

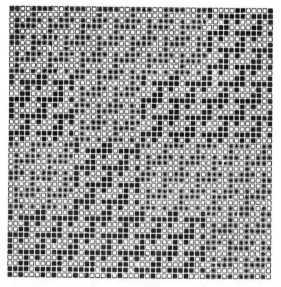

FIG. 1681.

At Fig. 1678 both face and back are woven plain. Fig. 1680 shows a basket and a plain weave. Fig. 1681 is a complete draft in which one texture is plain, the other a 2 up 1 down twill. The motif for Fig. 1681 is shown at Fig. 1679. These fabrics are usually set 1 fine, 1 coarse, 1 fine thread, or 1 worsted, 1 mohair, 1 worsted.

If the cloth is set 1 face 1 back, the weaves are arranged as already illustrated at Figs. 1638, 1639 and 1640.

There are transposed weaves in which each fabric is not woven with the same weave throughout, the weave being changed when the fabric is carried to the

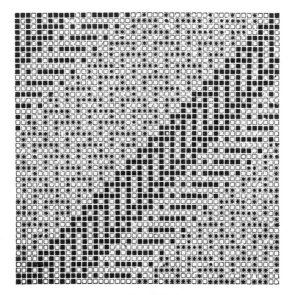

FIG. 1682.

opposite side of the cloth. Each fabric appears alternately on back and face, but shows in each case a different weave. No fixed rule can be laid down for drafting such weaves, the aim being to bring the transposition of the fabrics and the different weaves in the required order. The operation of drafting is facilitated by coloring the draft to indicate each weave.

An example of the last-named construction is seen at Fig. 1682. This is a 48-thread diagonal, of which 24 threads belong to each texture. One texture is woven with a 6 up 6 down twill when on the face and a 2 up 2 down twill when on the back, both twills running to the right, as the face of the cloth is held before the observer. The other texture is woven with a plain weave when on the face and with a 2 up 2 down twill to the left when on the back. On the face a plain weave alternates with a 6 up 6 down twill. On the back a 2 up 2 down twill to the right alternates with a 2 up 2 down twill to the left. Fig. 1683 represents the face and Fig. 1684 the back of this fabric.

Each of the transposed double textures thus far shown consists of two fabrics, each of which preserves its identity while passing alternately to the back and the face of the fabric. Each thread in the cloth be-

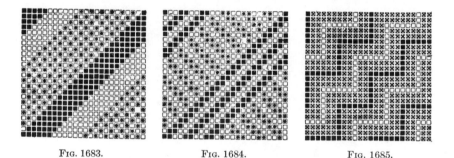

FIG. 1683.   FIG. 1684.   FIG. 1685.

longs to one of the two textures and does not pass to the other. This arrangement permits of but two shades to appear on either side of the cloth.

There are cloths, however, which are partially transposed fabrics, in which a portion of the threads of one texture change places, as it were, with threads of the other texture. By this arrangement it is possible to obtain three shades. For example, we may have one shade made by the crossing of black warp and filling, a second shade by crossing white warp and filling, while a third shade is a gray obtained by carrying the white warp across the black filling or black warp across the white filling. A tiger-skin pattern can be made in this way, the ground being a mixed shade, while the spots are made with light and dark colors.

An illustration of two plain weaves combined and transposed in this way is shown at Fig. 1686. The ground is a mixed shade, while the stair pattern alternates with a light and a dark shade. The motif is seen at Fig. 1685, each line of which corresponds to four threads in the complete draft.

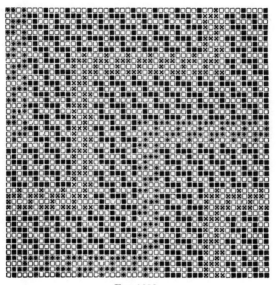

Fig. 1686.

CALCULATING THE NUMBER OF HEDDLES

When the warp is drawn in straight, the same number of heddles are placed on each shaft. For example, if 2400 threads are drawn straight on 8 shafts, each

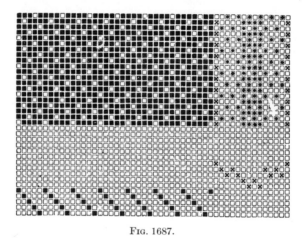

Fig. 1687.

shaft will carry 300 heddles. With many drawing-in drafts, however, it is necessary to vary the number of heddles on the different shafts to correspond with the draft. The number of heddles on each shaft is calculated as follows:

(1) Divide the total number of ends in the warp by the ends in a pattern to find the number of patterns in the full width.

(2) Multiply the number of patterns in the warp by the number of threads drawn on each harness in one pattern.

This method is illustrated by the following calculation based on the drawing-in draft shown at Fig. 1687, in which there are 50 threads in the pattern and 4000 threads in the warp, making 80 patterns in the full width :

Shaft 1, 80 × 2	. . . .	160 heddles
Shaft 2. 80 × 4	. . . .	320 heddles
Shaft 3, 80 × 4	. . . .	320 heddles
Shaft 4, 80 × 2	. . . .	160 heddles
Shaft 5, 80 × 2	. . . .	160 heddles
Shaft 6, 80 × 8	. . . .	640 heddles
Shaft 7, 80 × 7	. . . .	560 heddles
Shaft 8, 80 × 7	. . . .	560 heddles
Shaft 9, 80 × 7	. . . .	560 heddles
Shaft 10, 80 × 7	. . . .	560 heddles
Total, 80 × 50	. . . .	4000 heddles

THE INFLUENCE OF THE WEAVE AND COLOR PATTERN ON THE COLOR EFFECT

Patterns for cloth may be divided into three classes:

1. Color Patterns. A smooth, uniform weave with the pattern produced by an arrangement of threads of contrasting colors in either warp or filling, or both.

2. Weave Patterns. Warp and filling of the same color, the pattern being produced entirely by the weave.

3. Weave and Color Patterns. These are produced by combining weave and color patterns in the same cloth.

Varied and interesting effects are obtained by combinations of weaves and color patterns. Such combinations often change the appearance of the cloth completely so that the resulting pattern does not resemble in the slightest degree either the weave pattern or the color pattern which have been combined.

In sketching color effects the weave is drafted in the usual way. Then all warp risers on the dark threads are colored black. If, for example, the warp is dressed 1 dark 1 light, the risers on the first or black warp thread are colored black. The risers on the second or light warp thread are either left uncolored or colored a shade other than black, say red. The filling colors are next indicated by painting black the blank squares (sinkers) on the black picks. The blank squares on the light-colored picks are painted red.

The black color now indicates the black in both warp and filling, while the red indicates the light shade.

The effect depends upon the position and order of the differently colored threads. Frequently it is possible to obtain an entirely different pattern simply by changing the position of the filling colors so that the dark pick will come in the shed previously occupied by the light color. This enables many different patterns to be produced by simply changing the position of the color in the weave pattern.

As color effects are in extensive demand and designers are constantly called upon to supply new designs and combinations, it has been considered advisable to give a large number of examples, Figs. 1688 to 1874. In all of these drafts the warp colors are indicated at the top, the filling colors at the side.

Figs. 1688 to 1705 show color effects on a plain weave.

Figs. 1706 to 1741 are color effects on twill weaves.

Figs. 1742 to 1749 are color effects on basket weaves.

Figs. 1750 to 1873 show color effects on crêpe and similar weaves.

In many of these drafts the weave is shown at the bottom; the warp pattern at the top; the filling pattern at the left; and the color effect in the center. Following is a list of corresponding weaves and color effects which are shown separately:

COLOR EFFECT	WEAVE
Fig. 1692	Fig. 1693
Fig. 1712	Fig. 1711
Fig. 1715	Fig. 1714
Fig. 1735	Fig. 1734
Fig. 1751	Fig. 1750
Fig. 1753	Fig. 1752
Fig. 1754	Fig. 1755
Fig. 1756	Fig. 1757

Fig. 1688.

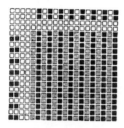

Fig. 1689.

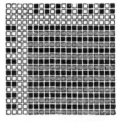

Fig. 1690.

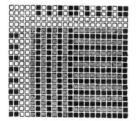

Fig. 1691.

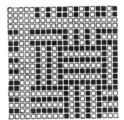

COLOR EFFECTS ON A PLAIN WEAVE

The plain weave is often used for the production of colored stripes. Fine hair lines running warpways

FIG. 1692.

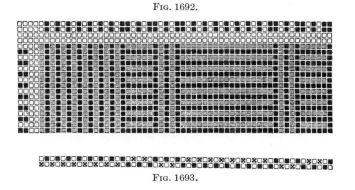

FIG. 1693.

are obtained by warping and weaving 1 light 1 dark, bringing the light pick in the shed where the light warp is lowered and the dark warp is raised, Fig. 1688.

The lines are made to run filling ways by weaving the same warp pattern so that the light pick is inserted when the light warp is raised and the dark warp lowered, Fig. 1689.

To alternate long with cross stripes, it is merely necessary to introduce two threads of one color and then continue the pattern 1 and 1 as far as desired, when the cross stripe can be changed to a longitudinal stripe by again inserting two threads of one color. For example, the color effects shown at Figs. 1690 and 1692 are produced on a plain weave by the following arrangement of colors:

WARP PATTERN FOR FIG. 1690

$$3 \times \begin{cases} 1 \text{ light} \\ \\ 1 \text{ dark} \\ 1 \text{ light} \end{cases}$$

$$\frac{2 \text{ dark}}{9}$$

WARP PATTERN FOR FIG. 1692

$$7 \times \begin{cases} 1 \text{ light} \\ \\ 1 \text{ dark} \\ 1 \text{ light} \\ 2 \text{ dark} \end{cases}$$

$$2 \times \begin{cases} 1 \text{ light} \\ 1 \text{ dark} \\ 1 \text{ light} \\ 2 \text{ dark} \end{cases}$$

$$\frac{}{27}$$

Both Fig. 1690 and Fig. 1692 are woven 1 dark pick 1 light pick.

By placing two warp threads of one color side by side it is evident that in the succeeding 1 and 1 pattern the light color will be brought on the shaft that carried the dark threads before the change, the dark color coming on the shaft that previously carried the light threads.

This is illustrated by Fig. 1693, which shows two picks of a plain weave for the color pattern at Fig. 1692. The crosses represent risers on the light-colored warp threads. The black squares are risers on the dark-colored warp threads. The first pick is a dark thread which comes to the face at the white squares. The second pick is a light-colored thread which comes

to the face at the white squares. It is evident that
for sixteen warp threads the warp risers and filling
floats of the same color will come in a perpendicular
line to produce a hair line effect. Then the two dark
warp threads cause a change by which the warp risers
and filling floats of the same color come in a horizontal
line to produce a hair line effect, which continues until
another group of two warp threads of the same color

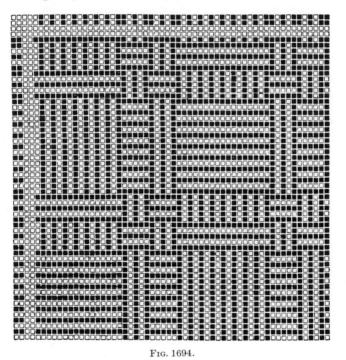

Fig. 1694.

changes the hair line from horizontal back to perpendicular. There are six changes of this kind in the pattern, producing three stripes of perpendicular lines and
three stripes of horizontal lines, as shown at Fig. 1692.

The reversal of the lines lengthways as well as
crossways can be effected by introducing two picks of
one color and then continuing the 1 and 1 pattern.
This method is illustrated at Figs. 1691 and 1694,
for which the warp and filling colors are arranged as
follows:

Fig. 1695.

Fig. 1696.

Fig. 1697.

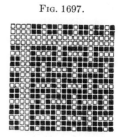

Fig. 1698.

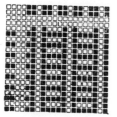

Fig. 1699.

Fig. 1700.

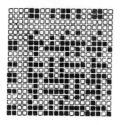

Fig. 1701.

Fig. 1702.

Fig. 1703.

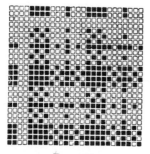

Fig. 1704.

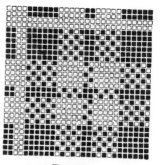

WARP AND FILLING PAT-
TERN FOR FIG. 1691

$2 \times \begin{cases} 1 \text{ light} \\ \\ 1 \text{ dark} \end{cases}$
$ 1 \text{ light}$
$ \dfrac{2 \text{ dark}}{7}$

WARP AND FILLING PAT-
TERN FOR FIG. 1694

$7 \times \begin{cases} 1 \text{ light} \\ \\ 1 \text{ dark} \end{cases}$
$ 1 \text{ light}$
$ 2 \text{ dark}$

$2 \times \begin{cases} 1 \text{ light} \\ 1 \text{ dark} \\ \\ 1 \text{ light} \\ \dfrac{2 \text{ dark}}{27} \end{cases}$

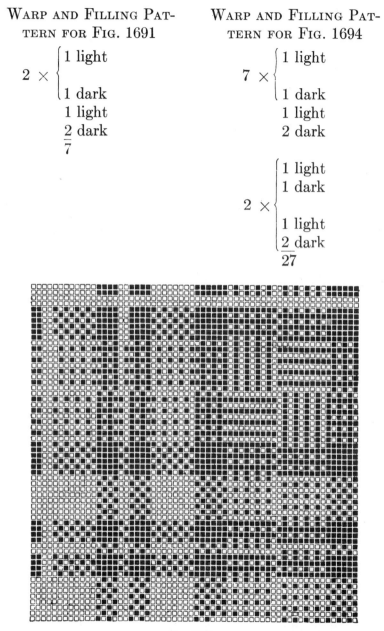

FIG. 1705.

Every pattern in which the lines are run in both directions, lengthways and crossways, must contain an odd number of threads, as in the examples given.

Other effects obtained with a plain weave are shown at Figs. 1695 to 1705.

COLOR EFFECTS ON TWILL WEAVES

The 3-leaf warp twill is used for stripes in which a thread of a contrasting color follows two threads of the ground color. The filling pattern is the same, the

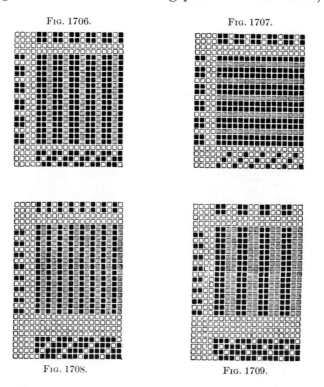

Fig. 1706.   Fig. 1707.

Fig. 1708.   Fig. 1709.

single pick going in when the single warp thread of the same color is down, Fig. 1706.

Cross stripes of this kind are made on a 3-leaf filling twill, the light-colored pick being inserted when the light-colored warp thread is raised, Fig. 1707.

In all 2 and 1 stripe patterns the single striping threads should come in the center of the pattern, which begins 1 dark 1 light 1 dark, the weave and pattern being adjusted accordingly, as shown at Fig. 1710, on which the weave is shown at the bottom. Fig.

1711 is the weave for the color effect shown at Fig. 1712.

In drafting large patterns the motif sketched on a smaller scale is first enlarged on the draft to the full size, a certain number of threads, depending on the enlargement desired, being made to correspond to each line of the motif.

Fine stripes or hair lines are often made on a 3 up 1 down twill by alternating 1 light thread with 1 dark thread in both warp and filling, as shown at Fig. 1708. The light pick is inserted when the light thread is down.

For a 2 and 2 stripe a broken 4-leaf twill is used, the warp dressed 2 and 2, the filling 1 and 1, Fig. 1709.

The 2 up 2 down twill is used for most of the color effects with twills. A stair effect, Fig. 1713, is produced by a 1 light 1 dark pattern in both warp and filling. Figured effects can be obtained with this stair effect by reversing the twill in either warp or

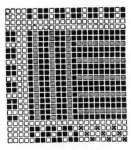

Fig. 1710.

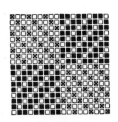

Fig. 1711.

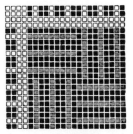

Fig. 1712.

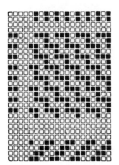

Fig. 1713.

Fig. 1714.

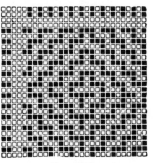

Fig. 1715.

filling or in both directions, as shown at Fig. 1715, the weave draft being shown at Fig. 1714.

The color effect produced by a combination of a 2 up 2 down twill and a 3 up 1 down twill, with a 1 light 1 dark pattern in both warp and filling, is shown at Fig. 1716.

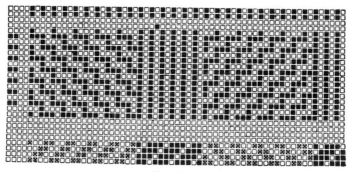

FIG. 1716.

FIG. 1719.

FIG. 1720.

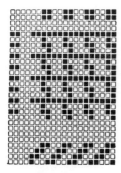

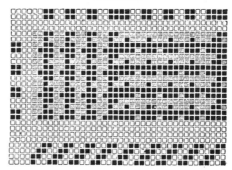

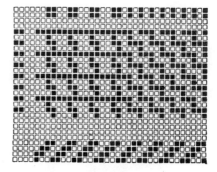

FIG. 1717.

FIG. 1718.

Frequently a 2 and 2 warp pattern is combined with a 1 and 1 filling pattern on a 2 up 2 down twill, producing the effect shown at Fig. 1717.

Pleasing effects are obtained by alternating a 1 and 1 group with a 2 and 2 group of threads in the warp to produce stripes, or in both warp and filling to produce plaid effects. An example of the former is shown at Fig. 1718.

Longitudinal stripes are obtained with a 2 and 2 pattern in both warp and filling on a 2 up 2 down twill by laying one of the light picks in the shed when both light warp threads are down, Fig. 1719. Cross stripes are produced by the opposite order, in which one of the light picks is laid in the shed when the two dark threads are down. These two effects can be obtained in the same pattern by inserting 4 threads of one color where the change from one effect to the other is desired, as shown at Fig. 1720.

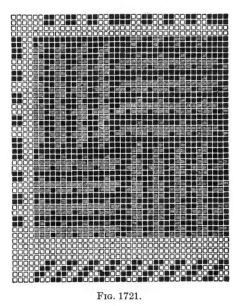

Fig. 1721.

Checked patterns can be produced by introducing 4 threads of one color at intervals in both warp and filling, as shown at Fig. 1721. The pattern which is marked at both top and sides is complete in 18 threads, while the color effect covers 36 threads.

In this class of patterns the 2 and 2 group can be made of any desired size. It is not necessary that 4 threads should be of the same color; the pattern may be 1 light 1 dark 1 light 1 dark, or 2 light 1 fancy 1 light.

An interesting effect is produced by introducing 3 threads of one color after a group in which the color pattern is 2 light 2 dark, as shown at Fig. 1722.   Here the pattern in warp and filling is as follows:

$$2 \times \begin{cases} 2 \text{ dark} \\ \\ 2 \text{ light} \end{cases}$$
$$\begin{array}{l} 2 \text{ dark} \\ \underline{3 \text{ light}} \\ 13 \end{array}$$

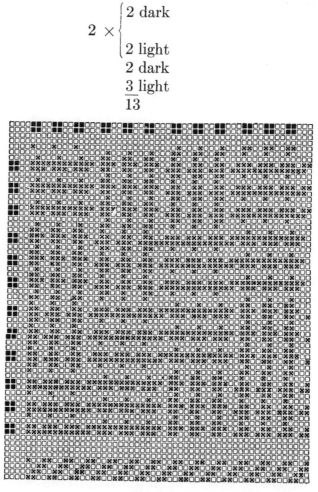

FIG. 1722.

Nearly the same effect is obtained by a 3 and 3 pattern in the warp and a 2 and 2 pattern in the filling on the weave shown at Fig. 1188.

Figs. 1723 to 1733 show various color effects produced on a 2 up 2 down twill with different color patterns.

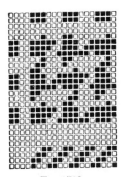

Fig. 1723.

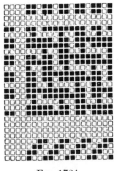

Fig. 1724.

Fig. 1725.

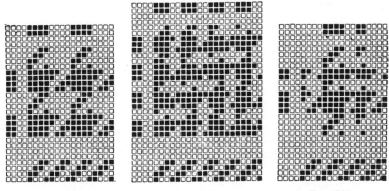

Fig. 1726.

Fig. 1727.

Fig. 1728.

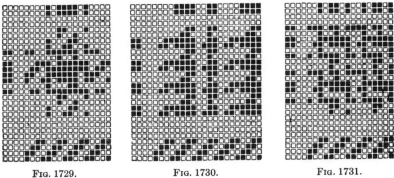

Fig. 1729.

Fig. 1730.

Fig. 1731.

If line effects are to be arranged to correspond with a given motif, the weave must be broken at the required points and arranged as shown at Fig. 1734. The color pattern in both warp and filling should begin 1 light 2 dark 1 light. The effect is shown at Fig. 1735.

The 3 up 3 down twill can also be used for color effects of this character. A difference of 1 thread between the color pattern and the weave pattern causes a gradual slant of the twill effect, as shown at Fig. 1736, in which there are 6 threads in the 3 up 3 down twill and 7 threads in the color pattern, the latter being 1 fancy 3 dark 3 light.

A peculiar effect is obtained by breaking and reversing the twill at regular intervals in warp and filling in

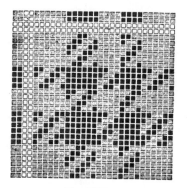

Fig. 1732.

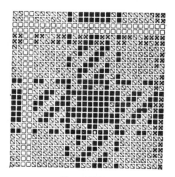

Fig. 1733.

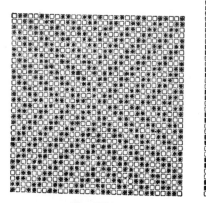

Fig. 1734.

Fig. 1735.

connection with a color pattern having one thread more or less than the weave pattern. An example is shown at Fig. 1737 in which a 3 up 3 down twill is reversed at the end of each 30 threads. The pattern in warp and filling is 2 dark 3 light. A part of the weave is shown at the bottom and side, the color effect being shown in the center.

The effect becomes still more interesting and complex when the twill squares do not include an even number of the color patterns; for example, a reversal of the twill at intervals of 36 threads with a 5-thread pattern, 2 dark 3 light, in both warp and filling.

Squares are produced by breaking the twill in both warp and filling

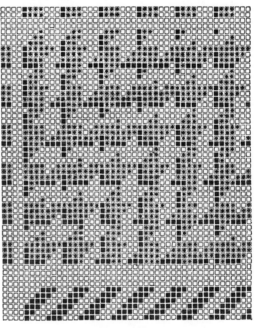

Fig. 1736.

and making the thread on each side of the break a different color from the body or ground. Fig. 1738 shows a 3 up 3 down twill reversed and broken every 4 threads; the color pattern is 1 dark 2 light 1 dark, a dark thread coming on each side of the break. Fig. 444 is often used for suiting patterns, the colors being arranged 1 dark twist 2 light twist 1 dark twist.

Similar effects can be obtained with the 4 up 4 down twill as with the 2 up 2 down or the 3 up 3 down twill, a coarser appearance resulting from the first-named

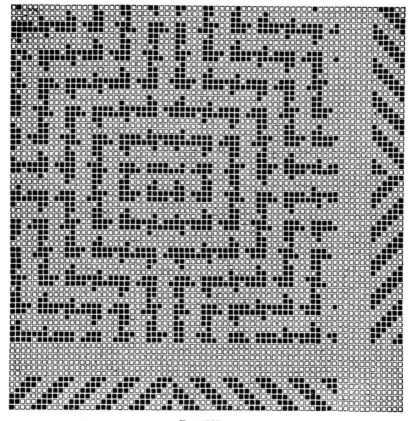

Fig. 1737.

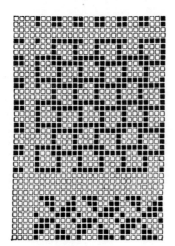

Fig. 1738.

arrangement. Fig. 1739 shows a stripe effect produced by a 4 light 4 dark pattern on a 4 up 4 down twill. Compare this with the stripe on a 2 up 2 down twill, Fig. 1719.

The stair patterns shown at Figs. 1740 and 1741 are obtained with a 1 and 1 color pattern on 8 and 9 shaft twills respectively. The stair effect runs in the opposite direction to that of the twill.

COLOR EFFECTS WITH THE BASKET WEAVE

All the color effects with a plain weave, Figs. 1688 to 1705, can be obtained with a basket or panama weave by substituting for each single thread as many threads of the same color as there are threads working together in the weave.

A variety of other color effects can be obtained by so arranging the color pattern that each color is brought into both squares of the basket. Several examples are shown at Figs. 1742 to 1749.

The basket weave gives many attractive color effects when the weave is so changed that the dark threads work together in certain places, while in other places they are divided, a part being raised when others are

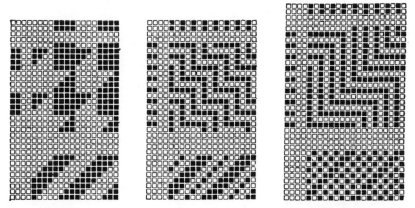

FIG. 1739.　　　　FIG. 1740.　　　　FIG. 1741.

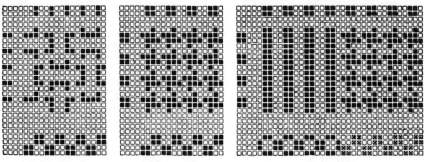

FIG. 1742.　　　　FIG. 1743.　　　　FIG. 1744.

lowered. Two patterns of this kind are shown at Figs. 1744 and 1745. Larger patterns can be obtained from a motif and with the corresponding arrangement of the weave.

Figs. 1746 and 1747 show the method of arranging the colors and weave to produce a combination of longitudinal and horizontal stripes.

Still another class of color effects with a 2 up 2 down basket is illustrated at Fig. 1748. The weave is rearranged in three different ways, producing longitudinal stripes, cross stripes and a mixed effect. The warp and filling pattern for Figs. 1743 to 1748 should be 1 light 2 dark 1 light.

Another kind of color effect on a basket weave is

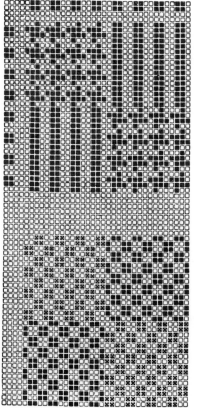

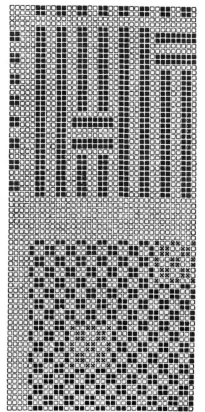

Fig. 1745.

Fig. 1746.

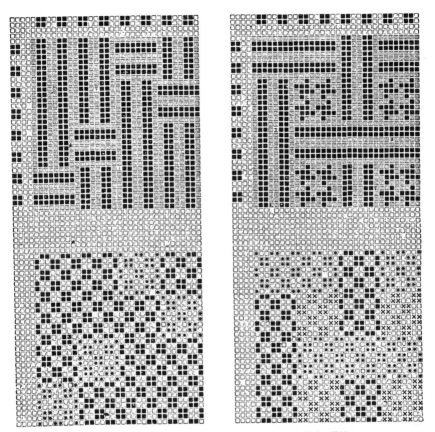

FIG. 1747.   FIG. 1748.

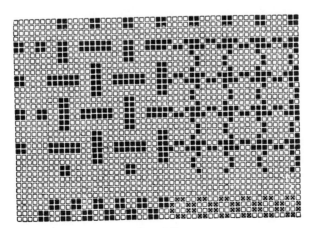

FIG. 1749.

Fig. 1750.

Fig. 1752.

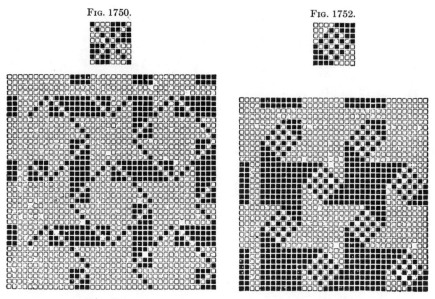

Fig. 1751.

Fig. 1753.

Fig. 1755.

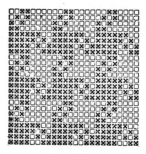

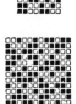

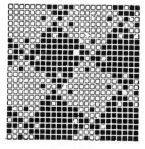

Fig. 1754.

Fig. 1757.

Fig. 1756.

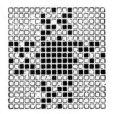

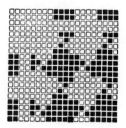

Fig. 1758.

Fig. 1759.

Fig. 1760.

shown at Fig. 1749, in which the warp and filling pattern is 4 light 2 dark, the weave being changed at intervals alternately to unite and separate the two dark threads in the shed.

COLOR EFFECTS ON CRÊPE AND SIMILAR WEAVES

Crêpe and fancy weaves offer a wide field for color effects. The most varied forms can be produced with

Fig. 1762.

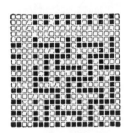

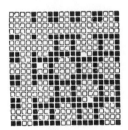

Fig. 1761.

Fig. 1764.

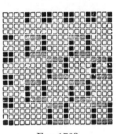

Fig. 1763.

Fig. 1766.

Fig. 1765.

Fig. 1768.

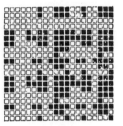

Fig. 1767.

Fig. 1770.

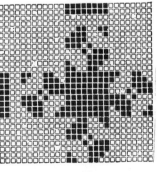

Fig. 1769.   Fig. 1772.   Fig. 1771.

these weaves by a suitable arrangement of the different colors. Examples are shown at Figs. 1750 to 1873. Fig. 1754 shows a square effect obtained with a 4

FIG. 1774.

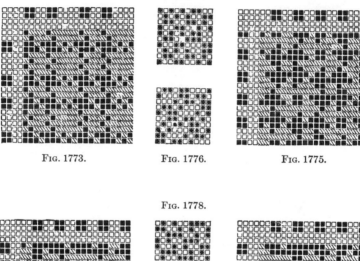

FIG. 1773.   FIG. 1776.   FIG. 1775.

FIG. 1778.

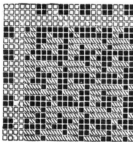

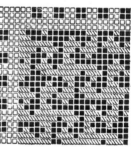

FIG. 1777.   FIG. 1780.   FIG. 1779.

FIG. 1782.

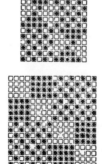

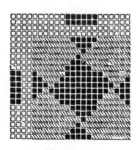

FIG. 1781.   FIG. 1784.   FIG. 1783.

dark 4 light pattern in warp and filling. The weave is shown at Fig. 1755.

The design shown at Fig. 1756 is made on the weave at Fig. 1757 with 6 light 6 dark in the warp, and 6 dark 6 light in the filling. If the pattern is begun in the same way in both warp and filling, 6 light 6 dark, the color effect shown at Fig. 1758 will be produced.

The patterns shown at Figs. 1787, 1789 and 1793 appear as if the threads had been woven in a diagonal direction. These weaves can also be used to advantage with 2 and 1, 6 and 6, 8 and 4 and similar patterns in the warp and filling.

The diagonal effect at Fig. 1795 results from a 3 light 3 dark pattern in warp and filling with the weave shown at Fig. 1796. Very attractive designs can be produced

Fig. 1786.

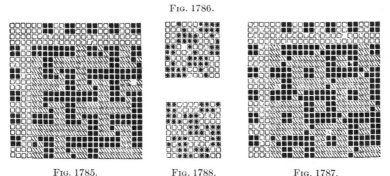

Fig. 1785.   Fig. 1788.   Fig. 1787.

Fig. 1790.

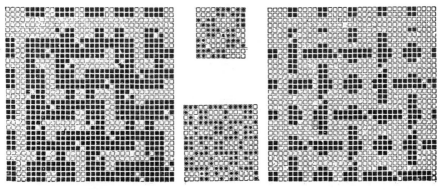

Fig. 1789.   Fig. 1792.   Fig. 1791.

by a regular transposition of this weave. Thus the color effect at Fig. 1798 results from a 3 light 3 dark pattern and the transposition of the weave, Fig. 1796,

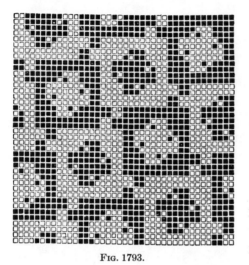

in plain weave order, as shown at Fig. 1797.

Fig. 1799 shows the color effect resulting from a transposition of the same weave, Fig. 1796, according to the motif shown at Fig. 936.

Promiscuous effects are obtained by the use of single and isolated threads of one color in the pat-

FIG. 1793.

tern. The color and weave patterns must not begin and end together, but must vary in size so as to bring the colors successively on all the shafts and picks of the weave draft.

FIG. 1794.

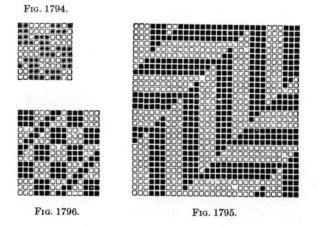

FIG. 1796.   FIG. 1795.

Two color effects of this kind are shown at Figs. 1800 and 1805; each has a 2 light 1 dark pattern in warp and filling. The former is an 8-shaft crêpe weave, Fig. 1800, the latter a 16-shaft crêpe weave, Fig. 1806.

A very attractive line of patterns can be made by

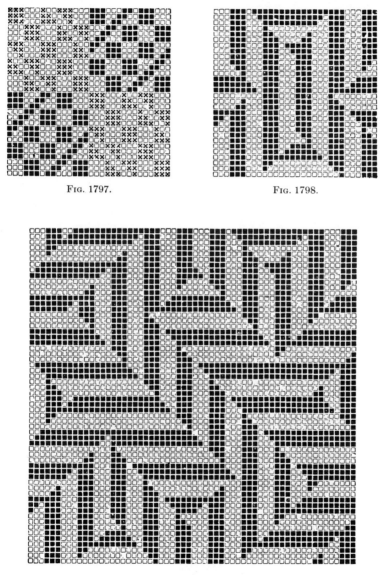

Fig. 1797.   Fig. 1798.

Fig. 1799.

combining a 2 up 2 down basket, Fig. 1801, with the weave shown at Fig. 1802. Fig. 1804 is the color effect

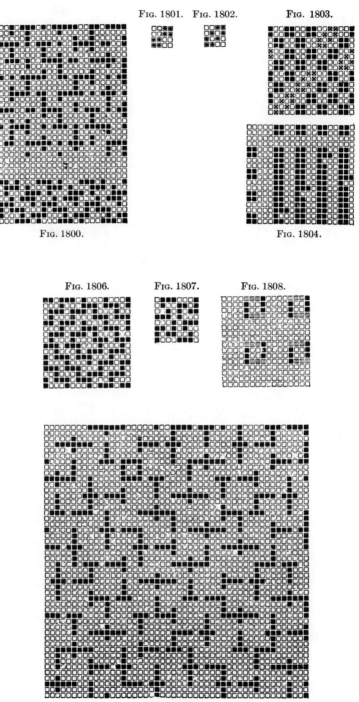

Fig. 1801. Fig. 1802.

Fig. 1803.

Fig. 1800.

Fig. 1804.

Fig. 1806. Fig. 1807. Fig. 1808.

Fig. 1805.

resulting from a combination of these two weaves in broken 4-leaf twill order as shown at Fig. 1803.

In Figs. 1809 and 1810 the dark spots in the light

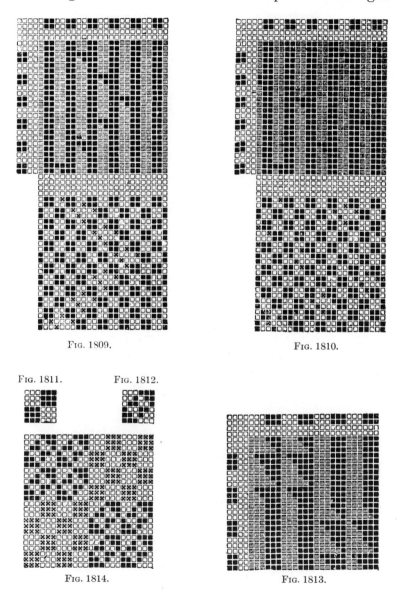

Fig. 1809.

Fig. 1810.

Fig. 1811.   Fig. 1812.

Fig. 1814.   Fig. 1813.

stripes are larger than those in Fig. 1804. An examination of the weaves and corresponding color patterns will show the method of producing them. Fig. 1809

Fig. 1815.

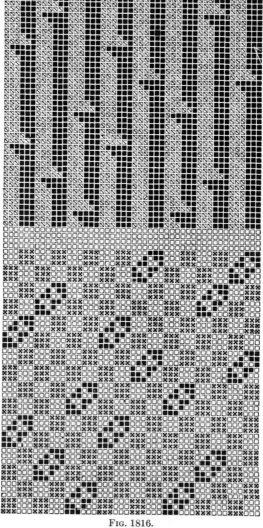

Fig. 1816.

shows the spots arranged in pointed form; Fig. 1810, in 6-leaf satin order.

With a 3 up 3 down basket weave, Fig. 1811, the

spots are produced by inserting the weave shown at
Fig. 1812. Fig. 1813 shows the effect obtained by
arranging the two weaves in checkerboard order, as

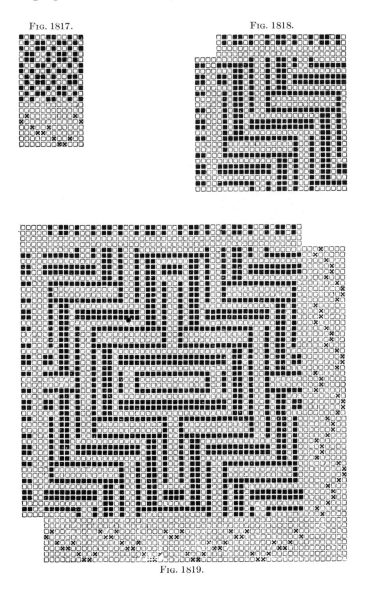

FIG. 1817.

FIG. 1818.

FIG. 1819.

shown at Fig. 1814. Fig. 1816 shows them arranged
according to the accompanying motif, Fig. 1815.

Another class of designs is illustrated at Fig. 1818,

in which the warp and filling pattern is 1 light 1 dark, 1 light 2 dark, 1 light 1 dark, 1 light, total 8. The weave is shown at Fig. 1817.

This design can be indefinitely varied by rearranging the drawing-in draft and picks. An example is

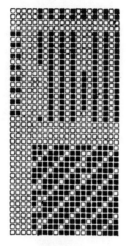

Fig. 1820.

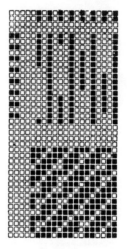

Fig. 1821.

Fig. 1823.

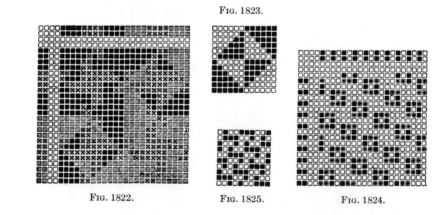

Fig. 1822.   Fig. 1825.   Fig. 1824.

shown at Fig. 1819, in which the color effect results from the weave at Fig. 1817 with the color pattern and drawing-in draft shown at Fig. 1819. The method of rearranging the picks of Fig. 1817 is shown at the right of Fig. 1819.

Streaked or spotted effects with a 1 dark 1 light

pattern in warp and filling are produced in the following manner:

A 4-leaf warp twill is first drafted over the pattern area. The risers are removed for certain distances from a dark warp thread, throwing the thread on the

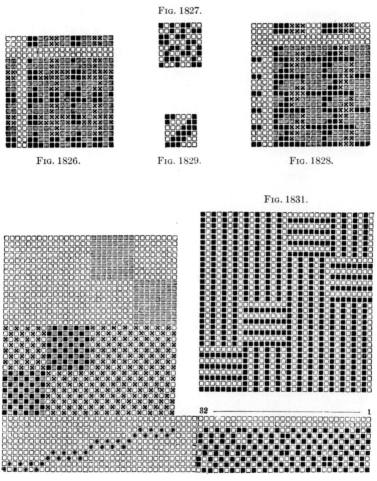

FIG. 1827.

FIG. 1826.

FIG. 1829.

FIG. 1828.

FIG. 1831.

FIG. 1830.

back in a 1 up 3 down order. This causes the light threads on either side to approach each other and make a more pronounced streak of the light shade in the cloth. Figs. 1820 and 1821 illustrate the method and the effect produced.

Other designs of this character are shown at Figs. 1822 to 1840.

Longitudinal and cross stripes on a plain weave can be obtained with a continuous 1 and 1 color pattern in warp and filling. It has already been explained that long-itudinal stripes are produced with this c o m b i n a t i o n of weave and color pattern by laying the light pick when the light warp thread is down; also that cross stripes re-sult from laying the light pick when the light warp thread is up. The stripe can be run in either di-rection by rearrang-ing the plain weave to raise or lower the light and dark warp threads in the re-quired order. The method of drafting is as follows:

FIG. 1832.

FIG. 1833.

1. The positions of the vertical and cross lines are determined and marked on the draft.

2. The cross lines are painted yellow.

3. A plain weave is drafted on the yellow lines to raise the light warp when the light filling is laid.

4. A plain weave is drafted on the remaining portion

Fig. 1835.

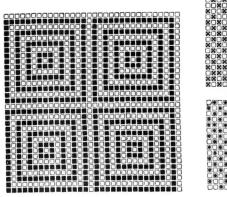

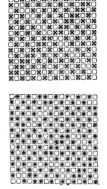

Fig. 1834.

Fig. 1837.

Fig. 1836.

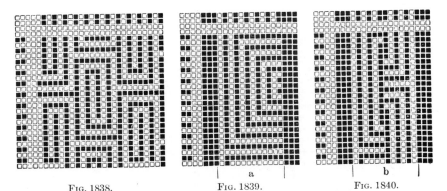

Fig. 1838.

a

Fig. 1839.

b

Fig. 1840.

of the area, where longitudinal lines are wanted, so as to raise the dark warp when the light filling is laid.

These operations are illustrated by the two examples shown at Figs. 1830, 1831, 1832 and 1833.

At the dividing line between the two divisions of the weave two

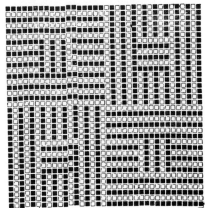

Fig. 1841.

risers or two sinkers come together, but this does not injure the pattern.

Several examples of this class of effects are shown at Figs. 1830 to 1844. Fig. 1836 is the weave for the color effects shown at Figs. 1839 and 1840.

FIG. 1842. FIG. 1843.

FIG. 1844.

When two threads of one color in patterns of this kind are placed together in warp and filling at the end of the weave pattern or at any other place, the light threads are changed to the position in the weave previously occupied by the dark threads, the dark threads taking the place previously occupied 'by the light threads. The result is that longitudinal stripes displace cross stripes, while cross stripes appear where longitudinal stripes were previously formed. This causes a complete transposition of the color effect, as may be seen by comparing the part, *b*, in Fig. 1840 with the part, *a*, in Fig. 1839.

Fig. 1845.

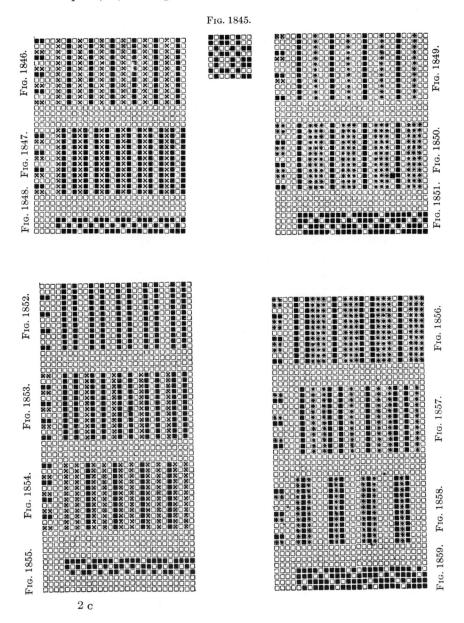

2 c

For the color effect shown at Fig. 1841 the color patterns are as follows:

WARP	FILLING

$$9 \times \begin{cases} 1 \text{ dark} \\ 1 \text{ light} \end{cases}$$

$$10 \times \begin{cases} 1 \text{ dark} \\ 1 \text{ light} \end{cases}$$

$$9 \times \begin{cases} 1 \text{ light} \\ \underline{1 \text{ dark}} \\ 36 \end{cases}$$

$$10 \times \begin{cases} 1 \text{ light} \\ \underline{1 \text{ dark}} \\ 40 \end{cases}$$

The line effects become still more interesting when, in place of the plain weave, that shown at Fig. 1845 is used, which has two threads working in reverse order, followed by two working together.

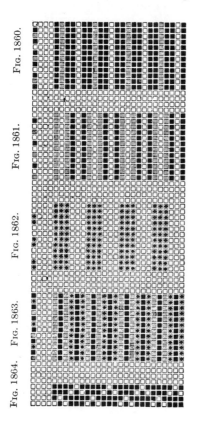

FIG. 1860. FIG. 1861. FIG. 1862. FIG. 1863. FIG. 1864.

FIG. 1865. FIG. 1866. FIG. 1867. FIG. 1868. FIG. 1869.

Figs. 1846 to 1873 show a number of additional examples of hair line effects. The weave is shown at

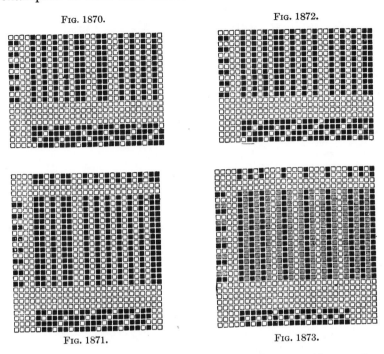

FIG. 1870.

FIG. 1872.

FIG. 1871.

FIG. 1873.

the bottom of each group of color effects. Above the weaves are the color effects obtained with various color patterns. The continuous lines of the width of one thread in these patterns are produced by inserting a pick of a given color when the warp thread of the same color is down. Thus when a black warp thread is down a black filling thread is inserted in the fabric.

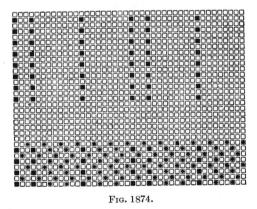

FIG. 1874.

Fabrics in which color effects are to be produced

should not be set excessively close in the warp, as it is desirable to have the filling colors fairly prominent.

The weave shown at Fig. 1874 is well adapted for clearly defined, but subdued, stripe effects. Each individual stripe, as well as the whole pattern, must comprise a number of threads which is divisible by 3. The warp pattern for the color shown at Fig. 1874 is as follows :

> 1 dark
> 2 light
> 1 dark
> 8 light
> 1 dark
> 8 light
> ――
> 21

"STRAIGHT LINE" ANALYSIS OF WEAVES, PATTERNS AND FABRICS

By SAMUEL S. DALE

It seems peculiarly fitting that a treatise on weave construction such as the "Handbook of Weaves" should be supplemented by an explanation of the best method of analyzing weaves and fabrics. The "Handbook" explains and illustrates the construction of weaves; that is, the manner in which warp and filling threads are interlaced to produce the effect desired. This supplement to that work will explain how the weave and the fabric construction of a woven cloth are determined, enabling a manufacturer to obtain the details of the layout for any sample of woven goods that may be submitted to him.

WEAVE AND COLOR PATTERN ANALYSIS

The method by which the weave is determined from a given sample is very simple, but the process itself is frequently difficult because of the felted condition of wool cloth, which prevents the separation of the threads in the fabric. Cloths composed of cotton, linen, silk, lightly felted wool, or other textile material ordinarily offer no serious difficulty in determining the weave construction.

A needle, scissors, pencil and cross section paper are the only appliances required. A slender awl, such as is used by machinists, answers well as a needle for this work.

A square or oblong sample of the cloth to be analyzed or, to use a common expression, "picked out" is cut with the edges running as nearly straight with warp or filling threads as possible. Three or four square inches of the fabric is a convenient size to handle and usually large enough to give several complete color and weave patterns.

The threads, usually the filling, are then withdrawn from one side of the sample for one half or three quarters of an inch, leaving the other set of threads (the warp, if the filling is withdrawn) projecting from the edge of the cloth. These projecting threads are clipped close to the filling for about half an inch at the left.

The sample with the face to the operator is then drawn firmly over the index finger of the left hand and held at the right between the first and second fingers. At the left, where the projecting warp has been clipped, it is held between the thumb and first finger, with the projecting warp threads pointing up.

One filling thread is loosened along the clipped edge of the sample and for a short distance beyond, care being taken not to withdraw it completely from the projecting warp threads.

Holding the cloth firmly over the first finger, the operator, beginning with the first projecting warp thread, notes carefully whether these warp threads are above or below the filling thread that has been loosened from the cloth. After the color of the filling thread has been marked at the left of the draft, the position and color of each warp thread are marked on the cross section paper, the color being indicated by a letter at the top of the draft. A cross in a square indicates that the warp is above the filling at that point of intersection, and a blank square indicates that it is below. This operation is continued until a record of the warp threads in one or more complete color and weave patterns for the filling thread has been obtained. This filling thread is then withdrawn and the same operation is repeated with the next filling thread, the work being continued until a record of the filling threads in one or more complete color and weave patterns has been obtained.

When it is impossible by the ordinary method to determine beyond question the order in which the warp threads lie in the cloth, the object can sometimes be attained by clipping some of the projecting threads and marking the short threads on the draft for identification. In this way a correct record for each warp thread is obtained. If in such a case the warp threads should be marked on the draft in the wrong order, it is often possible to correct these errors when the draft of an entire filling pattern has been obtained. It frequently happens, however, that this difficulty can be obviated by turning the sample quarter way around and raveling the warp instead of the filling thread by thread.

When the weave and color patterns in warp and filling have been determined, the weave draft, drawing-in draft, and color pattern are arranged in the form already explained in the " Handbook of Weaves."

Fig. 1875 shows the weave and thread drafts obtained by " picking out " a cross rib cloaking fabric. The 2-ply worsted warp threads are marked " W ". The 2-ply cotton warp threads are marked " C ". The marks at the left of the draft indicate the three kinds of filling: " 5-p ", 5-ply cotton; " 2-p ", 2-ply cotton; and " B ", carded woolen backing.

The warp pattern is:
2 worsted, 2 ply
$\dfrac{1}{3}$ cotton, 2-ply

The filling pattern is:
1 cotton, 5-ply
1 cotton, 2-ply
$\dfrac{1}{3}$ carded woolen, single

The face weave of this cloth is the full rib weave shown at Fig. 212 and described in the "Handbook of Weaves" under "Cross Ribs". The carded woolen back filling is stitched by the cotton warp in a 3 up 1 down broken twill order in an area of 12 threads square.

THE "STRAIGHT LINE" ANALYSIS OF WOVEN FABRICS

The best method of analyzing woven fabrics is that known as the "straight line," which is based on the convenient relations existing between ounces per yard, square yards per pound, width of cloth in inches, number of threads per inch, and the English basis for numbering yarn. Developed in the mill by the writer, it was first made public in October, 1902, and has since then been extensively adopted in American and foreign mills, always with complete success. The attention of the textile trade and the public in this and other countries was directed to this method of cloth analysis in 1913 when the United States tariff on cotton cloth was revised, with the ad valorem rates adjusted to a sliding scale based on the average yarn number, determined by the "straight line" method.

The essential feature of this method consists in cutting a rectangular sample of the cloth to be analyzed so that it will have an area of $\frac{1}{300}$th square yard (4.32 square inches). This is called the standard sample.

Every warp and filling thread in 1 square inch of cloth represents 1 inch of yarn, and also represents 4.32 inches of yarn in 4.32 square inches ($\frac{1}{300}$th square yard) of cloth.

If, for example, a woven fabric has 50 warp threads and 40 filling threads per inch, there will be 90 lengths of warp and filling yarn, each 4.32 inches long, in the standard sample of $\frac{1}{300}$th square yard (4.32 square inches). If this standard sample weighs, say 5 grains, it follows that the warp and filling yarn in the sample will have an average of 18 of these lengths (4.32 inches) per grain.

This number, 18, is the cotton yarn number because cotton yarn is numbered in all parts of the world to indicate the number of 840-yard lengths per pound, which is equivalent to the number of 4.32-inch lengths per grain.

It follows that the average number (by the cotton system) of the yarn in a woven fabric is equal to the number of warp and filling threads per inch divided by the number of grains in the weight of $\frac{1}{300}$th square yard (4.32 square inches).

The size or count of any particular kind of yarn in a fabric, for example, warp, filling, back warp, back filling, face warp, face filling, is found by the same method; that is, dividing the number of threads of the yarn in question per inch by the number of grains in its weight.

The result thus obtained indicates the size or count of the yarn (by the cotton system) as it lies in the cloth.   To determine the count of the yarn when spun it is necessary to estimate and make allowance for the changes in length and weight in weaving and finishing by reason of the take-up in twisting and weaving, shrinkage of length in finishing, and loss or gain in weight during these processes.

The weight per yard and number of yards per pound are found with equal facility by the "straight line" method.   The standard sample ($\frac{1}{300}$th square yard) is equal to a sample .12 yard (4.32 inches) long and 1 inch wide.   It follows that multiplying the grain weight of the standard sample by the width of the given fabric in inches will give the grain weight of .12 running yard of the goods.

The number of running yards of cloth per pound is equal to a pound (7000 grains) divided by the weight of one yard or to .12 pound (840 grains) divided by the weight of .12 yard.

It follows that the number of running yards of cloth per pound is found by dividing 840 by the product of the grain weight of the standard sample and the number of inches in the width of the cloth.

840 ÷ (grain weight of sample × width in inches)
= running yards per pound.

As there are $437\frac{1}{2}$ grains in an ounce, each grain in the weight of the standard sample is equivalent to 1 ounce per ($437\frac{1}{2}$ × 4.32) 1890 square inches. This is the area ($52\frac{1}{2}$ × 36) of a running yard $52\frac{1}{2}$ inches wide.

It follows that the number of grains in the weight of the standard sample (4.32 square inches) is equal to the number of ounces per running yard, $52\frac{1}{2}$ inches wide.

The number of ounces per running yard for any other width is found by proportion:

(grains × width in inches) ÷ $52\frac{1}{2}$ = ounces per running yard.

No special apparatus is required for the "straight line" system of cloth analysis. The cloth and yarn are weighed on an ordinary balance, such as is found in nearly every textile mill, with grain weights down to $\frac{1}{10}$th grain or smaller.

The standard sample (4.32 square inches) can be cut by a die, or with scissors or knife around a template of the required size. The sample may be of any convenient form so long as it is of the required area. 1.8 inches by 2.4 inches are convenient dimensions. If a smaller or larger sample is used, it can be made a fraction or multiple of 4.32 square inches.

Following are several sizes and corresponding dimensions:

Standard size ($\frac{1}{300}$ square yard) 4.32 sq. in.   (1.6 inches × 2.7 inches)
(1.8 inches × 2.4 inches)

Multiples:
Two (2) sizes ($\frac{1}{150}$ square yard) 8.64 sq. in.   (1.8 inches × 4.8 inches)
(2.4 inches × 3.6 inches)
(2.7 inches × 3.2 inches)

Three (3) sizes ($\frac{1}{100}$ square yard) 12.96 sq. in.   (1.8 inches × 7.2 inches)
(2.4 inches × 5.4 inches)
(2.7 inches × 4.8 inches)
(3.6 inches × 3.6 inches)

Fractions:

Three quarters ($\frac{3}{4}$) size ($\frac{1}{400}$ square yard) 3.24 square
inches   (1.8 × 1.8 inches)
Two thirds ($\frac{2}{3}$) size ($\frac{1}{450}$ square yard) 2.88 square
inches   (1.2 × 2.4 inches)
One half ($\frac{1}{2}$) size ($\frac{1}{600}$ square yard) 2.16 square
inches   (1.8 × 1.2 inches)
One third ($\frac{1}{3}$) size ($\frac{1}{900}$ square yard) 1.44 square
inches   (1.2 × 1.2 inches)
One fourth ($\frac{1}{4}$) size ($\frac{1}{1200}$ square yard) 1.08 square
inches   (.9 × 1.2 inches)

A convenient method for determining the threads per inch consists in dividing the number of threads on each side of the sample analyzed by the respective dimension. If, for example, a standard sample has 120 warp threads on the 2.4 inch side and 72 filling threads on the 1.8 inch side, the number of threads per inch in the warp and filling is found as follows:

$$120 \div 2.4 = 50 \text{ warp threads per inch.}$$
$$72 \div 1.8 = 40 \text{ filling threads per inch.}$$

The cotton count found by the "straight line" method may be reduced to any other system of numbering desired. Following are a number of formulas for such reductions:

Cotton No. × .52½	= Woolen Runs.
Cotton No. × 1½	= Worsted No.
Cotton No. × 2⅝	= West of England No.
Cotton No. × 2.8	= Linen No. (woolen cuts)
Cotton No. × 3.28	= Yorkshire skeins
Cotton No. × 840	= Yards per pound
Cotton No. × 1.693	= Metric No.
Cotton No. × .846	= French Cotton No.
5315 ÷ Cotton No.	= Deniers (for silk)
305 ÷ Cotton No.	= Drams (for silk)
1000 ÷ Cotton No.	= Grains per 120 yards
417 ÷ Cotton No.	= Grains per 50 yards
167 ÷ Cotton No.	= Grains per 20 yards
17.1 ÷ Cotton No.	= Dundee No. (for jute)

The "straight line" method of cloth analysis is illustrated by the following analysis of a heavy cross rib cloaking fabric composed of cotton, worsted and carded woolen yarn and the weave draft of which is shown at Fig. 1875.

ANALYSIS OF A RIB FACE CLOAKING

Made of cotton, worsted and carded woolen yarn

Counting the threads and weighing the different kinds of yarn in a standard sample of the cloth give the following results:

Warp, 2-ply worsted 61.2 ends per inch, 4.8 grains
2-ply cotton   30.6 ends per inch, 2.   grains
Filling, 2-ply cotton 18.3 picks per inch, 1.   grain
5-ply cotton   18.3 picks per inch, 5.2 grains
Single woolen 18.3 picks per inch, 13.6 grains
Total weight of standard sample, 26.6 grains

The loss of weight after the yarn is spun is estimated as follows: Worsted, 10 per cent; cotton, nothing; carded woolen back filling, 28 per cent.

The warp take-up is estimated at 12 per cent. No change in length of cloth in finishing. Slack of filling in loom, 5 per cent. Loom width, $66\frac{1}{2}$ inches for 55 inches finished. The shrinkage of filling yarn in length is, therefore, 21.4 per cent.

From the foregoing data the weight of the cloth and sizes of the yarn are calculated by the "straight line" method as follows:

Weight of Cloth

$(26.6 \times 55) \div 52.5 = 27.8$ ounces per yard, 55 inches wide
$840 \div (26.6 \times 55) = .574$ yard, 55 inches wide, to the pound
These results are verified as follows:
$27.8 \times .574 = 16$, ounces per pound

Sizes of Warp Yarn

$61.2 \div 4.8 = $ No. 12.7 cotton $= 2/38.1$ worsted
$38.1 \div .88 = 43.3$
$43.3 \times .90 = 2/39$ worsted, spun yarn
$30.6 \div 2 = $ No. 15.3 cotton $= 2/30.6$ cotton
$30.6 \div .88 = 2/35$ cotton, spun yarn

Sizes of Filling Yarn

$18.3 \div 1. = $ No. 18.3 cotton $= 2/36.6$ cotton
$36.6 \div .786 = 2/46.5$ cotton filling, spun yarn
$18.3 \div 5.2 = $ No. 3.52 cotton $= 5/17.6$ cotton
$17.6 \div .786 = 5/22.4$ cotton, spun yarn
$18.3 \div 13.6 = $ No. 1.34 cotton $= .7$ run woolen
$.7 \div .786 = .89$
$.89 \times .72 = .64$ run woolen, spun yarn

Summary of Results

Weight of Cloth:	27.8 ounces per yard, 55 inches wide .574 yard, 55 inches wide, to the pound
Warp:	61.2 ends per inch 2/39 worsted, spun size 30.6 ends per inch 2/35 cotton, spun size
Filling:	18.3 picks per inch 2/46.5 cotton, spun size 18.3 picks per inch 5/22.4 cotton, spun size 18.3 picks per inch single .64 run carded woolen yarn, spun size

Set of Finished Cloth: 91.8 ends per inch; 54.9 picks per inch

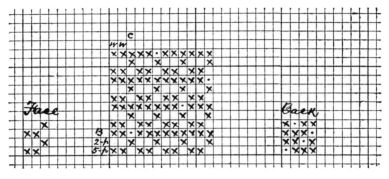

Fig. 1875.

INDEX

399